Maurice   with best wishes

Joe Nesoos

Sept 1993

The Littlewoods Organisation

100 Old Hall Street Liverpool L70 1AB   Direct Line: 051-235
Switchboard: 051-235 2222 Telex: 628501 Fax: 051-

Our reference:

Your reference:

3rd September, 1993

Mrs Marivic Visarutnantha
Manager
Littlewoods Thailand
127 Rajdamri Road, 3rd Floor
Narayana Phand Pavilion Building
Pathumwan
Bangkok 10330
THAILAND

Dear Marivic

Whilst your involvement with Littlewoods is relatively recent, I thought that you would be very interested in the biography of my father which has just been published.

In sending you a personally signed copy of the book, I know it will serve as a reminder to all of us that today is tomorrow's future, and many of the business lessons learned 70 years ago are still appropriate today and will be for ever more.

Enjoy the read.

Yours sincerely,

JOHN MOORES

Encl.   21-9-93

Directors: Sir John Moores CBE (President) L. W. van Geest (Chairman) Sir Desmond Pitcher DL (Vice Chairman) B. G. Dale (Group Chief Executive)
John Moores CBE The Lady Grantchester P. S. Guha W. Huntley M. A. Davidson J. D. Nettleton D. E. Cook J. W. Michie James G. Suenson-Taylor

The Littlewoods Organisation PLC Registered Number: 262152 London Registered Office: 100 Old Hall Street Liverpool L70 1AB

THE MAN WHO MADE
LITTLEWOODS

THE MAN WHO MADE
LITTLEWOODS

THE STORY OF JOHN MOORES

Barbara Clegg

Hodder & Stoughton
LONDON SYDNEY AUCKLAND

British Library Cataloguing in Publication Data
Clegg, Barbara
 The Man Who Made Littlewoods.
 I. Title
 338.04092

ISBN 0-340-57479-8

First published in Great Britain 1993

Published by Hodder and Stoughton,
a division of Hodder and Stoughton Ltd,
Mill Road, Dunton Green, Sevenoaks, Kent TN13 2YA
Editorial Office: 47 Bedford Square, London WC1B 3DP

Typeset by Hewer Text Composition Services, Edinburgh
Printed in Great Britain by
St Edmundsbury Press Ltd, Bury St Edmunds, Suffolk

For our mothers and our fathers

Contents

Family Tree		8
List of Illustrations		9
1	You Look After Your Own	11
2	Love, Marriage and 'Gambling Coupons'	23
3	The 'Royal' Family	33
4	First Million, Second Business	46
5	Expanding Horizons	59
6	Successes and Failures	66
7	Imminent Peril	76
8	'The Ordinary Man or Woman Can Do Anything . . .'	82
9	The Machinery of War	94
10	Count Your Blessings	105
11	Winning the Peace	116
12	The Message to Garcia	125
13	The Uncrowned Queen	140
14	'I Want Lucky People'	153
15	The Old Victorian Principles	168
16	Nothing But the Best	182
17	Doctor's Orders	196
18	Do Not Disturb	209
19	In My Beginning is My End	217
Acknowledgments		231
Index		233

John = Selina
1847–1907   1846–1901

John William = Louisa Fethney
1871–1919   1873–1959

five sons
two daughters

Hilda   Ethel   Arthur   Cecil   Charlie   Louise   Edna (Joy)
1894–1967   1897–1990   1900–1984   1902–1989   1906–1947   1908–1972   born 1910

JOHN = Ruby Knowles
born 1896   1894–1965

Betty   John Junior   Peter   Janatha
born 1925   born 1928   born 1932   born 1937
=   = (1)   = (2)   =   =
Kenneth   Sheila   Jane   Luciana   Patrick
Suenson-Taylor   Moore   Stavely-Dick Pinto   Stubbs

three sons   three sons   four sons*   one son   two sons
three daughters   one daughter one daughter one daughter   one daughter

[* two adopted]

List of Illustrations

A family wedding c. 1890. Louisa, second from left, with her three eldest children, John (in sailor's suit), Ethel (middle) and Hilda (far right). John William is in the back row, far right.

John with his two eldest sisters, Hilda and Ethel, in their teens, just before the First World War.

Ruby Knowles as a girl.

John in his early twenties, not in his naval uniform but the next best thing.

John and Ruby set off on a world cruise in the mid-Thirties.

John, Ruby, Betty and a very young John Junior at Cliftonville where Betty, in spite of her youth, was already at boarding school.

John steers Betty at an early Littlewoods sports day.

After spending three hours underground at Langwith Pit, south of Sheffield, canvassing the miners of Clay Cross in 1933.

The National candidate for Nuneaton, canvassing with his family in 1935.

Just before the fatal accident, John (far left), Ruby and Campbell Black (front row, third from left) watch as Miss Liverpool is christened with a bottle of champagne.

A family shooting party in Lancashire shortly before the Second World War. From left to right: Arthur, John, Arthur's first wife, Cecil, Lou and Joy.

This handsome studio portrait of Cecil was taken in the late forties.

This photograph, taken in 1953, hints at the dichotomy in John's character.

The massive undertaking of conversion to war work illustrated John's belief that 'the ordinary man or woman can do anything'.

Louisa with her four daughters at her seventieth birthday party, Easter 1943. From left to right: Joy, Hilda, Louisa, Ethel (recently widowed) and Lou. It was the women who kept the family together.

Ruby catches the largest salmon and John feels compelled to acknowledge her superiority.

At the British Industries Fair in 1951, John showed himself the ardent monarchist.

After the Hungarian uprising of 1956, Peter, then a student in Vienna, assisted in distributing aid from Littlewoods to the refugees.

John receives his knighthood in 1980. With him are three of his children; from left to right: Betty, Janatha and Peter.

The chairman joins in enthusiastically on a Motorists' Outing for Handicapped Children in 1962.

John congratulates David Hockney on winning first prize in the 1967 'John Moores'.
(*photo courtesy of John Mills Photography*)

John's ninetieth birthday in 1986. He was happiest painting in his studio.
(*photo by Don McPhee, courtesy of the Guardian*)

John in his nineties at a football match, wearing his famous hand-knitted Everton scarf.
(*photo courtesy of the News of the World*)

1

You Look After Your Own

On January 26th, 1917, a young man sat in a little office in Forster Square, Manchester, writing a letter. There was nothing particularly exceptional about his looks – he was wiry and athletic in build, although not very tall, and he had a shock of dark brown hair. It was the middle of a World War, but he was in a reserved occupation. He was a junior telegraphist, earning 18s a week, and would one day become a billionaire, reported by the Press to be amongst the eight richest people in Britain. His name was John Moores. It was the day after his twenty-first birthday, and he was writing a thank-you letter.

> 'Dear Mam,' he wrote, 'In fact, all of us. Thanks so much for all your good wishes. Knowing how sincere they are I value them beyond measure. I value them and view them not only as wishes (though that were enough) but as tokens of your faith and confidence that I *will* make good.'

Ambition, aspiration, the urge to 'make good' are common at twenty-one. But John Moores did in fact succeed, beyond most people's wildest dreams. Some luck must have been involved, but in a rise such as his, from poverty and obscurity to enormous wealth and power, more than luck was needed. There had to be a driving force, a force which never slackened and which took him through the bad times as well as the good; which kept him, after every success, always launching into a new venture; which never allowed him to sit back. What was it that motivated him?

He is something of an enigma, a very private man who has always avoided publicity; a man who has been described in a variety of ways. To one, 'His personality was the same as Jesus Christ's'; to another, 'He made Genghis Khan look like a civilised Christian man.' Different people had different impressions of him, but knowing him often altered their lives. Other people are the key; when we listen to what they say, when we look at the influence and effect he had on them, then we get a little nearer to the man himself. Their accounts may vary, they may produce different versions of the same event – our memories are usually biased and seldom objective – but from them a character begins to emerge, a complex and often contradictory character: John Moores.

Most of his own recorded words were spoken publicly in the context of formal speeches; very occasionally there is the bonus of a letter or an entry in a diary, although he seldom wrote directly about himself. This letter of nearly eighty years ago is an exception, and it still gives few clues as to what made him stand out. It is written in a beautiful copperplate hand, but then, at the beginning of this century, any intelligent youngster, even one leaving school at thirteen as John Moores did, would be likely to have good legible handwriting. The three 'Rs' were the basics taught. The spelling is accurate, too, and the phrasing is rounded and almost literary. His family's faith and confidence in him obviously mattered a great deal, for the letter goes on:

'Standing, as I do, on the brink of Manhood and my career, and facing the world, they are doubly cheering.

'They comfort me, they inspire me, strengthen me. And seem to bring to the top all that is good in me.

'Can I but keep them then I shall prosper; and can I but keep them, life will have been well lived – and worth the living.

'Give me them, then, now and always, and whatever success I shall have, yours will be the bigger share in it.

'I say *success*, and with all due gravity and confidence; not because I am strong enough to command circumstances, but because I feel that with such wishes supporting me, I must and will succeed, in so far as is good for me.'

A son nowadays would be more likely to ring home rather than write, but telephones then were far from commonplace. In 1910 there were still only 122,000 in use in the country, and although the number would have increased considerably by 1917, they would mainly be installed in the houses of the middle-class and better-off; there would certainly not have been a telephone in the Moores' family home in Droylsden, only twenty minutes' train ride from Forster Square. John had possibly spent a night away – perhaps working late, perhaps celebrating his birthday – for he normally commuted every day, often walking to save the fare. He still lived at home with his parents and his seven brothers and sisters. Now, at last, the letter gives its first clue, not simply because of what it says, but because of what it does not say. It never mentions his father.

John William was, however, still alive and only forty-five years old. He was a bricklayer; so was John's grandfather – yet another John

Moores – and so was his great-grandfather, Sidney; he came of a long line of bricklayers. Sometimes one of them would describe himself as 'master builder', but usually it was 'bricklayer (or bricksetter) – journeyman'. A journeyman was a man employed and paid by the day, not an employer of others, but was above an apprentice in the hierarchy. They were good solid Lancashire working-class stock. And more than that, they were Manchester working class.

Manchester had been the prosperous capital of the cotton industry since the middle of the previous century, an industry which included not only spinning and weaving, but bleaching, dyeing, finishing and manufacture of the necessary chemicals. Not only was it the big city to a hundred other towns such as Shaw, Bacup and Colne, and to industrial villages like Haigh and Appley Bridge; it was also the cotton and textile capital of the Commonwealth, the place where Indians and Egyptians came to learn the business and the language. It was a place, too, of small family businesses, of an aspiring middle class, sending their children to 'good schools'. Respectability reached down to many working-class households; there was a best room, used only on Sundays; there were strongly-held beliefs – 'Everything must be paid for', and 'You look after your own'. There was plenty of female employment. And there were standards.

The Moores men seem frequently to have married women who were weavers – not surprisingly, as it was a staple industry of the area. John's grandfather, an earlier John Moores, had gone one better and at eighteen had married a draper's daughter, Selina Rogers. His bride was a year older, slight and dainty, with a little fine-boned face, and she was practical and efficient. Her family are reputed to have owned a haulage and removal business as well as the draper's shop, and she may have brought a dowry with her, for the couple were comparatively prosperous. Selina drove about in her own carriage – the equivalent then of a family car now. Her husband, although trained as a bricklayer, had a small contractor's firm which did repair and maintenance jobs. They lived in Bradford – not the town in Yorkshire, but the Bradford of North Manchester, officially 'in the sub-district of Newton in the County Borough of Manchester'.

Family legend connects him with land in Bank Street, which was sold to the Newton Heath (Lancashire and Yorkshire Railway) Football and Cricket Club, later to become Manchester United. In addition he owned, or had an interest in, two pubs: the Brickmakers Arms and the Church Inn. There is a photograph of the couple in their middle years, taken on a victuallers' outing. He is seated; Selina is standing behind her burly, bearded husband with her little gloved hands on his shoulders, and there is no doubt who rules the roost. It was in the Church Inn in Eccles that their grandson, John, was born.

His father, John William, was their third son, born in 1871 into a world very different from the one we know. His mother, Selina, however efficient, could not write, and neither could either of his grandmothers. They 'made their mark' on birth certificates. The men of the family may well have been equally unlettered; there is no record. John William was one of eight children and he fathered eight in his turn. But the infant mortality rate was higher in his generation than in the next – one of his brothers died at two and a half, one at nine weeks. And judging by death certificates, the life expectancy of many adults appears to have been only the mid-fifties to mid-sixties: to reach three score and ten was an achievement.

Nothing brings the past to life more than an actual contemporary document. It is like looking at the piece of moon rock in the Science Museum in London. There it sits, in its glass case, a lump of grey-brown stone, solid and real, and suddenly all those moon landings which we have watched are not simply television programmes, they have reality too. In the same way, details of life and death written at the time, in a contemporary hand, even though the ink may have dried a hundred years ago, bring real people home to us.

John's parents married young. John William was only twenty-one when he took a young mill girl, Louisa Fethney, as his bride. She was spirited and intelligent, with a very pretty singing voice – she sang in the choir of Christchurch, Bradford, where they may have met – and had no money at all. The relationship was a turbulent and passionate one from the start. A daughter, Hilda, was born a year and a half after their wedding, and fourteen months after that, their first son, John. On the birth certificate, his father is registered as licensed victualler of the Church Inn, Eccles, but it is unlikely that John William actually owned it. He was still only twenty-four. In all probability he ran it for his parents.

In those days Eccles was a small country village thirteen miles outside Manchester, 'about as far as a horse could go, and so a place to make a day's outing'. The Church Inn was not simply a pub; it served meals and people could stay there. It had some ground, too, a garden at the front and a bowling green at the back.

But life for the young couple was not as idyllic as it might have been; John William was a possessive husband and there were violent quarrels. Worst of all, 'after he had been horrible to her and made her cry, he would expect her to be there all smiling to receive guests'. Very soon after young John was born, his parents split up. It may have been Louisa who had had enough and ran away, taking the baby and small child with her, or possibly it was John William who left them to see the world and seek his fortune. But the beginning of 1896 saw Louisa living with a married sister, Carrie, and taking in sewing to support herself and the children. John William was in America.

It was the year of the Klondike Gold Rush, and America was the land of opportunity. Whatever he was looking for, however, John William clearly did not find it. He travelled with his elder brother, Sidney, who stayed on in the States, but John William was back within the year, considerably poorer. Family tradition has it that he had come into some money, probably from the sale of family property, and that he had used this to fund his travels. He left taking his 'mess of pottage' with him, and he returned having spent the lot. Louisa took him back. As one of their daughters later remarked, 'Perhaps she preferred him that way. Poor.' She may have thought he would be less likely to order her about. If so, she was wrong.

Poorer they certainly were; Ethel was born nine months after the reconciliation, but they were no longer living in the comfortable surroundings of the Church Inn; his parents were still the proprietors, but John William and his rapidly expanding family had moved to a small brick terraced house in Openshaw of the *Coronation Street* type. It was a two-up, two-down, with one tap in the kitchen, no bath and a communal back yard with a row of outside lavatories. By the time John was eight they had moved to a better house in Clayton, near Edge Lane, which was three-up and three-down and had hot and cold water and a bathroom. It was here that the sixth child, Charlie, was born.

There had been two more boys in between, Arthur and Cecil. Louisa was delighted with the latest addition, and when remonstrated with for shortening his name from Charles, tossed him in her arms, laughing, and calling him 'My Bonnie Prince Charlie, my Bonnie Prince Charlie'. The eldest child, Hilda, at first refused to go and look at the new arrival. 'There are enough babies in this house already,' she said. There were to be another two before the family was complete – both girls, Louise and Edna.

All eight children survived infancy; they were bright and energetic, and Louisa had her hands full. She was strict and dealt out plenty of smacks, but they were a happy boisterous family, and they adored her. Girls had to share beds, and boys had to share beds, and as there was only one feather mattress, a certain amount of squabbling went on as it was dragged from one room to another. But everyone had turns. The children wore the traditional wooden-soled clogs with iron tips, and one of the excitements was to run along and then scrape the tip on the ground so that it produced a shower of sparks.

One daughter remembers that they were given a penny a week to spend, and on Sunday there was toffee, 'for which you didn't handle the money'. John, as the eldest son, was already in charge of that. He would make a toffee list, and you could choose what you wanted, but you were never allowed to change your mind. If you said 'mint humbugs', then mint humbugs it had to be; he would not alter it, even if he were still only writing it down. He was in charge in other areas as well. If he was being given castor oil, he made sure it was 'fair dos'; all his brothers and sisters had to have it too. He would line them up and his mother would dose the lot of them.

As was usual in that period, the boys were given priority. It was the girls who cleaned up after them and did the housework, who rocked the little ones to sleep in the family rocking chair, who doled out fresh hair ribbons and hankies. There were bedroom nights and ironing nights and cleaning nights. The floors were scrubbed on Friday nights; then papers were spread over them and not taken up again until Saturday midday after work. The boys were either playing football or fiddling about with bicycles. 'They could make one good bike out of four broken ones.' When Louisa came to look for her pie dish, it would be full of paraffin oil with a bicycle chain soaking in it. Worse still, when the boys had got the chain back on the bicycle, they would flick it round and round to make sure it was running smoothly, and oil would fly all over the whitened window-sill and up the window. And the girls would wipe it off and not dare to say a word to their mother.

If someone was coming to tea at the weekend, the two eldest daughters would tidy up the house and put out what clean towels they had in the bathroom, together with the best cake of soap – which would be put away again afterwards and replaced with an ordinary one. When everything was beautiful, in would come someone like Cecil, in his muddy football things. Cecil was usually the muddiest, apparently, and the best at football. 'Always dirty, but smiley.' He would have a bath and leave the tide-mark on the bath and mess the towels up, 'and it was no good complaining to Mummy, because you'd have a slapped face and the bath to clean as well!' Teasing her once, in later years, when she was in her eighties, her daughters informed Louisa that she had always spoilt the boys, that she had been 'man-mad'. She just smiled. 'I still am,' she replied.

Her husband was even stricter. He was a good parent by Victorian standards, insistent on honesty and thrift, though not always a good example himself of the latter virtue. 'A man who has nothing gets nothing in this world,' was Louisa's dictum. When young John badly wanted a cricket bat, he had to save half towards it himself before his parents would contribute the rest. It cost a guinea. Obedience was the major virtue inculcated. At half-past nine every evening, John William would rise to his feet and wind the clock on the mantelpiece. Without a word, his children – even in their late teens – would rise to theirs, say goodnight and go to bed . . . He certainly did not spare the rod, although, if it were their mother that 'put the guts' into them, as the children used to say, he never succeeded in knocking the guts out. Going upstairs one evening to whack the three youngest boys for some misdemeanour, he found them all in bed. Charlie got his beating, then Arthur. When it came to Cecil's turn, he managed to roll over; Arthur rolled back into his place and got whacked a second time by mistake.

Although he was a punitive father and they were sometimes frightened of him, he could be fun too, especially in the early days. He shared an interest in football. John never forgot being taken to watch Manchester United, and being lifted over the barrier and allowed to sit on the grass. And one daughter's favourite memory was of being carried on his shoulders to see the first electric tram, lit up and with hanging flower baskets swaying at its front and rear, a great change from the horse-drawn trams they were used to. They managed to accept his fierce discipline as a matter of course, but it was his treatment of their mother which they found hard to take. The relationship had never really changed; there was still a strong sexual attraction and John William was still possessive and jealous, even resorting sometimes to physical violence. A daughter described catching him with his hands on her mother's throat, and she remembered seeing the bruises there afterwards. Sexual passion can be misunderstood by a child, but there is no doubt that John William tried to dominate his wife.

Louisa loved fine china and one of her few indulgences was to collect pretty pieces, just one item every now and then, when she had saved up enough. After a particularly fierce quarrel John William picked up her most prized cup and deliberately smashed it on the floor. Louisa was not to be outdone. She went round the room collecting the rest, piece by piece, hurling each one down in front of him, until every bit of her precious china was in fragments at his feet. 'There,' she said, 'now you can't punish me any more. It's *all* smashed!'

This ability to stage a forceful demonstration was something which John inherited, or possibly it was a memory from his childhood. It was an ability which was to be put to good use in his business career.

If Louisa gave the boys preferential treatment, her mother-in-law, Selina, had gone much further with her sons. John William was well and truly spoilt. There is a story of how Selina once called round in the early days of the marriage to take the young couple out in her carriage, then stopped and pointed to her son's feet. 'Louisa! Look at his shoes, they're dirty!' Louisa had enough spirit even then to refuse to clean them. So Selina turned up her silk dress, went down on her hands and knees, and cleaned his shoes herself. 'No son of mine has ever cleaned his own shoes.'

Partly as a result of these ministrations, but also because it was in his nature, John William always seems to have taken a pride in his appearance. When not in working gear, he might have been described as 'a natty dresser', white handkerchief arranged in his breast pocket, bowler hat at a jaunty angle. 'He was a proud man. You could tell it in the way he walked. You could take off the way he walked,' a daughter said of him. He was also an extremely hard worker. He had to be, with all those mouths to feed; it was long before the days of child benefit. But Louisa was a thrifty housekeeper; the older children got jobs as soon as they were thirteen and handed their pay packets over to her. Some of them passed exams to go on to secondary school, but their earnings were needed and they never took up their places. John even took a part-time job at twelve and a half, doing a milk round as well as attending school.

They might have managed to get by, if John William had not started drinking. He was certainly under financial pressure and probably continued to drive himself too hard in a physically tough job, but there may have been family genes at work. His mother, Selina, had died in 1901, when John was only five and before her fifth grandchild, Cecil, was born. The cause was cirrhosis of the liver. She was fifty-four. She may have needed some consolation after the deaths of two children, and living in an inn cannot have helped, but even with a drinking problem she was still the one who ran things, the one with 'gumption'. After her death, her husband started to let things slide and he took to the bottle as well. Eventually the pubs had to be sold, and then the contractor's business. When he died six years later, he had gone back to being an ordinary bricklayer again. John William was following in their footsteps.

He still worked long hours, including overtime. The younger girls remember having to take him his lunch when they got home from school for their midday break. Their mother would give it to them in a basin with a cloth over it and say, 'Now run with it! I want him to have it hot.' In their early teens, the two older daughters had jobs in a shirt factory and used to walk to work together, while John was employed as a Post Office indoor messenger boy at 6s a week. 'Even in those days a good telegraphist could earn £4 to £5 a week with overtime,' and he was prepared to work to get somewhere. Some evenings he went to night school to learn telegraphy; the rest of his spare time was spent doing a correspondence course for the Civil Service.

His mother may have been comparatively uneducated, but she was a highly intelligent woman. She recognised his potential very early and gave him all the encouragement she could. 'You've got to get on! Work hard! Work hard!' Every evening the front room, otherwise sacrosanct, was opened up for him. If it was very cold and if Louisa could manage it, there would actually be a fire lit for him – an unheard-of luxury; otherwise he wrapped his legs in an old eiderdown. His writing desk was an ancient bamboo whatnot. Its cane top had gone, and it had a piece of leather–cloth stretched over it. There he would work every evening till late. Cocoa would be brought to him at some point and his sister, Ethel, would read him 'the long words for dictation and spelling, which helped me too,' as she said.

He put it down to his stubborn temper, but it was as much his sense of fair play as anything that led to his first setback. The postal messenger boys were on their feet all day, the only time they could sit down was when they took a turn at putting carbons between the flimsies for the cable men of the Press. In John's own words, 'One day, the head messenger decided young Moores didn't need a rest, and took me off the job just as I had thankfully taken the weight from my aching legs.' The head messenger, it appears, was not very much older than the boys, a thin sarcastic youth with an acid tongue. John objected and was taken in front of two Post Office officials. A short lecture from them would have been the end of it, but when the two lads were out in the corridor again the head messenger could not resist it.

'Now you've been damned well told off, young Moores, we'll have no more nonsense from you. In future you'll do as you're told.'

'I won't,' was the answer to that. And at the end of the week he was out on his ear.

It may have been a blessing in disguise, for soon after that he managed to get a job with the Commercial Cable Company as a trainee telegraphist. As he was to write later, 'Somebody worked it out that more millionaires have come from telegraphists than from any other trade. There may be something in it!'

He had done plenty of research into the subject. His book case did not only contain the required reading for night school, he was collecting an archive on 'success'. His youngest sister remembers it well.

'He wanted to read the lives of important men who'd got to the top. He wanted to know what they did, what they said. Always he wanted to know *how*. He couldn't be bothered with trivialities.'

Books were an expensive luxury, but Louisa would have done anything to help. She sank her pride, which was considerable, and borrowed some money from her two sisters, Carrie and Lizzie. It was a debt she never forgot, and in future years she was to help them as much as she could. When Carrie was dying of cancer at the age of sixty-seven, Louisa nursed her at home and gave her all the loving care of which she was capable.

There were other occasions, too, on which she turned to them for help.

John William's drinking bouts had become more frequent. At first they had only been sporadic, such as the occasion when some of the family had to spend the night out on the road. The three eldest children often used to go to St Andrew's Church for Evensong, and on one particular Sunday, after another quarrel with her husband, Louisa decided to go with them.

'When we got home again we were locked out, and so as not to stand around, we walked. We walked as far as Staley Bridge. We walked all night and he was inside the house drunk.'

Their father's drinking became worse, not surprisingly, when he was going through a particularly bad period himself. Sometime in 1907 they had moved from the better house in Clayton to Manchester Road, Droylsden. Louisa had opened a sweet shop to try to help the family's finances, and it was there that her namesake, Louise, was born; given the nickname Louie as a little girl, she was finally and for ever known as Lou.

John William was employed at Armstrong Whitworth at the time, and in an accident at work one day, fell down a hole and broke his wrist. He was off work for a long time on half-pay, and his enforced idleness at home had a disastrous effect. Half desperate, he used to help himself to money out of the sweet-shop till and go drinking, leaving Louisa to pay the bills. He still had a gold watch; unknown to him, one of the children would take it to the pawnbroker's in the middle of the week, and Hilda or Ethel would be sent to get it back in time for Sunday, when he wore it to morning church. Carrie or Lizzie had to be approached for the half a crown to redeem it.

Eventually the situation at the sweet shop became too difficult and they had to move once more, still in Droylsden, but to a house in Edge Lane. As a result of her husband's spending, Louisa left owing money. She paid off their debts by taking in sewing again, and Ethel used to help. Once, a customer had to have something ready by the crack of dawn the next day, so they sat up together till two in the morning, sewing in linings.

'Suddenly Mummy burst out laughing. She was hysterical. She went out in the back yard and sat there for twenty minutes or so, laughing and crying. When she came back she was all right, and sat down and finished the sewing.'

There was a particularly bad time when Louisa had to take in washing too. If it had not been for their father's propensity to drink, the family situation would have been considerably easier; the two older girls were in better jobs, Hilda working in the Co-op and Ethel in the Post Office; and it was now that John was earning the respectable sum of 18s a week in the little office in Forster Square. The only other employee there was 'a plump, pleasant man with spectacles, whose name was Mr Worrall'.

John described his day in an article he wrote over forty years later, when he was a millionaire.

'I worked from 8 a.m. to 8 p.m. with four hours free in the afternoon, except when Mr Worrall went on his annual three weeks' holiday, when I worked twelve hours a day. He taught me bookkeeping and how to run an office.

"See this," he said, showing me a neatly written memorandum sheet. "A sensible man makes one of these every day. It's called an epitome – anyway, that's what I call it. I write down everything I have to do during the day, and tick off each item as I've done it."

'Today I still make out an epitome just as Mr Worrall taught me to do, and so do all my department supervisors and store managers. So does every successful businessman I know.'

John was not only working his eight- to twelve-hour day in Forster Square; he was giving most of his wage to his mother, and the two of them were continually trying to think up new ways of making extra money. At one point he even had the idea of marketing Louisa's own home-made 'emulsion', a tonic which she spooned into the children when they were ill, until they decided that with such expensive ingredients – eggs, cream, and lime juice, which Louisa herself could barely afford – it would never be profitable. On occasions when he went home, as his father was no longer capable of it, he even had to administer the obligatory beating to one of his younger brothers who had misbehaved. It was a job which John hated. More and more he was having to take over his father's role.

As he sat writing that thank-you letter all those years ago, his future was already charted. That extraordinary dedication, that one-track

21

sense of purpose was locked in. He was resolved; he would not let himself be ruled by thoughtless passion; he would not drink; he would use his brain; he would work and work, and he would do what his father had never done – he would look after Louisa, he would look after the whole family. He would make their fortune.

Two years later, his father died.

2

Love, Marriage and 'Gambling Coupons'

In many ways John William's last two years were the hardest. He had long since recovered from his broken wrist, but he was what the family called 'off-colour'. He was back at work again, and back doing overtime; alcoholism apart, he was a conscientious breadwinner. He was the foreman on a site where Siemens furnaces were both built and dismantled. They were used for steel smelting, and they were brick-lined. After the smelting process was completed, John William's job was to break down the inner walls, and the brick dust from these must have got into his lungs. When, at the very end, he became too ill to go on working, he was described as having 'an industrial disease'. It was not silicosis, the miner's affliction – brick dust does not have the same effect on the lungs as coal dust. It does, however, irritate and weaken, making the lungs more susceptible to the tubercle bacillus. John William had TB.

The younger children were now sent off to bed before he was due home at night. All they remember of him is probably from weekends, 'very thin and very spent, lying on the settle, pale as death, with a little short-stemmed pipe in his hand, fast asleep'.

In another effort to keep the wolf from the door, Louisa started a fish and chip shop. This is a period which, for a long time, that generation of the family would have liked to forget. We may not live in a classless society yet, in spite of the hopes of politicians, but in 1918 it was infinitely more hidebound. To own a fish and chip shop, in the North of that time, was sinking low indeed. The second daughter, Ethel, nearly had her engagement broken off because her husband-to-be's family objected to the connection. Luckily he cared more for her than he did for their edict.

Every day after school, 'Lou and Edna had to get their clogs on and go down in the cellar and peel the potatoes.' Ethel herself had to buy the fish, before she went on to work. 'She had to get up, walk down to Manchester, go to the fish market, wait her turn, buy the amount of fish she wanted – possibly a stone in weight – have it boned and made into a big parcel, take it round to the tram terminal, and send it off on a tram, which her mother would meet. She then had to have a good wash in the public washrooms, slap on some cologne to cover any smell, and be in the Post Office for eight o'clock.'

When they were on duty in the chip shop the girls wore red and pink checked overalls which they had to wash and iron themselves, and the older ones often served until eleven o'clock at night, after a day's work in their own jobs. Louisa continued to run this establishment for several years.

John escaped most of it. First he was working a long day at his own job in Forster Square. Then, soon after his twenty-first birthday, although he was in a reserved occupation, he volunteered for the Navy and was posted to a shore station in Aberdeen as a telegraphist. The only other brother old enough, Arthur, was conscripted into the Army, in the last year of the war. An officer visited the Post Office where Ethel was working, asking for volunteer telegraphists to work at Army HQ and release men for the Front, and although she wanted very much to go, she was needed at home and her father said 'No'. All she remembers of that period is the constant stream of telegrams she had to receive and send which she punched out in Morse Code. 'Killed in Action, Missing, Died of Wounds, Killed in Action, Killed . . .' She could never forget it. Then, in 1918, after the German offensive on the Western Front, after the bombing of Paris, after the Allied offensive and the second battle of the Marne, the mutiny of the German fleet at Kiel, the war was finally over. On November 11th the Armistice was signed, and the German fleet surrendered.

John was not demobbed until 1919, shortly after his father's death. It was Hilda who registered this on behalf of her mother: 'Hilda Moores, daughter, present at the death'. Two things happened in the succeeding months. First, they sold the big, old oak settle on which their father had spent so much of his time in the previous two years. It was too painful a reminder. Secondly, and rather more importantly, John made himself head of the family. The first Christmas after their father's death, he gave his mother and each of his brothers and sisters a present, the best he could afford. Ethel remembers that hers was a purse with 10s in it – riches!

He had managed to save up in the Navy, in spite of sending money home, and these savings were soon to come in useful for other things besides presents. Back in the Commercial Cable Company, he was sent to their training school in Bixteth Street in Liverpool. It was his first contact with the city which was to become his home and the centre of his business empire, and to which he was to give his abiding loyalty. In those days it was the premier exporting port in the country, bigger even than that of London, and a major passenger port as well. The big liners plying between England and the States docked there. It imported raw materials and exported finished goods, and its docksides were lined with great silos and warehouses. Although the days of the notorious Liverpool Triangle were past – the days when manufactured goods from its hinterland were traded for slaves in West Africa, and the slaves in turn exchanged for sugar and molasses in the West Indies – much of its prosperity was based on this earlier pattern. It had its own shipbuilding industry too, and its business life was dominated by the great shipping families. There was still the long-standing joke about 'a Manchester man and a Liverpool gentleman'. The two places were very different. They had been the first two major British cities to be linked by rail – the Liverpool and Manchester Railway was built in 1830 – but Liverpool remained somehow isolated from the rest of Lancashire. It was a city of extremes, with far less of a relationship between the rich and the poor. And it had an aristocratic feel about it. It was also a city divided, and not just by the Mersey; the river still had to be crossed by ferry and the road tunnel was not built until 1934. Liverpool had some very wealthy families but it had too a large population of unskilled and semi-skilled workers employed on the seven miles of docks. Because of the nature of this work, it was male labour; there was very little female employment. There were rows of poor terraced houses, as well as the elegant houses of Rodney Street and Princes Park; there was overcrowding and poverty as well as a rich cultural life.

There was a divide in religion, too. Besides its Protestant population, Liverpool had the largest proportion of Roman Catholics of any city in Britain, due mainly to the very high level of immigration after the Irish famine in the middle of the nineteenth century – 300,000 Irish came to Liverpool in 1847 alone. As in many ports, there was a broad spread of races and of cultures. There was a sizeable population of Chinese, and there was a British black population of West African descent, a legacy of the infamous slave trade; there were a great many Welsh inhabitants – not for nothing is Liverpool called 'the capital of Wales'; and apart, possibly, from the Welsh, none of the immigrant populations was yet fully integrated. But it was a city, then as now, with a fierce pride in itself and with a distinct sense of humour. John took to it straight away.

Asked once why he had never moved south, closer to the national media and the hub of things, his answer was succinct: 'I have made money out of this area and I like the people here.'

His first stay in Liverpool was not a long one, however. When he had been taught to read cable slip and touch-typing, seventy to eighty words per minute, he was posted to Ireland.

The Waterville Cable Station was an isolated base in County Kerry, on the south-west coast, where the cable came out of the Atlantic. Its function was to receive messages from the Americas and re-transmit them to Liverpool and London. He described it as 'a kind of camp with married quarters for those who had wives, and the rest of us – about 150 bachelors – lived in a community centre, with shared bedrooms, a dining-room and a smoking-room'. John was sharing a room with Colin Askham, a friend made when they were Post Office messenger boys together in Manchester, so he was quite happy with the accommodation. The food, however, left a great deal to be desired, and after a lot of complaints and a protest meeting, the mess president was asked to resign. John was elected in his place. He had a shrewd idea why. 'Ex-servicemen will remember that this always happened to the chief spokesman of any group that protests about the way a mess is being run!' And he picked his committee from amongst the others whom he noticed being particularly loud in protest.

Their first job was to check on supplies. They weighed and counted everything as it was delivered and discovered they were being grossly overcharged by the local inhabitants. As soon as that was sorted out, John had another idea, and this was where the money he had saved in the Navy came in useful. He formed a little company called the Waterville Supply Company, had writing paper printed with a company letterhead, and started ordering goods direct from Dublin and England. There was no library in the camp, so he and his committee started one, importing bulk-purchased books.

There was, however, one local attraction nearby – a nine-hole golf-course. Sport of all kinds always interested him, so he took up golf, as a change from football, and practised his putting strokes into a tooth-mug in his bedroom. He became rather good at it. The difficulty was to get hold of golf balls, as there was no sports shop for miles. After a quick bit of lateral thinking, he wrote to Dunlop on the letterheaded paper, offering his company as their 'sole agent in Waterville for the supply of golf requisites'. They took him on. 'There was an interesting profit of about thirty per cent on golf balls in those days,' and as his was the only shop in the area where you could buy them, he did well. He also got the golf balls he had wanted for his own use.

Money was still a major concern; he was sending a good proportion of his wages to his mother, and trying to save at the same time. With telegraphy, overtime, the supply company and the golf shop, he was earning about £20 a week; an amount worth nearly £300 in today's terms. One of the perks of his post as mess president was free messing, and that was worth another £2, so he was managing a very reasonable income. 'It cost me fifteen to sixteen hours' work a day,' he wrote, 'but that left me plenty of time for sleep and exercise, so it was doing me no harm.' It also left him time for something else: long conversations with Colin Askham about ways of making more. When they were moved from Waterville eighteen months later and sent back to Liverpool, he had saved a thousand pounds. It was this sum which he used to start his next venture.

The thousand pounds was not his only legacy from Ireland. It seems to have been during this period that his distrust of Roman Catholicism began, a distrust that lasted well into old age. John has always been a man who demands total loyalty – to himself, to the team, to the ideals in which he believes. It may be that in Catholicism he discerned a different loyalty and one just as binding as the Protestant work ethic and 'fairness'. At one point, he discovered that a particular department head who was a Roman Catholic was only employing members of his own faith. It was common knowledge: 'You'll never get a job there if you're not a Catholic.' John may well have become concerned that members of any close-knit group within a larger organisation would have divided loyalties and would tend to give promotion and preferential treatment to their own. It is an accusation which from time to time has been levelled at others, at the 'Old Boy' network, at Masons, at Jews, at any minority group with a strong sense of its own identity. As a result, very few Catholics were to reach positions of power or authority in his empire for some considerable time. But he has never had any dislike of Catholics as individuals, and was happy to appoint a personnel director who was a Catholic, but whom he knew to be a man of impartial fairness, who would promote on merit rather than on religious belief.

The explanation for his distrust may be something simpler. There is a story, known to a few close friends and colleagues, that during his stay in Ireland an attempt was made on his life. It seems that he and Colin Askham stayed out later than usual one evening, and when they got back to camp, they discovered that several bullets had been fired through the window into John's bed. Whether these were intended to kill or whether they were warning shots it is difficult to say; even, whether the story itself is true. A further embellishment to it is that the bullets were a message to him to keep away from a young Irish girl whom he had fallen in love with and wanted to marry. She was a Catholic and her family were strongly opposed to the match.

There seems to be no way of verifying the story, but it was recounted at one point by his mother herself. One interesting additional fact is that John returned to the area at a much later stage in his life; he took his children to holiday nearby, at Parknasilla. The place must have held some pleasant memories for him, even if they were only of the golf and the beautiful scenery.

Back in Liverpool, John and Colin were joined by another friend from their Manchester messenger-boy days, Bill Hughes. The three young men were different in many ways; but what they had in common was a desire to make money. Discussing ideas and ways of achieving it was one of their favourite occupations after work had finished.

John had heard about something called a football pool being run by a man named John Jervis Barnard in Birmingham, but without any great success. Bill managed to get hold of one of Barnard's coupons, 'and late one night, when all the cable machines were quiet, we spread this thing out on his supervisor's desk and discussed it'.

Barnard had based his pool on the French *pari mutuel* system of betting, a long-established method in which ten per cent of the total stake is subtracted for management costs, and the rest goes to the winner, or is divided equally amongst the winners. John knew all about it, and for a while they amused themselves by working out just what Barnard would have to do before he started making a profit; how many coupons he would need and what the printing and distribution costs would be. It was not long before they decided that *they* could manage the whole thing much better.

Then suddenly they were in deadly earnest. The idea not only fired them, it had become serious – what was against them starting a football pool of their own?

One point against occurred to them almost immediately – it would be contravening the Cable Company's rules. No outside employment was allowed, and if they were caught setting up another enterprise in their spare time, they would be sacked. The Waterville Supply Company had been a risk, but at least it had provided amenities for Cable Company employees. A football pool would be incontrovertible 'outside employment' and against Cable Company policy. John obviously approved of their dictate, in theory; it was one which he was to incorporate in his own company rule book years later. A retired employee of his explained why it was a fair rule. 'You gave your all to the company. If you had a business outside, you would have worries there which would reflect on your work for the company.' John presumably learnt this from his own personal experience. But sitting around that supervisor's desk, the thought of not being able to give their all to the Cable Company was not a worry which concerned them particularly. What they were worried about was being found out. Clearly, they could not afford to use their own names.

'Well, John Smith's Football Pool is going to sound a bit dodgy,' said John. 'What name can we use?'

After a lot of discussion, they had a bright idea. Colin's original surname would do. His parents had died when he was a baby; he had been brought up by an aunt, a Mrs Askham, and later had adopted her name. But he had been born Colin Henry Littlewood.

Littlewoods Pools was started the next day. It was obviously going to be an expensive project and they decided that they would each have to put up £50 to start it off (£693 in today's values). Bill's job was to find them a printer who would not charge them too much, and even more importantly would be discreet enough not to give them away. They were lucky. Mr Bottomes was the perfect choice; he had a small printing firm in Duke Street, B & P Press, in partnership with a Mr Place, and from the start he took an almost fatherly interest in the three young men. History does not record what he thought of their hare-brained scheme, but at least they were prepared to sink their own savings in it. They were all 'rather pale with excitement' as they met at the bank, each to draw out his £50. John described the feeling. 'As I signed my own cheque, my hands were damp. It seemed so much money to be risking.'

The first expense was renting an office, a little room on the top floor at 38 Church Street, in the centre of Liverpool. That cost 25s a week, the weekly wage of the typist they engaged was about 30s (or £21 in current terms), and by the time everything was organised it was the middle of the season. Their first batch of coupons was to go out in February 1924, and they ordered 4,000 from Mr Bottomes for a start. They were to be distributed outside the football match by the Manchester Bill Posting Company, but a couple of days before, there was an urgent message from its manager. He had only just discovered that his firm would be distributing what he called 'gambling coupons', and he wanted one of the young men to call round immediately.

John's account of their meeting is brief. 'I went round to see him and discovered that he was a fervent Methodist. He looked at me as if I were a visitant from hell.' The manager refused point-blank to allow his company to be involved and there was nothing John could say to make him change his mind. A frantic search for an alternative distributor was unsuccessful, and before they knew where they were, Saturday morning had arrived. John took the coupons to Manchester United's ground himself. Because he had to keep a low profile, he tipped a number of little boys to run round and hand them out. 'I hovered on the fringe of the crowd, torn between the desire to supervise this rather haphazard operation, and fearful of being seen by any official of the Commercial Cable Company.' There was now more reason than ever to be worried about the possibility of losing his job, for a few months earlier he had got married.

Taking a job in Liverpool had meant that he could no longer continue to live with the rest of the family in Droylsden. It was too expensive and time-consuming to travel every day, and it was certainly too far to walk to save the fare, as he had often done in past jobs. Instead he found himself some very pleasant digs across the water with a family called Knowles. Taking lodgers was a new departure for them; they came of fairly prosperous farming stock who had once owned a sizeable acreage near Chester, at Ledsham. Pool Farm had been sold in 1904 by the executors of William Knowles, who was the last of the family to live there, and an old man and a widower when he died. Along with the land went a herd of over fifty cows, sixteen pigs, eighty hens, and ten horses – including 'Captain, dark brown cart horse, five years old, seventeen hands, fit for town work'. And the household items which came under the hammer included things as disparate as salt tubs, beetle-traps and a birch tester bedstead with hangings.

William Albert Knowles, his son, was a clerk in a shipping firm, and he married Annie Maria Margaret Latta. She was a widow with two children, Gertrude (Gertie) and Jack, so William Albert acquired two stepchildren at the same time; and before long he had two of his own as well, William (Bill) and Ruby. Annie Maria's mother seems never really to have accepted these last two grandchildren – like Queen Victoria, she disapproved of second marriages and considered that a widow should remain constant even to a departed spouse. Annie Maria herself died when the last of her four children was quite small and as a result, Ruby was brought up by her half-sister, Gertie. The family seems to have been a close one, however, and all four offspring were fond of each other and of their father. Bill emigrated to New Zealand at the end of the war, married and had a family there. But he and Ruby kept up a correspondence, writing to each other every week for over fifteen years, until they met again.

Ruby was fifteen months older than John Moores; she had been engaged once before, but her fiancé had been killed in the war. She was almost John's height (he was five feet six inches and she was an inch shorter), dark-haired and not conventionally pretty, but with natural dignity and charm. She had an unexpected sense of humour too, and on occasion could clown surprisingly well. Their first meeting was entirely by chance. John had gone for a meal to the State Café in Exchange Street, where Ruby and two of her friends were working as waitresses, and after a certain amount of 'chatting up', and several meals and visits to the State Café later, his attentions were clearly serious. The Knowles family did not disapprove, and when they took the unprecedented step of offering him lodgings, he jumped at it. Perhaps what attracted him most was Ruby's warmth and kindness and her strength of character. She had great integrity, and standards as strongly held as his own. It must have been difficult marrying into such a large and close-knit tribe as the Moores, all of whom almost worshipped their brother. Nobody could ever be good enough for John. But Ruby, although unassuming, almost self-disparaging, could hold her own. And when John proposed, she accepted him.

It is an interesting and continually recurring phenomenon in John's life that major steps in his career often coincided with important happenings in his private life. His marriage is a case in point. He was at the same time embarking on one of the biggest business risks he ever took.

Just how risky it was, and how chancy the outcome, became apparent to the three young men very quickly. Of those 4000 coupons that John had urged his schoolboy team to hand out, only thirty-five came back. The bets totalled exactly £4 7s 6d (the equivalent of £74 now) and the first dividend was £2 12s (£44). The ten per cent deducted did not even cover their expenses, and they had to make good the deficit themselves, but they were determined to try again. Next time they had 10,000 coupons printed, which were all sent to a big match in Hull. Only one came back.

Before long they each had to put another £50 into the kitty. Half-way through the 1924–5 season they were still nowhere near paying their own way; indeed the top gross receipt for that first half, on December 20th, was £79 15s 6d (worth £1,358 today), out of which their ten per cent gave them the princely sum of just under £8. Then they each had to put in another £100 to pay Mr Bottomes' printing bill. It was all getting too much.

Just before Christmas, Bill called an emergency meeting of the triumvirate over canteen lunch and, keeping their voices down, they tried to decide what to do next. Bill, at least, had already decided.

'Let's face it,' he said, 'we've lost nearly £600 between us. It sounded like a good idea, but obviously it will never work. I vote we cut our losses and drop the whole thing.'

Colin nodded. It was sad, but he agreed with Bill. They both looked at John and waited for him to speak. He swallowed and took a deep breath.

'I'll pay you back what you've lost so far – that's £200 each – if you'll sell me your shares in it.'

They both looked totally shocked.

'I still believe in the idea,' he said stubbornly.

In no uncertain terms they told him how rash he was being, and asked him to think it over.

…amily wedding c. 1890. Louisa, second from left, with her three eldest children, John (in sailor's suit),
…el (middle) and Hilda (far right). John William is in the back row, far right.

…n with his two eldest sisters, Hilda and Ethel, in
…ir teens, just before the First World War.

Ruby Knowles as a girl.

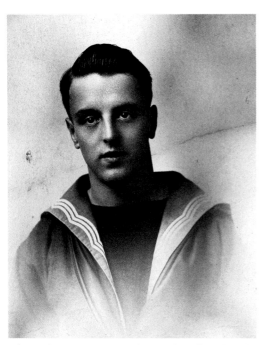

John in his early twenties, not in his naval uniform but the next best thing.

John and Ruby set off on a world cruise in the r Thirties.

John, Ruby, Betty and a very young John Junior at Cliftonville where Betty, in spite of her youth, was already at boarding school.

John steers Betty at an early Littlewoods sports

3

The 'Royal' Family

John was still mulling it over when he got home that night; arguments for and against had been going round his head ever since he had made his offer, and the person he wanted to discuss it with was his wife. They were living at 39 Hahnemann Road in Walton, and Ruby was expecting; she had had an earlier miscarriage but was now pregnant again. The baby was due in about six months, in June, so it was not exactly an opportune moment for the plan he was proposing; but she listened carefully. They went through their finances with a fine-tooth comb, but the only possible boost to their income that they could see was an extra £2 a week if John did overtime for the Cable Company on Sundays.

Ruby seldom told her husband what to do; she was a supportive wife who left major decisions to him. But on the rare occasion when she did put her foot down, she had real authority and, surprisingly, he always did what she said. Her advice now was unequivocal: carry on.

'If you don't,' she said, 'you will never quite convince yourself that another few months might not have turned the tide. I'd sooner be the wife of a man who has gone broke than a man who is haunted by regret.'

That clinched it. Christmas must have been a slightly subdued celebration that year, as belts had to be tightened. Colin and Bill were paid back their £200 each, and the first economy after that was to dismiss the typist – with some reluctance – and to stop renting the little office. In future, all the coupons would have to be checked and dealt with at home. The family rallied round immediately. Every Sunday for the rest of the season, a brother and sister would come over from Manchester and sit down with John and Ruby to do the marking. Between 7,000 and 10,000 coupons take a long time to check, and at the end of the session, his siblings would set off back to Manchester again, and John would go into the cable office for his turn of night duty. The gross receipt for the last week of that season, on May 2nd, 1925, was £54 8s 6d (£925), from which John took his ten per cent, exactly £5 8s 10d, to cover all expenses.

Their daughter, Betty, was born at the beginning of June, and there was great delight in the family over Louisa's first grandchild.

But the next football season was less than three months away and John's pools activity was still an expensive sideline, and still one which could threaten his main job with Commercial Cables. On Betty's birth certificate he enters his occupation firmly as 'commercial telegraphist'. Another decision had to be made – should they soldier on? The issue was never really in doubt, and by the autumn of 1925, brothers and sisters were again coming over to Liverpool on Sundays (John's wish was always their command) and Ruby was cooking meals for them as well as looking after a small baby. The enterprise was still losing money, but on one particular occasion when John went wearily to pay his usual enormous printing bill, Mr Bottomes had a suggestion to make.

'Mr Moores,' he said, 'why are you so intent on this ten per cent? Why don't you take out your actual expenses each week for printing, stamps and stationery, plus a little commission? At least you wouldn't be heading for bankruptcy if you did it that way.'

This comment struck John immediately. He always had a talent for listening attentively to what people said and picking on the vital remark. Indeed, he could have kicked himself for not thinking sooner of the obvious solution. He had been so obsessed with the *pari mutuel* system that he had been blind to the fact that his expenses alone would always be more than ten per cent. He put the idea into practice at once. Cecil was given the extra job of handing out coupons on Saturday at football grounds, as a bag of undistributed coupons had been found stuffed under a seat at one ground and John had decided that the schoolboy helpers were not reliable enough. He even risked his Cable Company job to join Cecil, and the two of them used to stand outside the Manchester United and Manchester City grounds handing out coupons to any of the spectators interested.

This was the time, too, John decided, to start making up a mailing list. Anyone who sent a coupon in had their name and address recorded, and a list was bought from one of the Sunday newspapers. The *People* had been running a competition to see who could forecast the results of various matches. The prizes were not enormous, so the competition was soon discontinued, but the mailing list came in very useful to John and Cecil. They even bought a primitive form of addressing-machine, which printed addresses from an ink roller onto the envelopes, while a treadle was worked – rather like an old-fashioned sewing-machine. Things were improving, and the last receipt of the season this time, taken on May 1st, 1926, was for nearly £258. It was also the day when, after a year of dispute between the miners, the Government and the mine owners, negotiations finally broke down and the miners were locked out. Two days after that, on May 3rd, the General Strike was called.

The strike itself lasted for only nine days, but the miners stayed out for six months. They went back eventually to longer hours and lower wages; there was no money left in the kitty for them to hold out any longer. Indeed, due to handing out strike pay, the funds of most unions had dwindled and union membership fell temporarily too. But wages generally were not affected, apart from those in the coal industry, and there was a more conciliatory spirit on all sides: a reaction against confrontation.

The next few years have been described by one historian as 'a golden age'. Production rose and unemployment fell. This was not particularly noticeable in Liverpool, which had its own unemployment problems, a legacy of its very rapid population increase earlier and a decline in the cotton industry; but one section of the population enjoyed itself. The younger generation, who had grown up since the war, thought that there would never be another, and that they were born to a new age. Women bobbed their hair and shortened their skirts as well. The popular songs were 'Makin' Whoopee' and 'You're the Cream in my Coffee'. (The Moores, and many like them, could seldom afford coffee, let alone take cream in it.) The vote had finally been given to women over thirty in 1918, and in 1928 it was extended to women over twenty-one, the age at which men could vote at that time. Shaw wrote *The Intelligent Woman's Guide to Socialism and Capitalism*, while in the same period Noël Coward was writing *The Young Idea* and composing and writing for Cochran's Revues.

The new style had remarkably little impact on the Moores family, and probably not a great deal on most of the working people of Liverpool. The man in the street took even less notice of certain movements that were stirring on the Continent. Mussolini had formed a Fascist government in 1922, and a year later had dissolved all non-Fascist parties in Italy. In 1924, the leader of the Italian Socialists had been murdered by Fascists, and the same year had seen the death of Lenin in Russia, and Stalin forming an alliance against Trotsky. In 1925, the first volume of *Mein Kampf* had been published.

Like most of his compatriots, John Moores was too busy earning a living to pay much attention. There was no television in those days to spread global news, and the media consisted of a smaller number of newspapers and the 'wireless'. The BBC, which stood then for the British Broadcasting Company, had been founded in 1920; it was not until 1927 that the British Broadcasting Corporation took over. There was still rivalry between the new medium and the Press, and the BBC was not allowed to broadcast news until seven o'clock in the evening. Its output consisted of programmes such as *Children's Hour* – with the presenters called Aunties and Uncles; *The Week's Good Cause* which is still going out and is the longest-running radio programme in the world. The BBC broadcast a great deal of music, both classical and popular, and its late evening dance music from the Carlton and the Savoy, with bandleaders such as Jack Payne and Geraldo, had the listeners at home rolling up the rugs and doing the tango and the foxtrot round their own living-rooms.

John was again working overtime on Sundays, and life was a hard slog. But the pools business was definitely growing; there were too many coupons now for the family to cope with alone, so he again rented a small office and advertised for school-leavers to help.

This office like the first was in Church Street, on the very top floor over King's Café; he took at that stage mostly boys – about ten or twelve – but only a few girls. Two of the boys rose to be directors in the firm. Frank and Eddie had the same surname, Jackson, and were known as 'Red' Jackson and 'Black' Jackson respectively because of the colour of their hair. Frank went to King's Café for a job interview when he was sixteen. His father was a printer who had done some business with B & P Press, who had told him that his son 'couldn't do better than to work for John and Cecil Moores. They were just starting up in business, were great people and you never knew where it might lead.'

He recalled going up the stairs at about half-past eight in the morning, finding the office door locked and sitting on the window-ledge to wait. There was a deep well through the centre of the building and all the floors had windows looking out into it. 'These fellows came up, stopped where I was and said, "Are you the new boy?"' One was Willie Simpson, the senior boy, the other was Bert Phillips, and they all stood there waiting. Suddenly, at about half-past nine, a young man in white flannel trousers and a sports jacket came up the stairs four at a time. This was Cecil – and he had forgotten the office key. The window to Littlewoods' office was at right angles to the one they were all standing by, so Cecil went into action. 'It was quite a drop, but he sprinted up, opened the window, got across and into the office.' The other three, rather gingerly, followed him.

The boys were between fifteen and sixteen; Cecil himself was only twenty-four, so as well as the hard work, there was a slightly madcap air about the whole place. There were also rats!

They may not have worried the boys too much, but the Moores sisters had to brave them as well. Hilda was particularly frightened of rats, and when she wanted to go along the corridor, Edna had to carry her. It was worse at night. If they were working late, the lights would have been put out downstairs, so while Hilda carried the candle, Edna carried Hilda on her back and banged on the iron grille of the lift door to frighten the rats away. She could feel them bumping into her legs. For the occasions when Edna was not available, Hilda kept a box of odd shoes in the office. She would hurl them ahead of her one by one to disperse the creatures, and then collect them up on her way in the next morning.

The fact that John was working somewhere else during the day so was not there all the time was a good thing, in some ways. There was a feeling of 'We'd better be careful, in case he comes.' John was only thirty himself, but 'he was quite frightening even then. He was the Boss.' And it was not long before John came to a momentous decision: not only was he going to take on more girls again, but he was finally going to take the plunge, give up his job with the Cable Company, and devote himself full-time to his own business.

He interviewed the girls himself, 'made sure their handwriting was neat, and that they were quick at figures. I judged their honesty from their faces, and in those early years was seldom wrong.' He gave them homework, too, sums such as twenty-two and a quarter divided by eleven and a half, and offered a prize of 2s 6d for the neatest correct answer. Then he would go home and work out the same sums himself, write the answer neatly, and pin up his version on the blackboard alongside that of the winner. 'Now,' he would say, 'which of us deserves the half-crown?' He also gave the girls very careful instructions never to accept cash for bets, because it was against the law. As long as Littlewoods refused to take ready money, he explained, it was an honest business; but the minute it did, they would all automatically become criminals. 'The girls were duly impressed by this, and made splendid little policewomen for me,' he commented.

It was just as well that he had made the point clear, for now that Littlewoods was becoming more successful it was rousing the interest of various anti-betting organisations. Gambling prompted much stronger reactions in those days, and it was no use explaining that a few pennies a week and an added interest in football would not really harm anybody. The first warning note was sounded when a man pretending to be a butcher came to the door, wearing a blood-stained apron, saying that he had missed the post, and asking if he could hand them his coupon and his stake of a florin. The girls had the sense to refuse, which was just as well, because the episode turned out to have been an attempted set-up.

Soon there was worse trouble on the horizon. The next move was made by the police, who brought a prosecution against John for contravening the Ready-Money Betting Act. Their claim was that a particular phrase in the Act – 'It is an offence to make payment on or for a bet to be determined thereafter' – meant that dealing in football coupons was illegal, and that it was actually against the law even to print them.

The evening before he was due to appear in the magistrates' court, John had a visit from his two ex-partners, Colin and Bill. They wanted to wish him luck and to tell him that they sympathised. They were probably slightly remorseful about having left him to face the music, but also extremely relieved that they had got out in time. They must have felt even greater relief the next day, for the magistrate, Mr Stuart Deacon, agreed with the police, and John Moores and his brother Cecil were convicted. John's stubborn nature was by now roused and he immediately lodged an appeal, to be heard at the next quarter sessions. The recorder considered the evidence carefully, and his appeal was upheld.

It seemed almost too good to be true. They were in the clear. And better still, they had received an enormous amount of valuable free publicity. The case had excited considerable attention and the name of Littlewoods had been spread around. The police, too, had been extremely fair, and had taken trouble to point out in court that although they considered the operation technically illegal, it was run with scrupulous honesty. Honesty is a virtue which John Moores possesses in abundance, and which was impressed on him by his upbringing.

His elder daughter remembers one particular illustration of it: aged about seven or eight, she had heard the post drop onto the mat, and ran to bring it to her father at the breakfast table. As she placed it proudly in front of him, she noticed that the letter on top had not been properly franked.

'Look, Daddy! That stamp hasn't been marked! We can take it off and use it again.'

Quite simply and kindly, he explained to her why this was out of the question.

'When you buy a stamp, you're paying for a service, you see – the delivery of a letter. We've had the service. The letter's been brought to us; here it is, so we can't possibly use the stamp again. That would be dishonest.'

His honesty obviously impressed the British public too, for the number of people doing the pools grew by leaps and bounds. Before the end of the season, in March 1927, there were four different pools; the week's gross takings had risen to over £2,000, and 20,000 coupons were coming in regularly each week. Within a year, that was to rise to 50,000 coupons and bets of over £4,000 a week.

John ploughed the profits back into the business, moved to a larger floor of offices at 44 Whitechapel Street, just across the road from the Post Office, and took on more girls again. Two of his younger brothers, Arthur and Charlie, had gone to try their luck in Australia; their sister, Ethel, had married and was helping her husband to set up his own business; but the rest of the family – Hilda, Lou and Edna, as well as Cecil – now worked full-time for their brother. The fish and chip shop was a thing of the past, and they had all moved to Liverpool. His mother, Louisa, at last able to indulge her passion for pretty china, had opened a china shop in Wallasey. The pools enterprise continued to snowball and in doing so it not only attracted more and more clients, it attracted something else as well – swindlers.

One Monday morning in 1928, while the girls were busy sorting, marking and tabulating, and John was doing his supervising rounds, he noticed something out of place. By a big pile of sorted 'unsuccessful' entries lay one solitary coupon.

'Who dropped this?' he asked.

There was no answer. A few of the girls nearest shook their heads or shrugged; nobody knew anything about it, so John picked it up to check. It was a winner. Every single match result was marked correctly on it and it could have netted somebody about £2,000. There was something odd about this coupon, however, and not just the fact that it should not have been there. In a second or two John realised what it was. If it had gone through all the correct procedures of being taken from its envelope, checked, rechecked, marked and sorted, it would have had pin marks in the top left-hand corner. There were none there; the paper was pristine. Someone had marked it after the match results had come through and tried to palm it off as the real thing. It was a cheat.

'I knew then,' John wrote, 'that what I had feared for four years had at last happened. One of these young girls – all fresh from school and apparently innocent – had succumbed to the persuasion of somebody outside to smuggle in a coupon, forge a "successful line", and had dropped it where she knew it would be found.'

He went into action straight away.

'I made Hilda a chief supervisor, and Lou and Edna, not long out of school themselves, were made into assistant supervisors over the young girl clerks.'

He wrote to his brothers in Australia and asked them to come back and help. 'I knew that I could not afford to be without them now.

It was all getting too big . . .' Then he and Cecil started to devise a security system that was foolproof. One brainwave of Cecil's is still used in the many checking operations today. He knew that it would be eventually almost impossible to stop a determined crook from smuggling a post-match coupon in with the legitimate ones. Thousands were being delivered by post in the proper way, and it would be the work of a moment for somebody in the right place to slip a bogus one in with the others; even to slip one into an empty envelope which had come through the post and been correctly franked like the rest. His solution was to stop the mail being delivered directly to Littlewoods and to have everything sent to the Post Office instead. There, every single item was fed through a special machine (another idea of Cecil's) which punched the time, date and registration, not only onto the sealed envelope, but right through onto the coupon and even onto the postal order inside. It was a modification of a postal franking machine with a metal spine instead of a franking stamp. Not until this had been done were the sacks of mail collected by Littlewoods and the envelopes finally opened.

Later still, when the firm had grown nearer to its present colossal size, it was to have electrified security checkpoints, guard-posts and patrols – its own police force, in fact; and on top of that its own investigation department, staffed by ex-policemen, detective-sergeants and inspectors, to investigate fraudulent claims. Typically, John analysed the psychological aspect of the situation and tried to devise a set-up which would 'eliminate the human element completely during working hours', as he put it. Each group of twenty girls had a supervisor; there was a chief supervisor over each group of supervisors, and an overseer over the chief supervisors. Each girl had her own working space and she had to stay in it; there was no wandering about permitted. A man was never allowed to be in direct supervision over a group of girls, and every male supervisor had to be at least three rungs up the ladder from the girls who actually handled the coupons.

Back in 1928, these sophisticated arrangements were still to come; then, it was the family doing most of the supervising, with one paid supervisor to help them out. Ruby's father was helping too. And Hilda's husband, George, had given up his job as a manager of a Co-op to join them. The two Jacksons and the other boys were even more useful now; they collected the sacks of mail from the Post Office across the way, two to a sack, and half-dragged, half-carried them up the stairs. 'Of course, we *would* be on the top floor again!' as one of them said.

There was the same sort of well in the middle of the building, with a rope and cradle apparatus to haul up loads that were too heavy to get up the stairs. One of the boys' amusements was to take it in turns hauling each other up and down, and it was quite a height.

'One day we'd got this fellow up to the top and were just about to lower him down, when Mr John appeared on the stairs and was coming up to ask us what we were doing. When someone said, "It's Mr John!" we tied the rope and left the chap hanging there. But Mr John just stood at the bottom of the stairs and shouted, "Come on, and get this fellow down before he falls down!"'

One of Edna's jobs was to lug the week's takings to the bank. They were quite a weight by then, but she was a strong girl. Then it was decided that this was no job for a woman, and it would be safer for a man to be in charge of the money. The job was given to George and the cash was put in a large leather bag and chained to his wrist. Edna said, 'Poor George! They thought it might be a good idea if I went with him – to scream or to protect him; because I was strong, I'd have fought for him.' She would have done, too.

Arthur and Charlie had come back from Australia in response to their brother's SOS, but instead of working on the pools floor, they had been put in charge of John's latest brainchild. Littlewoods now had a printing works of its own. Looking ahead as usual, John had decided that it was a waste of money to go on paying enormous printer's bills when they could be printing the coupons themselves. He had bought B & P Press, taken over the floor directly below their offices at 44 Whitechapel, had printing machinery installed, set himself and Cecil in partnership and appointed the faithful Mr Bottomes to run it. From this small start was to grow an enormous printing firm in its own right, J & C Moores, which by the Fifties covered 50,000 square feet in Edge Lane, printing up to 10,000,000 coupons each week. By the Nineties, it had become one of the largest printing companies in the North of England, printing not only for Littlewoods, but for many other organisations as well such as the Post Office, British Rail, various building societies and many major manufacturing firms.

It was 1928 that saw the inception of the printing firm, and it is hardly surprising to note that 1928 was also the year that John and Ruby were expecting another child. The baby, a son, was born on November 22nd, and he was christened John – after his father and grandfather – and as a result, was always referred to for many years as John Junior. On the baby's birth certificate, John Moores registered his occupation as master printer; there was no mention of the pools business.

It is difficult to see how any of the brothers could have received the necessary training as printers, unless they acquired it from Mr Bottomes as they went along. But a trusted and now retired employee, Miss Gaskin, who actually joined the organisation in 1928, remembers: 'We had printing works below in Whitechapel where they printed the coupons; Mr Arthur and Mr Charlie were down there.' Charlie in fact did the night-shifts. 'I think they were qualified printers; I think one of them served an apprenticeship in the printing trade. Mr John would go down and help set up the type if they were busy; he was very versatile and could do almost anything.'

She also remembers the day she was taken on, aged sixteen and three-quarters. Although she had certificates for shorthand and typing, it was difficult to get work in Liverpool at that time, and when she was offered a job by Miss Hilda at 17s 6d a week, she thought it was wonderful. 'Mr John kept his eye on everybody. He walked around while we were opening the post; so did Mr Cecil. They encouraged you to work hard, they were very kind and nice to you – but if you made a mistake . . .! I hadn't been in the company for long when I got a half-crown rise. That was a fortune. And it was always done so nicely. Miss Hilda came along with a little envelope and she said, "Mr John's very pleased with you, he's given you an increase in your wages," and so I got half a crown. I can remember that, it was my first increase I ever got.'

Weekend hours, when the match results were coming in and the coupons being checked, were very long.

'Saturday lasted to one o'clock on Sunday morning and you were back again at nine o'clock to carry on. Sometimes, not always, but quite a bit, you worked to the early hours of Sunday morning. You got overtime for it; you were paid for every quarter of an hour. By the same token, all the family worked as well. They went home after you left. They didn't ask you to do anything they wouldn't do themselves. If you were in a spot with the big sheets, and you couldn't make them balance, either Mr John or Mr Cecil would come along and help. They were working with you and it made you appreciate them.'

The boys worked even longer hours and often used to stay all night folding the coupons. 'It used to be Saturday morning and Mr John used to come out and collar us and say, "Look, we're behind with the billing and folding, could you come in tonight?" We always used to say we could.' In fact one of the Jacksons had made a deal with his mother: she was to get the whole of his 10s a week wage if he was allowed to keep his overtime money. He had heard how much it was likely to be.

As a break in these long shifts, everyone was given four hours off on Saturday afternoon. They were supposed to go home to bed, so that they would not be too tired later that night and on Sunday, but they were nearly all young people and the break was seldom used for that purpose. Boys like 'Red' and 'Black' Jackson would go off to Anfield to watch the match there, and John and Cecil used to play football themselves.

'I don't know where it was or what club they played for, but they used to come back in their football gear, and of course they were all dirty. We had a boiler-man named Joe Clark, who used to take boiling water from the boiler and a tin bath up to the office, and they'd have a bath. Then they would be spruce enough to go on the pools floor on a Saturday night. You see, they had to be there, because as soon as the results came through on tape, they had to take them down and give them to us so that we could get on with the marking.'

The two younger sisters had organised their own Saturday afternoon routine. Another early member of the firm, Miss Price, described it: 'Miss Louie and Miss Edna used to go up to Sissons in Bold Street and buy all those gooey cream cakes we wouldn't dream of buying; they were too expensive for poor little typists. They'd bring back boxes and boxes of them on a Saturday. We supplied our own tea and we took our own sandwiches, but at nine o'clock, when we were still there on a Saturday night, these cakes were handed round, and boxes of chocolates, which we'd never thought about buying. Miss Louie and Miss Edna, if you didn't like a thing, they'd want you to say you didn't like it. They were always ready to listen, they were always keen to please you. I think the whole family was like that.'

At the end of each football season, John would take the whole of the work-force to the local cinema as a treat; he made sure they had a Christmas party too, at which the usual high spirits were unleashed. 'The boys (Clifford Appleton, Frank Jackson and Clifford Clare) were the worst . . . because they'd throw pens at the dartboard; we used "dip pens" in those days. Clifford Clare used to chase you round the cloakroom to get a kiss under the mistletoe. When Mr John came on the floor, we used to sing "Oh, Johnny! Oh, Johnny! How you can love!" He liked it. He always came to our parties. We used to have the odd bottle of port in those days, but he told us to be very careful when the youngsters were around. He would supply the drinks, but I never saw Mr John with more than a glass of wine.'

43

Another matter to which John turned his attention was organising something for the slack period between the end of one football season and the beginning of the next. He could not afford to keep on all his young typists doing nothing, and to get rid of them for three months every year would have been treating them as part-time or seasonal workers; added to which they were all extremely keen to stay in the job. A good interim employment seemed to be to turn the organised pools system to other forms of betting.

Dog-racing was one of the options he tried, and for a while Cecil used to go off to Stanley Greyhound Track as a temporary bookie and set up a large board with the name of Littlewoods emblazoned on it. He was accompanied on these occasions by a Mr Smith. 'Smithy', as he was nicknamed, was an ex-bookmaker's clerk and knew the ropes. 'He was quite a character,' as one contemporary remarked. 'You never saw a fella with such beautiful handwriting.'

It was not long before John had decided to drop the dog-racing and set up a racing business on the horses. It was kept quite separate from pools and called H Littlewood Ltd. The racing season filled the gap perfectly, from the Grand National to the Manchester November Handicap. Smithy was to be put in charge of the operation which included instructing the others, as he was the only one who knew how to calculate the bets. In those days there were no betting shops and ready-money bets on horses were only legal in Scotland; the racing business in England was a credit business. Unfortunately Smithy's skills as a teacher were not quite up to his racing know-how. John had to take on the job of instructor again – explaining the intricacies of singles, doubles, trebles and Yankees.

Frank Jackson commented, 'Mr John had such a good brain, he could do it and pass it on to us. As a teacher he was very good and very precise. There was a mixed bag of us, females and males. He was very patient with the one or two who didn't cotton on – they just did typing.'

The able did both. Miss Gaskin, for example, was quite capable of picking up the betting calculations. Her clearest memory is of her boss standing by the blackboard and saying, 'Sixpence each way on Acorn.' She remembered it particularly because she thought it was a very funny name for a horse. Typists like her were put onto the accounts machine and had to work out bets as well. 'It was sort of two jobs at once.'

Girls who had not been trained as typists were offered a secretarial course at a college in Bold Street. They had to go in the evenings in their spare time, but John paid for them. Most were only too pleased to grab the chance; a commercial course was expensive and more than they could have afforded themselves. John could never bear talent to be wasted or people to be denied opportunity. And, of course, chances offered to members of his work-force often benefited him indirectly as well. As in every good relationship, even a marriage, both sides have to be getting something out of it for the relationship to work. And this one worked very well.

John had created a powerful team, helped by his family, of course – indeed, his family were its strength.

'He was a man that inspired loyalty,' one worker said. 'The whole family did. We called them the royal family – we used to refer to them like that.' And John always referred to his female employees as 'my girls'. As one of them said, 'We got to the stage years later that we were rather elderly girls, but he still called us "girls". He was an excellent man to work for.'

This was the team that he was leading into the Thirties, into a growth and expansion so rapid and enormous that even he must have been surprised by it. At the same time, the country was heading into the great Depression.

4

First Million, Second Business

The world slump of 1929 to 1934 was worse than any that had been seen before; prosperity and employment plummeted. First, round about 1928, there had been a fall in agricultural prices. Competition from Soviet Russia caused a drop in the value of timber; over-production of wheat in the USA and Canada affected farmers world-wide. There was speculation on various exchanges and a financial collapse, notably in the USA, with the panic of the Wall Street Crash in 1929. The withdrawal of American money from Europe affected French bankers, who in turn were forced to cease short-term loans to a major Austrian bank, which was then unable to meet its obligations. Its collapse hit Central and Eastern Europe, and the German banks postponed payment of debts to foreign investors, a great many of them British bankers. There was a heavy run on the pound.

Lack of capital meant that there were fewer imports. This hit the export trade and factories had to be closed; and as fewer goods were being transported, shipping and shipbuilding were affected. Country after country abandoned the gold standard. Everywhere there was mass unemployment – 13.7 million in the USA, 5.6 million in Germany, 2.8 million in Britain – one man in every three was out of a job in Liverpool alone.

In the same period, John Moores was taking on more and more staff every week. Littlewoods was not yet the biggest employer on Merseyside that it currently is, with a UK work-force of 30,000, but even in those days it provided jobs for over 10,000, which helped the unemployment problem. The length of the dole queues and the hardship that many were enduring seemed to have no effect on the rush to bet on the pools; it may even have been a small but necessary distraction for a lot of people. In the 1929–30 season, the total weekly pool jumped to over £19,000 for two weeks running; by 1931, it was nearly £47,000; by the 1934–5 season, it was over £200,000 – the equivalent of more than £4m. in modern terms.

The obvious popularity of the enterprise began to attract imitators, and soon there were competitors in the field. Vernons Pools was started in 1929, also in Liverpool; three years after that, Soccer Pools, in Leicester; a year later, in 1933, Zetters Pools in London; and in 1935, Empire Pools in Blackpool. None of them affected the popularity or the growth of Littlewoods, and probably the competition was good for all of them. It was certainly good for the industry as a whole.

One effect this speedy expansion did have on Littlewoods was to produce a continuous and urgent need for more and more space. The office at 44 Whitechapel was used for only about eighteen months before it became too small for the firm's requirements; then the horse-racing section was transferred to a building at 34 Pall Mall, previously the Palatine Engraving Company. The printing works was moved to Brownlow Hill, and the football pools went to Hood Street. A whole building was taken over here; it had been a tobacco factory and at first seemed very spacious, but soon another had to be acquired, just across the street from the first. There was an underground tunnel connecting the two properties, and this turned out to be infested with rats with long greasy fur – obviously Liverpool's endemic rodent in those days. Lou, who was helping to run Hood Street, used to describe them as 'tobacco rats'.

The previous year's coupons had been stacked in a storeroom in the first building, and when the second building was bought John suggested that Edna get the girls to store the coupons over in the new premises. As this meant carrying them through the tunnel, he was obviously rather chary of asking the girls himself. It took several journeys, and Edna led the way each time with loud Red Indian war whoops. 'We used to run down and across with the bundles, making a noise to frighten the rats, and we'd get across to the other side all right. Once, we found all these nests of baby rats; the place was infested.'

The tunnel was cleared of rats as soon as possible, and a connecting bridge was built over the road between the two buildings. The Hood Street premises stayed in the firm for many years, but extra property had to be bought as well. New buildings were constantly being acquired, and either kept for long periods or disposed of fairly quickly. They would be used for one particular activity for a while and then another would take over; often several activities might be going on in the same building. Williamson Street housed a subsidiary of Littlewoods called Bonds Pools, run for a while as a stand-by. Premises in Leeds Street were used by the horse-racing section, H Littlewood Ltd, which in March 1938 took over a small engineering works in Walton Hall Avenue, later to become the headquarters of the pools. Finally Edge Lane was built, larger pools premises still, and almost opposite an enormous printing works was set up for J & C Moores.

This continuous movement was paralleled in the private lives of the Moores family members. John led the way, as usual. In 1930 he bought a modest four-bedroomed house to the north of the city in Freshfield, which is an extension of the middle-class suburb of Formby. Although it was only half an hour to the city by train from the small country railway station, Freshfield was still very much a village. John was a rich man by now, but he was as careful as ever with money, and bought through a building society.

The house, called Fairways, was pleasant, but not particularly aesthetically pleasing. He once said, 'What more does a man want than three square meals a day and a roof over his head?' Which generally summed up his approach to architecture at the time. The house was at the end of a cinder track with few other houses nearby. It looked directly over the golf-links – hence its name – which were only a few yards away across the road, and it backed onto an expanse of open uncultivated land or waste ground. It was also a few minutes' drive from miles of sandhills and unspoilt beach. John always loved the sea – not to travel by, as he is not a particularly good sailor, but to walk beside.

Soon afterwards he bought a house nearby for his mother, very much of the same type, and installed Louisa there. It was within walking distance in Larkhill Lane, nearer still to the sea and in an even less built-up area. As the land drains that ran along it were still open ditches, the entrance to the house was over a little bridge. The pine woods started at the end of the back garden and stretched right down to the sandhills, half a mile away. The woods were the home of a colony of red squirrels, and still are – although the species is becoming rarer and rarer in Britain.

The rest of the family followed him; and for the next few years all of them were constantly moving house; always up-market. Cecil had married in 1930, and he and his wife Doris finally settled in an Edwardian mansion with extensive grounds in Victoria Road; Hilda and George in a large house in Birkdale, nearer to Southport; Lou and her husband Len in a big detached house with a newly-built oak-panelled 'music room', very near to Cecil's house. Some houses had built-in cocktail bars, which were considered smart at the time. All had grand pianos, too, and one even a pianola.

The family were definitely 'moving up', mainly at the instigation of the women members, as is frequently the case. They were always proud of being Lancashire, and were not in the least snobs, in the usual sense of the word. They never considered themselves 'above' anybody; but they were ambitious, they had a certain style, and they were learning. Auntie Carrie and Auntie Lizzie became Aunt Carol and Aunt Beth. Manchester accents were modified slightly. Edna was a talented amateur actress and she learnt to dance as well as to speak 'musically'. Her name also underwent a change, and from then on she was called Joy, the nickname she had been given at dancing class because of her *joie de vivre*.

John remained aloof from these upwardly mobile home removals. He stayed where he was, at Fairways. Ruby was neither fashion-conscious nor status-conscious, or if she had ever shown either of these tendencies, John had discouraged them. And the house was perfectly placed for him. It was a few minutes' walk from the prestigious Formby Golf Club, which he joined in 1931 (gaining membership could be tricky even as late as the 1960s).

Although he continued to play football until he was forty, golf was now the game which interested him most. 'It was a science to him, it wasn't just learning how to play. He had to work out how the pros did it, and he got good at golf like all the other things he did.' And Fairways had a golf-course on the doorstep. The approach to Formby's seventeenth green lay parallel to his front garden, and as he passed his home on his way to the last hole at the end of his Sunday morning round, he would wave. Ruby or someone in the household would be looking out for him, and lunch could be timed exactly. Ruby herself was always warmly hospitable to any of the work-force who delivered or called for anything, and her idea of welcome was tea in the kitchen, while she kept her apron on. And she still warmed John's slippers and put them out for him when he got home at night.

Although he hated any form of showing off – 'a man has to know how to carry corn' – and even when an eighty-year-old billionaire, still insisted that he was 'an ordinary working man', John was an expert at having his cake and eating it. It was not a conscious ploy, but somehow he always managed to remain a man of the people while at the same time always getting exactly what he wanted.

He did, indeed, continue to live unostentatiously, but his 'modest four-bedroomed house' was added to over the years and became a somewhat larger, if still unassuming, residence. The garden grew in the same way. An adjoining field to the south was bought in 1933, a strip to the east in 1939, and the 'large field to the east' as late as 1955. A series of ornamental ponds was made at the end of one of the lawns; there was a hard tennis-court, and nearby a separate building which housed a squash-court. It was still far from being the palatial millionaire's home that people might have expected, but it was the way he wanted it. In the early years, although John was already wealthy, it was he and his family who helped to make the gardens themselves. There were countless weeding sessions over the lawns which were gradually replacing the field. When her grandmother and youngest aunt were visiting Fairways, Betty used to be sent in by her father to call them out to work. 'Daisy-picking, Granny!' was the summons.

What he wanted, when he wanted it – these were the perks his money brought him. His wants were still simple even when he became rich and powerful, as he has always claimed. What he has perhaps never acknowledged, even to himself, is that by then, simple though his wants may have been, they were always immediately gratified. If he mentioned a particular sort of paint-brush which he needed, for example, it would be there – even if a minion had to be despatched to Brussels to the only firm that could be traced which made them.

Now he and the family were beginning to enjoy more of the pleasures of life, John made sure that his work-force – in a way, his extended family – were being looked after as well. The move to Hood Street saw the installation of a canteen: bright, clean, airy, with good food at rock-bottom prices – subsidised prices, in fact. Everyone ate there, from managers to the newest office-boy. There was free milk for everyone on winter mornings, and orange juice in the summer. A welfare department was established.

'That wasn't the normal run of things in those days,' as one of the firm's early employees said. 'Only people like the Levers or Cadburys or Frys or those big firms, mostly Quakers, had welfare departments and canteens, so we felt it was something really good.' They did, of course, work extremely long hours at certain times of the week, and needed hot food and somewhere comfortable to sit, but it was not only this side of their welfare that John considered: 'Anything to do with sports and social he was keen on.' He bought a sports ground, the White Star Sports Ground at Picton Clock, Wavertree, where the staff could play football, bowls, cricket and tennis. There was a social club too, in Bold Street over Smart's, the furniture shop. Alcohol was not obtainable on the premises, but a host of other things were, from ballroom dancing to snooker matches. And the membership fee for both clubs together was 3*d* a week. All these activities were to grow and proliferate during the Thirties, but even in their small beginnings they were an oasis in the bleak Depression years at the beginning of the decade.

It was the hardship and poverty prevalent in these years of unemployment that were to lead to John's next venture.

According to his own account, he was playing golf one day with his brother Cecil. 'It was a fresh, lovely day and I was counting my blessings. I had a pleasant four-bedroomed house near my favourite golf-links. I had a nice car waiting for me at the clubhouse, to whisk me home. My wife had a maid to help her with the housework, and could have had two if she wished.' He was only thirty-five and he was already a millionaire. But something was bothering him, and he confided in his brother.

'Cecil, do you think we've been rather lucky? Was it all a fluke? If we'd gone into any other sort of business, d'you think we'd have done as well?'

This amused Cecil, but he could see that his brother was serious. There was obviously only one answer, he said, and that was to start from scratch in another line altogether and see how that business went. Which was exactly what John decided to do. He remembered the little mail-order firm he started as a telegraph clerk in Ireland, the Waterville Supply Company, and he made up his mind there and then that mail order would be his next venture. If he could make another million from nothing, then that would prove it was more than luck.

Success had to be due to application. It could not simply be the result of luck, because that would call in question the work ethic, and hard work has always been one of his great creeds.

'Any person who is prepared to work five or ten per cent harder than the next man is bound to succeed. The man who wants to get on in life must be prepared to put in that bit extra. The man who gets on does so not only because of the quality of his character, but also because of his readiness to sacrifice himself and to impose upon himself self-discipline.'

Many years later, when he was knighted, he was still standing by his conviction that it was enterprise rather than luck which matters. The motto he chose for his coat-of-arms was 'Opportunity made, not found'.

His story of sudden inspiration on the golf-course is dramatic and entertaining, and although a reaction against 'luck' may have been the trigger for the new venture, the nature of the enterprise and the form it was to take must have been growing at the back of his mind for some time. There were already eighteen small but flourishing mail-order firms in the country. Great Universal Stores was just starting up – in fact these two giants have been friendly rivals ever since. But the way John was thinking of running his mail-order firm was not one of the usually accepted ways, and he wanted advice.

His first step was to go to the public library to see if there were any books on the subject. He found one by a man called Max Ritson, an advertising agent, who lived in London. John was on the train to London the next day. He wanted to ask the expert whether he should organise a mail-order business for cash or credit like the others, or whether 'to try and form thousands of little clubs, where the members paid, say, one shilling each and drew lots as to who should receive the first pound's worth first'.

The idea of clubs had been around for centuries. The earliest were those run by the Church, enabling people to put enough by each week to ensure that they had a decent burial. The guilds founded by different trades were a form of club. The Co-operative movement, started by the Rochdale Society of Equitable Pioneers, was in a sense a club: it was cheaper for a group to collect money together and buy direct from the factory. Another institution which helped the poorer working class, particularly in the textile areas of the North, was the tallyman. He would have a group of customers in a district, rather than a club with members, and would knock on doors to sell the housewife bedding or clothing, collecting a shilling a week and charging a little extra for credit. It was the only way that many poorer families could keep their children in shoes or have enough blankets on the bed.

John knew all about the difficulties of a large family and a low income from his own youth. His originality lay in applying a mix of the club or tallyman principle to a large-scale business enterprise. The idea came to him partly because he wished to help others. He has always been a caring man, particularly in areas which he could understand from his own experiences; but with that extraordinary range of observation which is typical of him, he saw too a vast untapped market. 'An enlightened self-interest is the best interest anyone can have,' is one of his maxims. The pools, although thriving, was always at risk from the anti-betting lobby, which was a continual worry. He was also not unaware of the fact that the enormous mailing list from his pools business could come in very useful when building up a mail-order clientele.

Max Ritson immediately seized on the opportunities the list provided. It could be used to find out what people wanted. Mail order for cash or a club system? People could choose. 'Why not take two batches, each of 10,000 names, from amongst your football pool clients and ask then through the mails which they'd prefer?' he suggested.

John took his advice. It was, in fact, an early example of direct mail testing, now a widely-used method. One colleague from that period recalls that as well as acting on it at once, he also expressed his appreciation: 'Max Ritson – see he gets £500 a year.' The results of the questionnaire were fascinating. 'They showed overwhelmingly that the "twenty-week-club" idea was preferred.'

John had demonstrated his customary shrewdness in assessing the situation; now came the job of putting his idea into practice. The details were worked out meticulously. Letters were to be sent inviting people to become 'organisers', and each organiser was to collect a group of relatives and friends, up to twenty in number, to form a club. Members would pay one or two shillings weekly, and each week the organiser would collect their payments and order one to two pounds' worth of goods. Members had to draw lots to decide in which order they were to receive their merchandise – which led to the clubs being called 'turns clubs'. The mail-order company would receive cash with the order each week, and all members, except the one whose turn was last, would get what they ordered before they had finished paying for it. The organisers' perk was a discount off the value of their own personal order. Littlewoods' perk was that they were dealing with a series of cash transactions, and financing credit for nobody.

As usual, all the family were to be involved. And, also as usual, John was embarking on this new enterprise just as Ruby was about to have another child – their third.

Littlewoods Mail Order Stores was incorporated on January 23rd, 1932, two days before John's thirty-sixth birthday. On April 9th, another son, Peter, was born. John handed over the running of the pools to Cecil; their brother Arthur was deputed to get catalogues flown in from mail-order companies all over the English-speaking world. John himself made sure that they had a catalogue from each of the eighteen British mail-order companies which Max Ritson had told him about.

As John recalled: 'We took all these catalogues to our mother's house. I asked the rest of the family to be there too. It was almost like the old days, when we all used to gather round the fire in the winter evenings, marking football coupons, while mother brewed tea and made sandwiches for us. Only now we were millionaires . . . But at mother's sensible, unaffected fireside, one could easily forget that. And the whole art of being happy, although a millionaire, is not to think too much about it, I have found.' What followed was typical of the man. He had already planned the steps of his campaign. The people involved may have been members of his family; campaign headquarters may have been his mother's house; but his approach was a structured and ordered one. In its own way, it was the formal research and development of a business project.

The first thing John wanted was all the boys' clothing and

menswear advertisements cut out of the catalogues. There was no table big enough, so everyone got down on hands and knees on the floor and went into action with scissors. The next step was to paste all the cut-outs onto sheets of cardboard. Finally came the choices. The women in the family were each asked what they would choose from the boys' wear for their sons, and the men were asked what they would pick for themselves from the menswear. Having got that sorted out, John took the results and set off with them for Leeds; for the simple reason, as he said, 'It seemed to me the place where such goods were mostly made.' His list of wholesalers was taken from the *Classified Directory*, which he consulted in the Post Office when he arrived. 'Surprisingly, most of the firms were patient with me, and I arranged to buy various batches of garments, two or three dozen at a time.'

Arthur was given the job of preparing an illustrated catalogue. He did this by picking all the items from other firms' catalogues which had been admired by the family, checking that the wholesalers could still supply them if ordered, and building the catalogue around them. It was a much smaller version of the ones that were to follow later, about the size of a library book, but like all those early catalogues, its price structure was determined by the fact that each organiser would be spending 20s a week, so the bulk of the goods had to be either 5s, 10s, 15s or 20s. Looking at it today, it is amazing to see oak dressing-tables at £1, fox fur stoles also at £1, smart day frocks at 10s each, and folding push-chairs and carpet-sweepers at the same price.

Like the later catalogues, it had John's photograph at the beginning and a personal message from him. It was Arthur who insisted on this. He was determined that a 'personality' was what was needed, and John was dragged unwillingly to the photographer's. The first effort looks extremely posed, and John's hair is slicked down, smooth and flat.

'You've got it scraped back like an old-fashioned school-marm,' Arthur said. 'Here, borrow my comb and loosen it up, then for heaven's sake let's try again.'

Later catalogues show him in more characteristic casual attire, and more relaxed in his message. On that first title page he faces the reader, pen in hand, his stiff collar and carefully knotted tie impeccable, and underneath, in a reproduction of his own handwriting, is the message: 'I personally invite you to become a Littlewoods Club Organiser – John Moores.'

The catalogue was only one of the things that had to be organised. There was also the question of staff and premises. Edna was asked to select four sensible girls from the pools division, and John himself picked a cash department supervisor, called Miss Carr. They bought a typewriter, and rented a room in Whitechapel at £3 a week. John was determined to see what he could do, starting from scratch, although it has to be mentioned that this time he did start with a share capital of £20,000.

That first week, 20,000 letters were sent out in a recruitment drive. There were 245 replies asking for more information. After details had been posted, there was a long pause – then seventeen organisers announced that they had formed clubs. The first week's takings from those seventeen clubs was £35. It was just like the beginning of the pools all over again, except that this time John found it easier to stick with his hunch.

'And instinct proved again to be correct, for within a fortnight, out of 245 original enquiries, nearly eighty more had formed the necessary clubs with no further urging from me. All they had needed, apparently, was a little more time.'

John was enjoying himself. He was a great leader and liked nothing better than inspiring a small team to fight against the odds, but he did think that perhaps at this stage he needed to employ an assistant more experienced in the field. Harry Gemmell applied, and remembered his interview well.

'For a start I couldn't get up the stairs because a fellow with his coat off was struggling up them with a crate of crockery or something. I asked him who he was and he said he believed he was the head buyer. Then I was shown into a room containing a desk and a table. "This table," I was told, "is the boardroom and that desk is the buying office." You could have bought the lot for £30.'

But Mr Gemmell took the job and stayed on to become an executive.

The top floor of a building or rooms up a flight of stairs always seem to have been the sites John selected for the start of his enterprises, perhaps because he had discovered that they were cheaper to rent. Another early arrival had a tale to tell on that score. In July, six months after its start, Frank Mumford joined the mail-order firm at the age of fifteen, and was taken on as a porter. He had done a shorthand, typing and bookkeeping course at Barrow-in-Fleet Technical School – known in the recession as the Dole School, because it was patronised by large numbers of the unemployed trying to acquire new skills in the hope of getting a job. He was certainly qualified enough to be a porter, but apparently there was one particular qualification you had to have, otherwise you were not taken on. You had to be able to carry two spring mattresses at once up a steep flight of stairs, and you were tested to make sure. Frank was physically strong enough and he got the job on a fortnight's trial. His interview was with the warehouse manager, but he met the Boss in the first week.

'I was staggering up these narrow stairs carrying a settee on my back, just a bit too much really, and I felt someone helping at the back. So I said, "Thanks very much, mate," and staggered on up. Who was it at the back? Mr John. That gave me an idea of the company I was in.'

Frank's fortnight was soon extended, and his next job was helping to transfer merchandise to the new warehouse, none other than 34 Pall Mall, Liverpool, which the horse-racing section had vacated to make room for it. After the very cramped office suite which had been used for warehousing in Whitechapel, it seemed amazingly spacious. 'The warehouse itself would fit into one floor of the mills we've got now, but we thought it was spacious then.'

Soon he was promoted to order picker, a job which entailed pushing a very large trolley round the floor of the warehouse; loading it on the way with merchandise selected from the racks to meet a particular batch of orders; and then pushing the lot to the despatch section, unloading it and sending the items down a chute. The trolley carried about half a ton of stuff at a time and could only just fit between the racks full of sets of china, cobblers' tools and heavy goods. As it was very weighty, it took some heaving to get going; worse still, once it was moving, it was even more difficult to stop.

'So I'd got this thing going – I was doing a fair pace because we were on bonus, of course, and the faster we worked, the better – and to my horror, a figure came round the corner of these racks, engrossed in thought, and didn't hear this thundering trolley approaching. I couldn't see properly because it was loaded too high, I was just pushing, you know, shouting "Gangway! Gangway!" And as I tore past, I saw this figure dive into a blanket-rack head first.' When Frank managed to stop and turn back, he discovered that the man he had nearly run down was his employer. 'I thought, "Oh well, I've had it now. Might as well pick up my cards at once." But when I'd helped him out, the only thing Mr John said was, "Thanks very much. Keep going!"'

It was like the beginning of the pools business all over again – a good team, with everyone mucking in, bosses included. It was hard work; all orders had to be cleared before the staff went home on Friday, which meant sometimes working until eleven o'clock at night; but at the end of the hard work, everyone would enjoy themselves together. Christmas was the special time, and Cecil would come over from the pools division and join in. Frank Mumford had what he called a 'fond memory' of it.

'We never had any means of throwing a party of any kind, so what Mr John and Mr Cecil used to do was buy a few bottles of port and sherry. We'd bring some glasses out of the stock, clean them, and Mr John and Mr Cecil would pour it out and we'd have a drink. I remember vividly that once, Mr Cecil was left without a glass and he said, "Don't open another box." He drank out of the teapot which was being used to dispense the port. Out o't'spout!'

Just as the pools business had done, mail order too was taking off. At the end of the first year the turnover was £100,000. John sailed for New York, the first of many trips to the States, and went to see Sears Roebuck and Montgomery Ward of Chicago, which he had been told were the biggest and most prosperous mail-order firms in America. He had no contacts and no letters of introduction, but both companies were enormously helpful. 'They were delighted to think that a businessman from England should have come, as they put it, "all that way", to see how they did things.' They showed him everything. He was very impressed by their enormous warehouses 'where youths on roller-skates whizzed along the shelves, picking out items from bins that bore grade labels like some vast library index'. When he came home, his suitcase was full – 'with samples of their mail-order indexes, tickets, systems, charts – everything'. By the end of 1934, their second year, the Littlewoods mail-order turnover had risen fourfold to £400,000.

John decided to give a party in London for the club organis-ers. Several dozen names were picked at random, and a splendid cross-section responded to the invitation. 'One was a charlady from Yorkshire. There was a council labourer and his wife, a baker's wife from Islington, the wife of a solicitor, and a clergyman's housekeeper,' amongst others. What impressed John most were the reasons why each of them enjoyed being an organiser. There were many testimonials to the financial side: 'When I draw this commission I will have earned enough money to pay for having my home laid on with electric light'; 'I have four sons . . . I could not afford to buy some things out of a week's wages and that's where I find the commission very useful'; 'I have had a new sewing-machine with my commission . . .' But even more than this aspect of the role, what they enjoyed was the social side – the weekly meetings, the people they got to know. As one of them said to John, 'My doorbell seldom used to ring, but it goes constantly these days. I've made scores of new friends, and we've always got something to talk about.' There was an even better testimonial: 'Through the common interest of running Littlewoods mail-order clubs, I met a girl whom I'm about to marry very shortly.'

John was not slow in altering his publicity and his method of appeal. People were no longer approached to 'form a Littlewoods club and make money'; they were asked to 'organise a Littlewoods club and make friends'. The symbol of the handshake and the 'Happy Circle' was born.

John summed it up. 'Money, you see, is not everything. I had known it for years, but it was nevertheless enlightening to discover that so many other people knew it too.'

Not 'everything', possibly, but by early 1936, mail order was grossing £4m. a year, and John had made his second million. So much for luck.

5

Expanding Horizons

As the Thirties progressed, so did the Moores family. Their horizons expanded, and their world became a bigger and more exciting place. They still remained provincials, but rich provincials who visited London fairly frequently, and whose hotels were the Savoy or the Dorchester.

The London of those years was an even more fashionable city than it is today. Britain had recovered from its financial crisis ahead of the United States and France, and rich Americans in search of pleasure found London, with its Season and its Court occasions, irresistible. The great fashion houses were still in Paris, but French couturiers opened branches in London, and there was even an indigenous but internationally-known designer called Norman Hartnell, with a salon in Bruton Street. Opera was going through a revival at Covent Garden, under the artistic directorship of Sir Thomas Beecham. There were concerts conducted by Sir Henry Wood and Toscanini, there were theatrical first nights with Noël Coward, Evelyn Laye and Gertrude Lawrence; there was tennis at Wimbledon, rowing at Henley, and racing at Ascot, Newmarket and Goodwood. There were smart restaurants such as Pruniers, Quaglinos and the Ivy. There was plenty to enjoy, although it was the racing, the restaurants and the fashion which appealed to the Moores most at this stage.

Fly-fishing was John's latest sporting interest, shared by Cecil and very soon by the rest of the family. A long lease was taken on Loch Grannoch, a trout loch in Galloway, and fishing holidays became the order of the day. The place was very popular with the children of the family too, and they and their young cousins used to be taken up to Scotland in batches in the summer. The drill was to drive up to Gatehouse of Fleet, have a large meal at the Galloway Arms, then drive to the viaduct, which was as far as the road went, and leave the various cars parked there for the duration. The party would then set off on the climb over the moors and down into the dip between the hills where the loch lay. It was hard walking for nearly three miles, with a pony and small two-wheeled cart to take the luggage. Louisa was getting a little too old to tramp the distance, so when she accompanied any of her offspring and their families, a chair would be placed in the cart for her and she would sit in that, sometimes with a sunshade up, but more frequently with an umbrella to protect her from the rain. Very small children would make the trip in panniers on either side of the pony.

There was a cook in residence, once they reached the lodge, and two ghillies, but it was a slightly primitive and far from luxurious holiday – which was probably what appealed. When dusk fell, the lighting was provided by paraffin lamps. And although the bathwater was hot, it was dark brown in colour; it came from the burn which flowed through peat and it was the softest, silkiest water in the world. The children's job, if they were big enough, was to bring in the peat for the fires. That, and freshly-caught trout for breakfast and the chance to run slightly wild, made it irresistible.

Holidays were taken farther afield too, and the South of France was the favoured area. Cecil was the leader in this, and a man of great *bonhomie*, but where he would take his family and friends to the fashionable Cannes, John patronised Bandol, a small town of no great distinction on the Mediterranean coast. He was always less ostentatious than Cecil and he was always more penny-pinching – or penny-wise, depending on one's point of view. Cecil was generous to a fault; at one time, if he offered you a cigarette and you accepted, he would immediately grab four or five from his cigarette-case and press those on you too. He always seemed to know if impecunious young nieces or nephews were doing Europe on the cheap, and they would get a call at their Left Bank *pension*, asking them out to a splendid dinner. As one of them said, 'He was what uncles are supposed to be like.' John often gave quietly, and would give time and thought as well as money. He tried to help people to help themselves. If someone was in debt, he would pay off half the amount for them, on condition that they saved enough weekly to pay off the rest themselves. The brothers' holiday styles were equally different: Cecil went for what he could enjoy, John for what he could learn.

To begin with they were all innocents abroad. Two of the sisters had been taken to France for the first time by their mother, along with two sisters-in-law. They had stared in amazement through the windows of their sleeping compartment when the train stopped at a station, at the sight of French soldiers, each with a long loaf under his arm, queuing for a *pissoir*. Then, to the girls' horror, they took the bread inside with them, 'and you could still see their feet!' The 'girls' were all married women, but they got down from the window immediately when sternly told to do so by Louisa. By the end of the decade, however, they had become more sophisticated.

John's trips to America were on business, although he often took Ruby with him; his explorations of Europe were intended as holidays.

He was always a great walker and had been on several walking tours in France with Colin Askham – what we would now call backpacking. Ruby had been left at home on these occasions with the small children, but with help in the house. When John did start to take the family on holiday, it was never exactly for relaxation. His world cruise in 1935 included Ruby, her father, two of their children, his mother and his youngest sister, Edna, or Joy as she was now called. In her mid-twenties and not yet married, she had stopped working at Littlewoods because she had refused to 'clock on'. John had only latterly introduced the clocking-on system, and having toiled all hours for her brother since leaving school, Joy jibbed. She took it as a lack of trust. In fact, it was an expression of John's obsession with time. Time is even more important to him than money, and it must never be wasted.

The system was in operation at Littlewoods as late as 1980, and everyone clocked on, from top directors down. As it happened, Joy's leaving when she did probably suited him very well, as it meant that she would now be at home with their mother, and Louisa would have someone to drive her about and look after her. Her inclusion in the cruise had the same sort of all-round benefit: Joy saw something of the world; Louisa, who loved cruises, had a beloved daughter to keep her company and look after her; while the children, aged six and nine, got an unpaid nanny. The youngest child Peter, aged three, was left behind in the care of various relations, so Ruby also got a slight break; more importantly, and for her one of the main objects of the expedition, she was at last able to visit her brother and his family in New Zealand.

The family party did not see a great deal of John. He swam with his children in the canvas pool on deck, and he made sure they were taught to dive. Both children continued to be good swimmers as they grew older, and he continued to encourage them – often by a system of rewards: '£1 for a mile swim, £1 for a quarter of a mile crawl, £3 if you did two miles, and so on'. Learning was his god; and money spent on encouraging 'self-improvement' he did not consider wasted.

Apart from swimming, they saw him at meals; but his conversation was never animated, as his mind was on other things. His day would be spent meeting people and playing bridge. There were a number of Americans aboard – one of the reasons he had picked that particular cruise: he was always fascinated by the American ethos and by American business methods. He had learned bridge especially for the trip, with that in mind; Americans played bridge, so he was going to play bridge too. Like everything else he did, it was treated as a science and he mastered it quickly. His exceptional memory was always an asset, and when challenged during one game that he had done something against the rules, he was able to quote Culbertson, the American authority, to prove that it was perfectly permissible. He quoted not only Culbertson's exact words, but the particular edition of *The Bridge World* and the number of the page on which they appeared.

Skiing was another sport that the family discovered round about this time. John was keen; it was another skill for them all to master and it was athletic. Although not a natural athlete like Cecil – he would never allow himself to rely on an instinctive reaction; conscious mental control was all-important – he was, nevertheless, a more than adequate performer. St Moritz was the place chosen for their first winter sports in 1936, and a large family party all stayed at the Palace Hotel. This venue was probably picked by Cecil, but John for once allowed himself to enjoy some luxury. The party consisted of the two brothers, their wives Ruby and Doris, sisters Hilda and Joy, and a woman friend of the family. The holiday was a great success. There is a home movie of them skiing; the men in plus-fours and caps, as though ready for golf, the women looking more suitably attired in dark trousers and skiing helmets, but all of them remarkably proficient for novices.

Possibly the most formative of their Thirties' holidays was the first – a motoring trip through Germany and Austria in 1934. They joined an organised tour, but as the small coach allocated was already fully booked, a car was laid on for them and they were to share the same itinerary and couriers as the rest of the party. Dollfuss, the Austrian Chancellor, had just been assassinated by the Nazis, and the *Daily Mail*'s leader the day the Moores contingent was due to leave was headed, 'Keep out of Austria!' It did not stop them. Nor did the fact that they had to find a last-minute substitute when one of their party was pronounced not well enough to travel. The expedition had been planned for the two brothers and their wives, but Doris, Cecil's wife, was taken ill and Lou stepped into the breach. It was the first time any of them had flown, and also their first European journey together.

John kept a diary, and his daily entries reflect his particular interests and idiosyncrasies with great accuracy. His lack of sophistication is revealed, but at the same time he is never put down by this; he stands firmly on his own two feet, trusts his own judgement and observes the world with great perspicacity.

The party stayed the first night at the Savoy, and got off to a bad start next day when they nearly missed their flight. They had spent time buying brandy at the hotel, in case of airsickness, and then were driven to the office of Imperial Airways, the first British national airline, in John's own car, with their luggage going by taxi. The airport bus had already left when they arrived and their nonchalant attitude quickly changed when they were told that they would probably miss their plane. They had not even realised that the airport was some considerable distance outside London, at Croydon. Fell, the family chauffeur, was sent away with the car and they all piled into a taxi, thinking quite correctly that the taxi-driver would know the quickest route. He drove 'as if for dear life, swaying his body about as though helping the taxi along with his own vitality'. And 'by the grace of God and a lot of luck on the green lights', they made the airport with a few minutes to spare. In the hurry, Ruby slipped and hurt her thigh, but they jockeyed her along telling her that she was just frightened of flying and frightened of going to Austria. There had always been a hearty, knockabout streak in John's sense of humour.

To their surprise they discovered that brandy was available on the aeroplane and that lunch was actually served as well. 'A very nice cold meal, and the trip was very pleasant.' It became slightly less so about ten minutes from Paris; 'the aeroplane began to bump a little' and John was airsick. He had always been a bad sailor too, but he was delighted to find that almost as soon as they landed, he began to feel all right again; 'airsickness is evidently not half so terrible as seasickness'. The airport, as in London, was unfortunately on the outskirts of the city, and it took them some time to reach the centre of Paris. And although they chartered a taxi to drive them around and show them the sights, the driver's English was 'non-existent'. They visited the *Folies Bergère* that evening, which, John wrote, was 'a little hotter than I had expected'. It was probably not the temperature to which he was referring.

The lack of English spoken on the Continent is a continual theme of the diary. They visited a cinema in Brussels, thinking that part of the film would be intelligible, but it turned out to be all in Flemish or French, so they left. A music-hall in Vienna gave one or two sketches composed of 'nothing but German dialogue', which was a little trying. But his desire to understand, to be able to communicate, was already aroused. The name of every place they visited has an entry by it to show how it should be said: 'lunch at Senlis (pronounced Sollis)'; 'just before lunch came to Mainz (pronounced Minz) and the Rhine'; 'we arrived at Cologne and are surprised to find it spelt Köln and pronounced Kurlen'.

In his description of learning to dance the csárndás in Budapest, he refers to it simply as the 'chadda'; presumably because he had never seen the word written, this was his phonetic equivalent. His urge to learn languages was born. There were obviously people who could speak several and, apart from anything else, it roused his competitive spirit. He did not like to be beaten by anybody, at anything, and there is a touch of envy as well as humour in his description of their guide in Budapest. 'I am told she speaks ten languages. She is a widow. It must have been a trial for her husband.'

This trip also saw the beginning of his interest in painting. There are detailed and glowing descriptions of castles and of scenery, which he obviously enjoyed, but it is the art galleries which rather unexpectedly claim his attention; the gallery in Dresden, the private collection of the Liechtenstein family in Vienna, the Rubens and particularly the Van Dycks and Tintorettos in Munich. He complains bitterly whenever any of the guides is not knowledgeable enough to 'explain' the paintings.

The seeds of two of his great passions, painting and languages, were sown now, although they were to lie dormant for many years; it was not until the incredibly frenetic pace of his life slowed down somewhat, and he was much older, that he found time to indulge them. But there is also another current to be discerned running through his diary. Many of the entries are concerned with practical or trivial details – brief but succinct character sketches of the other members of the tour; continually recurring complaints about the way waiters pester them to buy wine and then overcharge; his distaste for garlic, which meant that he preferred the American 'hot dog' to real frankfurters; but underlying the description of daily events is a feeling of his growing awareness of Europe.

The tour took place just after the death of Hindenburg and four days of national mourning had been proclaimed in Germany, so there was very little night life, and flags were being flown everywhere in token of respect. Oswald Mosley had been holding Fascist meetings in England, and people at home were just beginning to open their eyes to the new Nazi Germany, although they still did not realise all its implications.

John admired the German character in many ways, preferring it to the French or the Belgian. 'Immediately we cross the border a change of atmosphere can be almost felt. Here are a people of triers and workers.' He obviously approves of the women too. 'After the heavily made-up girls of France, the lack of make-up on the German girls is very noticeable.' Lou, always very chic and fashionable, is even stared at and causes giggles in Cassel because of her rouge and lipstick. But as they progress, John becomes more doubtful. 'Uniforms are very apparent. Brown shirts abound by the

er spending three hours underground at gwith Pit, south of Sheffield, canvassing miners of Clay Cross in 1933.

The National candidate for Nuneaton, canvassing with his family in 1935.

t before the fatal accident, John (far left), Ruby and Campbell Black (front row, third from left) watch as ss Liverpool is christened with a bottle of champagne.

A family shooting party in Lancashire shortly before the Second World War. From left to right: Arthur, John, Arthur's first wife, Cecil, Lou and Joy.

This handsome studio portrait of Cecil was taken in the late forties.

This photograph, taken in 1953, hints at the dichotomy in John's character.

score. Even children have their brown shirts too.' But he can still sympathise to some extent – the castle in Heidelberg is 'mostly in ruins, having been destroyed by Napoleon. German history is so full of tales of destruction by the French that I begin to appreciate why the Germans don't feel too friendly.' They are a people he respects, but he also respects their potential as possible adversaries. His strongest reaction is recorded in Prague.

'One of the most astounding sights is the Jewish Cemetery. The Jews in ancient times had so little room granted to them in the city that they had to bury their dead on top of each other. Gravestones are crowded on top of each other; even the most famous Jewish men were given a tiny grave. The cemetery has been closed for 200 years. Its oldest stone is the year 600-and-odd. Many of the graves bear inscriptions of a dog, horse, etc., as the Jews were not allowed a name until they were able to purchase one. A sight of the graveyard would tell more of the persecution of the Jews than a thousand books.'

All the way through there is a feeling that John is aware of a darker groundswell under the fun they were all having.

Holidays were far from a major part of his life, however, and most of it was still dedicated to work, work, and more work.

6

Successes and Failures

Back home in Liverpool was where the main business of John's life went on. As he had anticipated, the anti-betting lobby was still gunning for the pools. At one point, in 1932, an entire batch of over ten thousand coupons had to be taken out of their envelopes as they were about to be sent off, on the advice of his solicitor Holland Hughes, so that one word could be altered. However carefully he tried to stay strictly within legal limits, there were still those who disapproved. In 1933 a Royal Commission on Betting actually recommended the suppression of the pools, but there was a public outcry and the prohibition was withdrawn.

The legal status of pools was clarified by the Betting and Lotteries Act of 1934, and in the same year the Pools Promoters Association was formed. Next was the turn of the Football League itself to go on the offensive, and in 1935 they forbade the pools companies to print fixtures on their coupons, claiming that they were copyright. The Pools Promoters Association made an offer of £100,000 a year for the privilege, but it was refused. They would have been prepared to go even higher, up to £500,000 a year; there was no betting tax in those days, so they could have afforded it. And as John said, 'We'd have been very happy if they had accepted it, because then the pools would have secured the blessing of the governing body, and we could have been helping sport.' But payment offered for permission was refused, and even the Football League's own advance publication of the season's fixtures was withdrawn. Luckily for the pools business, all this had such a bad effect on attendance at matches that before very long the campaign was dropped. Several Members of Parliament were still active in the attack, however; in 1936, R J Russell introduced a private member's bill calling for the abolition of pools which was defeated at the second reading; and the bill brought by A P Herbert in 1938 was also thrown out.

They were worrying years, and although John had handed over the running of the pools to Cecil, he was still very much involved. On Saturday night, when the dividends were being declared, he would always put in an appearance; and he and Cecil and a few of the others would play cards while the results were coming in. One compensation for the continual harassment was that the popularity of the pools continued to grow. A total pool of over £460,000 was reached one week, and the Penny Points Pool, which had been launched in the 1936–7 season, regularly attracted a stake of over £100,000. The number of dividends declared mounted continually – first three, then four, then five and finally, in 1937–8, six. It had been decided that compensation prizes would be paid to 'near winners', as well as the first dividend to the correct solution. This could be as much as £30,000: even a second dividend might be over £3,000, and a fifth dividend over £30. When one considers how much these sums would be in today's terms, the consolation prizes were consoling indeed.

John's main involvement at this time, however, was with the growing mail-order business. By 1936, its headquarters were at Crosby, where an old mill once used for cotton-spinning had been acquired, reconditioned and enlarged by a two-storey extension. This was only four years after the start of the business, and according to the people who were involved then, it was not a very comfortable place to be. Everyone was pushed to their limit.

With John's driving force behind it, the business was expanding at an enormous rate, and he was incisive and ruthless. 'Ruthless, but fair' seems to be the consensus. And as one retired long-time employee said, 'Although it reflected on the man on the ground, he was ruthless with his executives. If anything went wrong, he didn't slate the poor fellow on the floor down there, it was the management.' He encouraged people who were able and ambitious, but he would expect more of them. Two of his favourite sayings illustrate that: 'If you live on high hills, you must expect high winds,' and 'If you can't stand the heat, stay out of the kitchen.' They were both used frequently.

Friday night was the time everyone feared, because that was when you would find out whether you still had a job or not. 'In the early days at Crosby the personnel manager would walk round doing an inspection and people would hide in the toilets to keep out of the way, in case they were blamed for something. If you were receiving £5, you were in the private wage category, so you tried to keep below £5 because otherwise you were vulnerable and could be sacked.' Or, as another retired employee put it, more succinctly, 'PWA (Private Wage Account) and next week PAC (Public Assistance Committee)' – a common expression in those early days.

John's brother, Arthur, had a great deal to do with running the business, but John looked after most of the buying and was particularly interested in the buying office, so buyers were amongst the most nervous. 'One Friday before the war, we had thirteen buyers, and by four o'clock we had three. One of the survivors was Joe Neary, who bought rainwear, but right to the day he retired, every Friday up to four o'clock Joe used to get agitated.'

Everyone was kept at full stretch, which was good, but there was also an underlying feeling of fear, which was not. At the same time, John himself generated enormous personal loyalty amongst the staff. In later years, people who met the brothers would be tempted to think of Cecil as the one with charisma, and John as the brain. Yet John was also a born leader, perhaps due to a mixture of apparent simplicity and approachableness; coupled with an excellent analytical mind, the ability to make quick decisions and above all, to take responsibility. The buck always stopped when it got to John. All the early employees refer to him admiringly as 'the Old Man', not a reference to his age, but a common term for 'the Boss'. All of them begin any discussion about the company with the firm statement, 'I'm a John Moores man . . .' It is fascinating to try to discover the secret of this compelling appeal.

'He was a hard taskmaster, but he had to be, to build this business.'

'He was strict, but fair. When you came out of work, he was a friend, and you could have a little joke with him about football.'

'He never forgot his roots.'

'He was the brain and the driving force.'

'He had very high principles.'

One of those principles was, as it had always been, a rigid honesty. All dealings must not only be completely above-board, they must be seen to be so. His innovative buying system is an example. He made buying and stock control two different departments, 'so that the buyer could concentrate on finding the right goods at the right price, and the stock controller could decide how many to contract for'. In other words, he separated the selective from the purchasing side of buying. He was very much ahead of his time in this, although most of the major mail-order and chain-store companies now operate on the same principle. From a business point of view, it has the advantage of placing merchandising in the hands of financial experts who can plan around a financial budget. And it has one other advantage, which particularly appealed to John. If it is the job of the buyer to select goods for the catalogue or store, and of the stock controller to estimate the number to be sold, then it is the stock controller and not the buyer who places the order with the suppliers. In this way 'back-handers' from the supplier, which are sometimes regarded as a buyer's perk, are kept to a minimum. Any suggestion of bribery was anathema to John, and he applied the same rigid standards to his own behaviour.

'The Old Man had a pair of £1 19s 11d shoes from the Littlewoods catalogue. His excuse was it was all he could afford. So one day he sent for the shoe buyer, Harry Bettle, and said, "Can you get these soled and heeled for me?"

'The buyer contacted one of the suppliers and sent him the shoes. "These are for the Boss; get some Bolton calf and make a really nice pair of shoes for him."

'In due course the shoes arrived and John was presented with them, but his reaction was not as expected.

'"These are not my shoes!" said the Old Man.

'"No, they're Bolton calf. Best shoes you can get."

'"I can't afford that!" was the response.

'"They're a gift from the supplier, Mr John."

'That did it.

'"I don't take gifts from suppliers! Take them back and get my shoes soled and heeled."

'The buyer then rang the supplier and asked for the original shoes back, mended, and was appalled to discover that they had not been considered worth the labour and had been thrown into the furnace. Frantically, the supplier went the rounds of the staff, until he found a man in the factory who took the same size and had a similar mail-order pair.

'"Give us your shoes!" he said.

'And they soled and heeled those and gave them to Mr John who accepted them without suspicion, and everyone was happy.'

'A hard taskmaster' he may have been, but he was harder on himself than on anyone else; and if he pushed others to their limit, he treated himself in the same way. This is the period of some of his failures, as well as of his greatest successes. Nothing tests a man like failure, our Anglo-Saxon forebears believed; even the old Norse gods must finally fall to show how they comport themselves in defeat. An attempt at a Parliamentary career was one of John's few areas of failure.

His first try for Parliament was in 1933, during the state of national emergency. He stood as National candidate for Clay Cross against Arthur Henderson, Labour, and Harry Pollitt, Communist. As one paper reported, 'Mr Moores, the Government candidate, admits that he used to be a Conservative; but is now "definitely appealing to people of all parties to support a Government consisting of all parties". The inference that the cynic will draw, not unfortunately without fair ground, is not that Mr Moores has ceased to be a Conservative, but that the distinction between a Conservative Government and Mr Moores' "Government of all parties" is hardly worth making.'

The Cabinet, in fact, consisted of four Conservatives, four Labour members and two Liberals, with a Labour Prime Minister, Ramsay MacDonald. It had been endorsed by the Liberals with only one dissent, and by the Conservatives unanimously. Labour was in opposition.

John was not ashamed of his allegiance. As he said, 'In the days of party politics I was a Conservative, but since the state of national emergency came, I have been an out-and-out supporter of the National Government.' And in a safe Labour seat, which in the previous election had seen a Labour majority of over 10,000 and no Conservative candidate even standing, to be a National candidate was a more realistic option.

He was considerably more cagey about his business connections; in the usual newspaper cartoon of the contestants, he is described as 'Mr John Moores, National, who is connected with the printing business'. Printing did not provoke the adverse reaction which 'pools promoter' might have done in some anti-gambling circles.

Arthur Henderson, drawn with angel's wings in the same cartoon, is described as 'The Peacemaker at home and abroad'. In Germany, Hitler had been granted dictatorial powers and the first concentration camps were being erected. Goebbels had been made Minister of Propaganda. In Clay Cross, the candidates' views on disarmament were a main issue in the campaign. Henderson had been President of the World Conference on Disarmament; he was a firm advocate of the League of Nations, and one of his statements was that 'the Governments of the world have renounced war as an instrument of national policy'. He was speaking just six years before the outbreak of the Second World War.

On the other hand, one journalist wrote, 'Mr Moores' views on disarmament are rather vague.' John's reply to this was immediate: 'I believe in disarmament just as much as Mr Henderson, but I wish to make it clear that my first concern is the bread and butter of Clay Cross miners.' He canvassed actively amongst them, going down at least ten different pits and spending over three hours underground at one, Langwith Pit. 'I am urging that coal does not depend so much on politics,' he said, 'as upon trade.'

Arthur Henderson won the seat.

Undeterred, John was back two years later fighting Nuneaton, another safe Labour seat. Again he lost. This was the year that

Mussolini invaded Abyssinia and in Germany the Luftwaffe was being formed. It is more than likely that John would have tried a third time, had not world events stopped him. What he did do, more successfully, was to stand for local government. He served as a Conservative City Councillor for Kensington Ward, Liverpool, from 1933 to 1937 and from 1937 to 1940 as a representative of the then Sefton Park Ward.

As legend goes, during one of these campaigns he heard that an employee of his, Jimmy Jones, was standing against him for Kensington Ward as a Communist candidate. Jimmy was summoned to the Old Man's office, and went defiantly, expecting his cards.

'You'll need time off to canvass. How much paid leave are you going to want?'

John's work as a City Councillor was not the only way in which he expressed his feelings for Liverpool. In September 1936 there was an air-race from England to South Africa. It was sponsored by Schlesinger, the South African magnate, to commemorate the Golden Jubilee of Johannesburg, but the pilots themselves had to find backers to provide their planes. One of them was Tom Campbell Black, a famous long-distance pilot who with Charles Scott had recently won the England to Australia Air-Race, and the backer he found for the South African race was John Moores. The plane was a Percival Mew Gull – Campbell Black had decided to make this a solo flight – and it was to be named Miss Liverpool.

The race was to start from Plymouth, but John was insistent that the 'christening' should take place in Liverpool; the name of the aircraft and his backing had been designed to boost his chosen city. Campbell Black had no objection, indeed the opportunity to 'handle' the plane a little more before the actual race was probably an attraction. The ceremony went well and drew large crowds. John broke a bottle of champagne against the nose of Miss Liverpool, and a banquet was given that evening in Campbell Black's honour.

His wife was Florence Desmond, the well-known actress and impersonator, who was playing in variety at the Holborn Empire in London and rehearsing at the Victoria Palace for a new review called *Let's Raise the Curtain*. She had therefore not been able to accompany her husband to Liverpool. He rang her from the Adelphi Hotel, while he was dressing for dinner, to tell her how things had gone. It was the last time that she ever spoke to him.

Next day, at Speke Aerodrome, his plane was taxiing out at ten or fifteen miles per hour, prior to taking off for London, when an RAF bomber which had just landed ran straight into it. The Mew Gull was a small plane, and the bomber's propeller sliced right through the cockpit. Campbell Black was badly injured and died half an hour later. It transpired that the pilot officer, who had been taking the aircraft on a short test-run, had circled the field prior to landing and seen that it was clear. As the bomber's wheels touched the ground, its nose came up and from that moment until it actually stopped, the pilot was unable to see in front of him and had to watch the ground on either side. It was apparently during these few crucial minutes that Campbell Black's plane taxied out of its enclosure. One witness thought Black had been glancing at a map, which was later found on the floor of the cockpit. It certainly seemed as though he did not see the bomber until a few seconds before the crash, because his machine swerved at that point. Not, sadly, in time.

News of the accident was relayed to Florence Desmond while she was rehearsing, and a quick telephone call to the hospital by the stage manager brought the shattering revelation that it had been a fatal one. It was John who rang her with the actual facts and with more details; and when she travelled up to Liverpool next day with Tom Campbell Black's parents and brother, it was John and Ruby who met them at Lime Street Station. Florence Desmond described the scene:

'There was a large crowd of people at the station, as well as reporters and photographers. Two figures dressed in black disengaged themselves from the crowd and came forward to meet us. They were John Moores and his wife, Ruby. It was a difficult meeting. I had never met the Moores before, but as they stepped forward and gripped my hands, I felt that here were two kind and very real people. At this stage I dared not trust myself to speak. Mrs Moores said, "John and I will take you to the hospital." I just nodded my head.'

After leaving the hospital, they drove her to Speke Aerodrome, as she wanted to see Tom's plane.

'It was under guard in a hangar. One wing had been smashed, and the cockpit was completely cut out, as if a circular saw had ploughed through it. The engine was quite untouched. If the collision had occurred one foot farther away from the cockpit, the chances are he would not have been touched.'

Through all this, Florence Desmond exerted the most superb self-control, but she was in something of a daze by the time that she and Campbell Black's parents were being driven out to Formby. They were to stay the night at John's house, and the Moores did everything that they could to help.

'After I had made a feeble attempt to eat dinner, Ruby Moores took me up to my room and stayed with me until I got into bed. She kissed me goodnight and begged me to try to get some sleep. After she left the room I lay in the bed with my eyes wide open. I felt cold and lifeless, and then I began to tremble; I remember crying out and sobbing. Ruby came running into the room; she was in her nightgown. She got into bed with me, and took me into her arms. After crying myself into a state of exhaustion, I suppose I must have fallen asleep. When I awoke it was morning, and Ruby was creeping out of the room.'

John continued to help others where he could, and not just in Liverpool. Sport of every sort had always interested him, and this was an area where he would often provide assistance. One of the problems for many sportsmen as they came to the end of their sporting careers, often at a comparatively early age, was to find another livelihood; they generally found it difficult to know what they could do. Several were already employed by Littlewoods; John had seen to it that they were offered jobs and this practice continued to be company policy. It is reputed that Liverpool's goalie once worked on stock control; the stock man in Chester was a member of the Boxing Board of Control; and Dixie Dean, the footballer and record goal-scorer, was well looked after. Several ex-boxers were employed, including Joe Tarleton, Nel Tarleton's brother, who was an order picker. (A fellow employee remembers asking him how he got through his order-picking so quickly. 'Used to flush them down the toilet,' was the answer.)

Cocky Moffat was another, a well-known local boxer who was employed on general duties. He was very strong, and once, when another car had unwittingly been parked behind John's and boxed it in, 'he bounced it, bumpitty, bumpitty, bump, until it was out of the way'. He had the job too, of looking after people who had been working late – a not uncommon occurrence – and he would escort the girl employees down a 'jigger' (scouse for alley) and round to Exchange Street. The long-time chief commissionaire, Bob Sergeant, used to call, 'There's another bundle of ten coming down!' and Cocky would 'dissuade' any drunks from annoying them and see them safely on their way. He was still with the firm in the mid-Fifties and as a nephew said, 'He absolutely adored Uncle John – thought the sun rose and sank with him.' Cocky's party piece was a performance on a weird musical instrument he had made himself from a biscuit tin and a broom handle. The strings just made a 'plunk' sound but when he played it at Christmas parties, as he regularly did, the girls used to shout and cheer. The high spot was that he always stopped half-way through and called, 'Mr John! Mr John! Here, Mr John!' And John would go up on-stage and finish the act with him. It brought the house down every time.

Surprisingly, it was in the area of sport that John had his only other failure: baseball. He had been very taken by it on his American trips, where he had met John Heydler, President of the National Baseball League, and Babe Ruth, the famous player, and where he had seen matches played by the New York Yankees, the New York Giants and the Chicago White Sox. He was convinced that baseball would go down well in England and decided to bring some baseball players over. The two he selected were Canadians, Alan and Jack Ritchie; they were employed at Crosby in the mail-order business, but their real job was to teach the game at the Littlewoods Sports Ground at Wavertree, where the amenities now included not only tennis-courts and a bowling-green but a nine-hole golf-course as well. Baseball was already played in England, but with a revised code; the American game was much faster than the English one. John hoped to establish a new league which would play the game as it was played in the States – with more 'pep'.

It never took off. John had made one of his few misjudgements and although he persisted for a while, even he eventually had had enough. It was obviously not a game which suited the national temperament.

Another area in which he encountered some opposition, and this time from close associates, was one even nearer to his heart. Involved as he was in mail order, it was not John's sole business interest; he was working up to a new venture.

The economy began to pick up in the latter half of the Thirties, although this was not the case in Liverpool; transatlantic liners were now docking at Southampton instead, with subsequent loss of trade to Liverpool. However, the spending power of most of the country had risen dramatically. John had set his sights on another American retail idea – chain-stores; and as usual his business timing was impeccable. It was a logical progression from mail order in many ways, as he and his executives already had contacts and buying experience; unlike his other two businesses, however, this was a much more costly enterprise. Instead of being conducted by paperwork through the post, chain-store retailing was face to face with the customer and meant an enormous expenditure on sites. It was also, this time, not an innovative move; he would be entering a field in which there was stiff competition – Woolworth and Marks & Spencer were already established leaders. His brother, Cecil – an exceptionally shrewd man; his trusted accountants 'Tommy' Roberts and Ingram Legge and indeed most of his advisers, were dubious about the whole enterprise. But John pressed on.

His method, as always, was enormously detailed analysis followed by total dedication, total concentration. Four stores were opened in 1937 – Brixton, London's Oxford Street, Blackpool and Birmingham. The following year there were twelve more, in 1939 there were another nine; while further sites had been acquired and were awaiting planning and building programmes.

This enormous expansion took place in under three years; it was a well-mounted and full-scale attack. And the year of its launch was also the year that there was another addition to John and Ruby's family. Janatha, their second daughter and the last of their children, was born on July 4th, 1937, and the first store was opened in Blackpool two days later on July 6th.

7

Imminent Peril

A new baby, a new business. For this pattern to repeat itself four times must be more than coincidence. Several explanations are possible; perhaps the answer is a combination of all of them. It may be that new offspring, like new enterprises, were conceived during peak periods of creativity, both mental and physical; or simply that once an enterprise was launched, he had more time to give attention to his wife and family – until the business was running smoothly, when he would need something new on which to expend his mental energy. It may have been an unconscious urge not to be totally sucked in by his family, but to have his own area, his own empire.

Perhaps, after all, it was his basic competitiveness again. Certainly, all men of ability were competitors in his eyes, even his sons. Many, many years later, when old and very frail, he firmly refused to sign a power of attorney when they asked him to and struggled to his feet, saying, 'They want to take away my power!' He was quite happy to sign it later for one of his daughters and a trusted woman lawyer. Men were either competitors or devoted followers. The women in his life seem to fall into two categories as well: maternal, supportive figures; or young girls, like daughters or nieces, to be cherished and looked after but not taken too seriously. Career women, who as times changed and progressed reached executive positions in his firm, were treated like men; wives were in a different category. There was one area, however, in which wives could present a challenge and claim the major share of the limelight – that was in the area of childbearing. A new business venture counteracted this and re-emphasised the supremacy of the male world.

The only recorded instance of his wife ever objecting to this secondary and supportive role was, surprisingly, concerned with fishing etiquette. She was expert at dry-fly fishing and more than once caught the largest salmon of the trip. They were salmon fishing on the River Spey, and the unwritten rule was that you had a stretch of water to yourself each day until the following lunch-time, when you moved down to the next. John started fishing a pool on Ruby's stretch – a favourite pool of hers – before her time had expired, and when she objected that it was her water, he took no notice of her. She walked away and flatly refused ever to fish that pool again.

As a rule, Ruby saw to it that her husband was given priority, and the household very much revolved around him. He was a loyal husband and a devoted father although, as was the case on the world cruise, his family did not see a great deal of him. Work claimed most of his time; he would leave for the office early and get back late most days. His younger son remembers, as a small child, trying to stay awake as long as possible so that he could hear his father arrive home and call out for him to come up and say 'goodnight'.

There were plenty of small cousins around now, and as most of them lived in the same area they all saw a fair amount of each other in the holidays. There were regular family get-togethers too. The tradition was for everyone to meet at Louisa's on Christmas Day, and when all the children were still very young, the party would be at three o'clock in the afternoon; then, as they got older, it was moved to the evening. Boxing Day was reserved for an evening party at John and Ruby's. This was family practice and it never changed.

Another part of the ritual was that everyone did 'turns'. It was not unusual in those pre-television days for families to entertain themselves, and the Moores enjoyed it. Louisa would sing – she still had a very pretty voice – and 'Love's Old Sweet Song' was the family favourite. Arthur played the violin. So did Ethel's husband, Bert, and the couple both recited as well. George played tunes on his teeth with a pencil; and John's party piece was the boy's poem, 'If I durst – but I durstn't!' He was not a naturally talented performer, but he was keen and he worked at it. The evening always ended with a general singsong. The children of the family were not really old enough to perform yet, although many of them were having piano and dancing lessons. John and the whole family believed that every bit of talent must be developed and worked at.

His elder daughter, Betty, remembers her father's encouragement. 'If I wanted extra lessons in the holidays, I only had to ask. He would be delighted.' In term-time, Fell, the family chauffeur, would collect her from school and drive her to dancing class, to tennis coaching, to swimming lessons. The journey to school itself was made by public transport; John did not believe in spoiling his children. Every morning Betty would walk the length of Shireburn Road to the station and remembers, on one or two occasions when she was late, begging a lift from the milkman in his milk float. It was only for 'extras' that John allowed chauffeuring. She says of her father, 'He really wanted us to do the best for ourselves. He never gave us the impression that we were just going to sit around and be nice young ladies.' He still shared the generally-held view, however, that once a woman married and had children, her entire attention must be given to her family.

There were other celebrations, too, towards the end of the Thirties, and the nation's troubles seemed to be over. People everywhere had mourned the death of George V; had worried over Edward VIII's involvement with Mrs Simpson; now Edward had abdicated and been named Duke of Windsor, and his brother was to be crowned George VI. Like the rest of the country, the Moores family joined in the excitement of the Coronation. John took a house in Kensington – for himself, his three children and their nanny. Ruby stayed behind in Formby as she was expecting the latest arrival. The Coronation took place on May 12th, 1937, and Janatha was born less than two months later. Louisa and her daughters were all in London for the occasion, in hotels or rented flats; and as the Littlewoods store in Oxford Street had windows looking out directly onto the route of the procession, it was there that they spent the day of the Coronation itself.

The rest of the visit to London was divided into strictly male and female activities – the men were in business meetings during the day and at business dinners in the evening. The women of the family enjoyed themselves, going twice to the theatre – once to see *George and Margaret* and again to see Jack Buchanan in a musical. The latter was on the eve of the Coronation itself, when the streets of the capital were crowded and people were sleeping out on the pavement in order to get a good view next day. There was a disturbing incident after the show, when the driver of their hired car was threatened by a couple of drunken revellers who jumped on to the running-board and attempted to hit him through the open window. Louisa, sitting at the back in a car full of women, had to be forcibly restrained, as she tried to heave herself forward to defend him. 'Let me get at them! Let me get at them!' she kept saying.

In spite of advancing years, Louisa never lost her physical courage or her fighting spirit. She was always game. That same year saw yet another instance. When her youngest son's marriage broke up and he was left with three small children, the youngest only a baby, Louisa took them all home to live with her; and although Charlie was always involved with their upbringing and took them for holidays as they grew older, it was Louisa, at the age of sixty-four, who reared them and loved them dearly.

The final festivity of the decade, as far as the family was concerned, was Joy's wedding in January 1939, with six of her small nieces as bridesmaids, in cherry-red velvet. Joy was marrying an Army officer, ADC to a general, and in future was to live in 'the South', near Maidenhead, but the wedding naturally took place in Formby.

A contingent of pools girls with whom she had worked were amongst the most honoured guests. John, as her eldest brother, gave her away.

It was not only the family who enjoyed themselves during this period; John regarded his work-force as his extended family and their welfare mattered too. As well as other benefits, in 1937 he produced a pension scheme for employees. 'A marvellous thing at that time,' as one retired director said, and it was certainly unusual then. He saw to it, however, that there was fun as well as work.

The Littlewoods staff outings were well known both in Lancashire and farther afield. In the early days, they would go to Llandudno, and sometimes to the Isle of Man. Ferry boats were chartered and filled with pools girls and mail-order workers. John nearly always accompanied them. One retired manager remembers 'going on the *St Sieriol* to Llandudno and there was a really heavy sea rolling; everyone was green. Mr John was present and did his best to cheer everyone up, but he was green too!' In view of what a poor sailor John always was, it is hardly surprising that before long, the outings became trips to Blackpool or to the Lake District – by coach. By coaches, would perhaps be nearer the mark. The number varied from five coaches in the early days to the hundreds required later for the annual outing to Blackpool when the whole work-force, 12,000 strong, were taken there and back in the day. They would arrive in a gigantic convoy and all the entertainments of the Golden Mile plus lunch would be provided. On the way home, the coaches would stop for everyone to buy fish and chips; 'if they weren't in newspaper, they weren't nearly as good'. John enjoyed them with the rest; 'he never lost the common touch', which was one of the reasons for his popularity. He literally joined in all the fun of the fair.

One retired secretary recounted a pre-war 'go' on the dodgems. 'I had bought a hat which cost three guineas. At that price, it was a terrific hat! We all went in hats, dressed up. Well we were in the dodgem cars, and the next minute all the people, including Mr John, got into the cars. You can imagine who was the target! My hat ended up round the pedals of the car. We did enjoy ourselves.' John's enjoyment of mild horseplay was obviously shared by his work-force. He shared his own triumphs and pleasures with them too.

'We were all on one outing, sitting having dinner. When he'd made his little speech and welcomed everybody, and hoped we all had a nice time, Mr John said, "I've got something to tell you – I've got my first Rolls-Royce at the door." We all went and had a look at it. He was so proud.'

This was before he acquired JM1 as his car number – but when he did, that gave him equal pleasure. It has always seemed surprising that a man as modest as John Moores – a man who spends very little on his clothes and who dislikes outward signs of wealth – should go in for a personalised number plate. When a comment was made to this effect to a retired employee, he rounded on the speaker in defence of the Old Man. 'That was his little treat!' he said supportively. One of his two loyal secretaries of many years' standing has a simpler explanation. 'Mr John put his head round the office door once and said, "What colour's my car?" He hadn't got a clue.' It would be changed for a new model every three years, and as cars were never a great interest of his, the personalised number plate helped him recognise his own.

Treats, outings and celebrations there may have been, but they could not disguise a growing unease throughout the country. People may have been singing 'Jeepers Creepers' and 'A Tisket, A Tasket', or dancing the new dance, the rumba, but there was often this sneaking worry at the back of their minds. They enjoyed buying *Picture Post*, a magazine which had not been out long; it was still fun to go to the 'pictures' – to see *Snow White* or *The Lady Vanishes*; because even after the Munich crisis and in spite of all the signs to the contrary, no one believed a war could really happen. Of course there were contingency plans to evacuate schoolchildren; gas-masks were ready to be distributed; but the policy of appeasement had been in operation for two years, ever since Lord Halifax had visited Hitler in 1937. War would be averted somehow.

On August 24th, 1939, the Littlewoods annual outing to Blackpool was under way. It was usually spread over two days, so enormous were the numbers involved, and this was the second day's contingent, consisting of 200 coachloads. The festivities were in full swing, when they were interrupted by a wireless announcement. The country was 'in imminent peril of war'. Several of the coaches were commandeered, but there were no complaints. Everyone squashed up together in those that where left and managed to get back to Liverpool. The drivers had call-up papers in their pockets and were picking up other reservists and transporting soldiers as detailed.

An urgent message was sent to Maisons Lafitte just outside Paris, where John's two eldest children were on a holiday course in French with a woman tutor and they were hurried back to England.

September 3rd came. The whole country listened to Neville Chamberlain's broadcast. Young Moores cousins were on their usual summer holiday in North Wales, and two of the small boys were only just retrieved in time. They had been standing, open-mouthed, watching, as crowds of evacuee schoolchildren arrived; some harassed adult had assumed that they were evacuees too and had marshalled them into a group. Bus-loads of children were being rushed out of Liverpool as fast as possible, and distributed around families that had room for them – families in areas less at risk. All the big cities were evacuating their children, because nobody knew when the air-raids were going to start. War had been declared. After all.

8

'The Ordinary Man or Woman Can Do Anything . . .'

John, of course, had seen it coming.

'After Mr Chamberlain had come beaming back from Munich with the message, "I believe it is peace in our time," I think you will remember that we divided into two camps in England. There were those who believed he was right and those who did not. I was among the latter.'

As early as August 1938 while John was staying at Loch Grannoch, the remote fishing lodge where the family holidayed, a telegram had been delivered to him suggesting that the Government might wish to buy, or commandeer, the thousands of blankets awaiting sale in Littlewoods' warehouses. Later there had been news on the wireless of Chamberlain's impending visit to Munich. John had driven back to Liverpool that night, and by nine o'clock next morning he was on the telephone to Whitehall. They wanted blankets urgently; how many could he let them have?

'The lot!' was John's answer.

Within forty-eight hours the entire stock was on its way south and Littlewoods' buyers were looking for replacements. At the same time, after a quick conference, John and Cecil offered all their premises to the Government, should they be wanted, in the event of war.

The Munich conference took place in September 1938, and by October 10th, Germany had occupied the Sudetenland. In Britain some people had already started to consider air-raid precautions and to form what they called ARP organisations. John Moores was amongst their number; he organised an ambulance division at his own expense and enrolled as an ARP ambulance officer.

The year dragged on. Eden resigned in protest against Chamberlain's policy; Duff Cooper resigned as First Lord of the Admiralty. President Roosevelt appealed to Hitler and Mussolini to settle European differences peacefully, but by Christmas both the USA and Germany had recalled their ambassadors and broken off diplomatic relations.

In 1939, Germany occupied Bohemia and Moravia and placed

Slovakia under 'protection'. England and Poland signed a treaty of mutual assistance; and when on September 1st Germany invaded Poland and annexed Danzig, there was no turning back.

Less than forty-eight hours after hostilities had been declared, the Government censorship department moved into the pools building at Edge Lane which had only been completed earlier in the same year, and it was handed over entire, with all the desks, extra telephones and teleprinters that had been installed.

In the same way, John placed a great many of Littlewoods' vehicles at the disposal of the ARP to be used as ambulances, and he himself was appointed divisional ambulance officer for the north-west area, where he continued to visit ambulance stations regularly. At first, the drivers were all Littlewoods employees, but as the weeks passed many of them were called up. Their call-up papers may even have been printed by J & C Moores, for the Littlewoods Edge Lane printing works had previously turned out seventeen million National Registration forms in the space of three days at the Government's request. The ambulance drivers were gradually replaced either by men over the age of conscription or by women. At that point conscription was limited to men between the ages of nineteen and forty-one; but in 1941 the call-up age limit for men was lowered to eighteen and a half, and at the same time conscription was extended to single women between the ages of twenty and thirty.

All the firm's employees who went into the Forces received certain assurances. The first was a letter from the personnel manager, telling them that they would be getting a weekly allowance from the company during their first ten weeks in the Services, and that they could have a refund of all the contributions they paid into the company pension scheme, if they wished; or they could leave the money in the scheme and, on their return, continue where they had left off. 'In the event of your decease while serving with the Forces, a circumstance which we earnestly hope will not arise, all your contributions left in the scheme will be immediately payable to your wife.'

Within a year came the second offer; this was a letter promising a weekly allowance on a regular basis 'to certain members of the staff serving with the Forces for their dependants (other than a childless wife who is able to work)'. The amount was calculated on a sliding scale, and staff were asked to fill in a questionnaire. They were also able 'to continue in the pension scheme as a member entitled to benefit under Grade A', and in addition would be covered immediately for £100 life assurance, provided they were not serving with the Royal Air Force, for 'flying risk cannot be covered with the assurance company . . .' It was signed, 'With best wishes for your health and safe return, Yours sincerely, John Moores'.

Better still was the brief missive, also from John Moores, which contained the paragraph, 'We would like to assure you that your job will be kept open for you and when you are demobilised, please communicate with the office, when you will be reinstated.'

Retired commissionaire Bob Sergeant remembers that when he came back from the war in 1947 and called at the personnel office, he was asked how he would feel about going down to London, as the particular chain-store where he had worked was no longer in operation. The idea did not appeal to him. As he explained, there were already about 500 men from the corps of commissionaires in London.

'It was only a thought,' they said. 'Don't worry.'

Bob's reply was immediate and made with complete confidence. 'I'm not worried! I've got Mr John's letter here!'

Backing the fighting men and women, and giving assistance to Government departments was obviously not going to be enough for John, however. He wanted involvement and action. He and Cecil called a meeting, and over a cup of tea they examined their various options. They could try and carry on business as usual; they could close for the duration and hand over the rest of their buildings and equipment to the Government; or they could convert to war work. It took about two minutes for them to make their decision.

'But – good heavens – we know nothing about manufacturing munitions and such!' was the reaction of one executive.

'Then the sooner we learn, the better,' Cecil replied.

John's next step was to contact a Government equipment inspector in Liverpool and ask what kind of armaments were most urgently needed. He was given an address in London to apply to, but the inspector was not very encouraging.

'You can go and see them if you like,' he said, 'but I doubt if they'll be very helpful.'

The youngest Moores brother, Charlie, and a cousin, Cyril Hodkinson, who also worked for the firm, were sent to see what they could find out. What they discovered was an empty house, as the department had been evacuated to Harrogate. They were on the next train to Yorkshire. At the Grand Hotel, they found a Colonel Disney who headed one of the Air Ministry's production boards. Again they did not get a particularly enthusiastic reception; neither the Colonel nor anybody else seemed to believe that a firm dealing in mail order, football pools and chain-stores was capable of turning over to mass-production. Charlie and his cousin were not deterred and very shortly, John received a telephone call from them to say that parachutes were the prime necessity and that the Air Ministry was ready to place an order with the company.

'How many do they need?' John wanted to know.

The reply staggered even him: 20,000. And that was just to start with. At that point the firm had neither the materials nor the machinery; nor, most worrying of all, the know-how.

The contract was duly signed. Mail-order and chain-store buyers were briefed, and while some were deputed to scour Liverpool and snap up every sewing-machine they could lay their hands on, others were sent to buy cloth, webbing and cotton wherever they could find it. The rest were given the job of scouting round for expert seamstresses to teach the work-force. The Hanover Street building was cleared; at one time it had been used as a warehouse, but was practically derelict. Now it had to be equipped with special ventilation, heating and lighting; a power plant was installed and an air-raid shelter built. But as the sewing-machines, benches, jigs and templates were moved in, the floors began to buckle and sway. Stanchions had to be erected quickly from the basement up to steady them. The factory was prepared one section at a time, and as each section was ready, a group of pools girls would move in to be instructed by the experts and set to work. They had to learn cutting, sewing, rigging and assembly, and they were able pupils. The first parachute was produced on December 11th, 1939, only a month after work had been started on the actual building itself, and one month after that, the first 20,000 parachutes were delivered to the Air Ministry, with not a single fault in the whole batch.

More contracts were to follow in rapid succession. There were eventually 400 sewing-machines in operation, but this was not enough to cope with the orders. The obvious answer was to work a night-shift, and although at first the Air Ministry vetoed this, by the time it had changed its mind Littlewoods already had the shift in operation. Within five months of the first parachute being produced, there were three shifts working round the clock, consisting in total of over 2,000 staff, which turned out parachutes for launching mines, bombs and rockets. Hanover Street had become one of the leading parachute centres in the country.

John had always believed in giving credit where credit was due, and he was not slow in apportioning praise. Some of the success, he considered, was due to 'methods of setting about things tried and tested in our pools and mail-order experience'. Sub-contractors, for example, who could not supply on time were helped to iron out their problems instead of being jettisoned, with mutual benefit all round. Meticulous initial planning was another asset.

'I had previously made in America a thorough examination of time study, and continually proved its value throughout our organisation, particularly as production developed. Progress charts showed everyone where he or she fitted into the machine, and it was always our policy to encourage and lead rather than drive our workers . . . I believed in seeing everybody and allowing everybody to see me; for the principal who sits in his office has the wool pulled over his eyes. I like to think that all our workers trusted us not to give them impossible jobs, and knew that Cecil and I would never ask them to do anything we would not do ourselves.'

It was the workers, in fact, who received his chief approbation, especially the girl supervisors in pools, whose 'command of staff and adaptability were wonderful'. Many years later, in peacetime, he was to say categorically, 'Supervisors are the engine-room of a business.' The girls themselves impressed him enormously too, and he admired the loyalty and enthusiasm they brought to the job. It vindicated his long-held belief that 'the ordinary man or woman can do anything if they want to badly enough'.

He soon had an opportunity to test this further, for even while the parachute division was expanding, John had decided that it was time to diversify. Barrage balloons were urgently needed, as the Government was expecting severe bombing-raids to start at any moment, and a Major Nixon of the Barrage Balloon Section was contacted and given every detail about buildings and staff. Men were to be sent to Dunlop's factory in Manchester for a ten-week crash course in balloonistics, and John hand-picked them himself – young men who he knew from his reference file had 'shown initiative and possessed personal drive and enthusiasm'. The first order for barrage balloons was received in January 1940, before a suitable building had been prepared and before the men had even returned from their course. Twenty or thirty balloons were to be turned out each week. It was crisis time. Germany had invaded Norway and Denmark. Chamberlain had resigned and Churchill had taken over.

John quickly decided that the Littlewoods Canning Street building (acquired around 1936) was tall and spacious enough for the job in hand, and within a week all the pools equipment had been moved out, transported by the firm's vans, and stored in the Alexander Dock warehouse. Jigs and tools for balloon-making were moved in, and as the newly-qualified 'experts' returned from Dunlop, they instructed other workers. All was not plain sailing to begin with, and some balloons went through an initial stage when their fins, rudders, tails or mooring patches were attached in the wrong places. As usual, John took responsibility for this himself.

'When the trainees returned, I made the mistake of allowing them to transmit their knowledge to others instead of starting on the job themselves, for at Dunlop's they had only watched and had no practical experience.'

As with each new project, he became personally involved, and his eye for detail was unerring.

'Making balloons is a much more difficult task than making parachutes. It calls for a very high degree of precision in every process, and particularly in that of sticking the seams together with rubber solution. To start with we were given five sets of balloons to assemble by the three operations of sticking, sewing and then taping . . . To make matters more difficult, some of the special 3-ply balloon fabric, which was also being made by firms new to the work, was not properly biased and some of it was faulty. Consequently we had a terrible time with the first few balloons; after rejected work had been pulled apart once or twice, it looked a most untidy mess.'

Before long John had moved into his office in Canning Street permanently, and started 'sleeping on the job – in a bunk at the factory'. There was chaos for about a month. 'In those days I used to get up at 5 a.m. to see the night-shift depart, help clean the place before the day-shift arrived, and see the supervisors before 7.30 a.m. I seldom got to bed before 11 p.m. and then would be called at 3 a.m. to see how things were going, before turning in for a final nap. I also started a night school in the factory at that time, so that the girls could practise the processes on scrap pieces of fabric.'

Miss Price, who retired as assistant manager in pools, and who was actually one of the girls whom he had taught how to work out racing bets in earlier days, remembers his involvement. He was always there, seeing how things were going and coming up with new time-saving ideas. She described his kindness on one occasion, when she was in some pain. Working on balloons necessitated wearing very flat rubber shoes, so that there was no danger of the fabric being damaged, and as she had fallen arches, this type of footwear caused her considerable discomfort. Although there were over 500 operatives employed in balloon-making, John noticed her difficulty.

'Now look, Miss Price, I'll send you into hospital at my expense to have them treated.'

'No, thank you very much!' Miss Price replied. 'If I didn't have my fallen arches, I couldn't argue with you.'

That made him laugh, and Miss Price still smiles at the recollection.

With the Boss on the spot, things improved rapidly, and in a couple of months, all was running smoothly. The operation was divided into manufacture at Canning Street and assembly and testing at Irlam Road; when an inspector, sent by Lord Beaverbrook to examine the set-up at one point, saw fifty balloons in various stages of manufacture, he remarked, 'Fine; we will have those tomorrow.' The deadline may have been a little optimistic, but the balloons were delivered in a remarkably short time. The first balloon had come off the production line in May, the month of the Dunkirk evacuation which started on May 27th and went on until 4th June. Only six months later, in December, the thousandth balloon was produced.

Lou's husband, Len, who was general manager of the balloon division, was determined that this should be the perfect balloon to celebrate the occasion, and his staff had worked on it meticulously, each piece of fabric being hand-picked and each panel hand-cut.

'A long time afterwards, two members of the balloon division met a corporal from a balloon site who claimed that his unit had the finest balloon ever made, and that for nine months it had flown without the constant topping-up which most balloons need. Out of curiosity, they asked him for the marking numbers on the balloon, and when he gave them, it was discovered that this was none other than the handmade, thousandth balloon.'

The thousandth is also particularly remembered because of a narrow escape had by John, Cecil, Len and a great many of the firm's executives. A dinner was given at the Adelphi in Liverpool to mark the occasion and John was presented with a silver salver. Most of the company's top brass and various Ministry officials were present. In the middle of the meal, a high-explosive bomb fell just outside the building. The room was wrecked, but luckily there were no casualties. John recalled looking up and seeing the stars overhead, so the ceiling must have been badly damaged. He also saw that everyone else had got under the tables, and heard Cecil saying, 'Come on, then! Let's hear the rest of the speech!'

Air-raids were now intensifying, and work often had to be halted for a dash to the shelters. As was often the case, these were situated under the building itself and a supervisor remembers that during one particularly heavy raid, they had only just evacuated all the girls and were about to go down themselves when they met the whole work-force pouring back up the central staircase.

'What's the matter?' they asked.

'There are rats down there! We'd rather have bombs!'

Rats again.

The shelters were not always popular and on another occasion, although work had to be stopped, some of the girls simply crouched in a little outer office. One of them was petrified, and kept asking whether it was reinforced. 'Yes,' said another. 'Best reinforced plywood you can buy.'

On top of the air-raids, there were fire-watching duties. Staff volunteers, from managers to the most junior clerk, took turns in patrolling their particular building all night, usually two or three to a floor. There would be a free breakfast provided in the canteen, and then a day's work to do as usual. Very often, of course, those who were not fire-watching for Littlewoods were fire-watching at home, or acting as ARP wardens in their own neighbourhoods. And there were the inevitable fatalities. John's secretary, Miss Dew, was killed in one of the air-raids. (The advent of Miss Mitchell took place not long afterwards; she was joined later by Miss Richards, and the two remained his secretaries for over forty years. They made a formidable team and without the protection of these two guardian angels, John's business life would not have been so smooth-running.)

The family, also, did not escape unscathed. Ethel's husband Bert, a keen member of the Local Defence Volunteers, later called the Home Guard, died of a heart attack after particularly strenuous Army exercises, and Ethel and her two children moved in with Lou and Len. She continued to run her own display material factory, which had also converted to war work; commuted to Manchester every day and also took turns with her sister in patrolling the garden at night, on the look-out for incendiaries. Len was often absent on duty as an ARP warden in Liverpool, where he was in charge of the docks area. The family air-raid shelter was at the far end of their large garden and when the sirens went, small children used to be bundled into 'siren suits' made by Ethel and piggy-backed there as fast as possible. It was the same sort of routine as that going on all over the country.

On one occasion, when Len had just returned from a particularly bad night of fires at the docks and had collapsed asleep on the top bunk, Lou rushed in from patrolling the garden, shouting, 'Paratroops! Invasion! Paratroops!' In the moonlight she had mistaken the puffs of smoke from anti-aircraft fire for descending parachutes. Len leapt from his bunk immediately, landing fair and square on the family help, Dorothy, whose camp bed was on the floor between the bunks. Luckily there were no casualties. It was the same mix of terror, slightly hysterical laughter and sheer hard slog and perseverance which was common everywhere during the raids.

John's daughter, Betty, and several of the cousins were now away in term-time at boarding school. But in the holidays, the women saw to it that the children were in the safest place available. The rest of the Moores family members, all with large houses, took evacuees from the Liverpool blitz into their homes, so there were often a great many children to get to shelter. Lou was a prime mover in converting the village hall into a canteen and running it for the young conscripts in the Army camp, Harington Barracks, which had been built in the fields by Larkhill Lane, opposite Louisa's house. Ruby was doing the same thing in the Gild Hall, in Church Road, at the other end of Formby, and she was also one of the mainstays of the local WVS. Like a great many women, Lou and Ruby both spent their spare time bottling fruit and preserving eggs in isinglass. Rationing had started, and the family's tennis-courts and gardens had been turned over to poultry and pigs, and the flower beds to vegetables. Servants and staff disappeared, one by one, to more important jobs. John's younger son Peter, at the age of twelve, found his erstwhile nanny making munitions. Louisa, now in her late sixties and, like everyone else, without petrol, was unable to walk to the shops from the end of her long country lane, so she bought a large tricycle and rode about on that.

The men of the family were all heavily involved in munitions production at Littlewoods, which was growing apace. The parachute division had continued to expand, and in July 1940, Oldham Place had been added. This was a former pools building which had been used as a paper store since the beginning of the war, so tons of paper had to be moved out to the Alexander Dock Warehouse before the parachutes could be moved in. About the same time, Walmer Manufacturing Company in Chapel Street, Manchester, closed down; their rather dilapidated premises were taken over by Littlewoods in June and re-equipped as a war factory, although still keeping the Walmer name. The first Government order was for pyjamas for the troops, but by the autumn it was full-scale parachute production; and so successfully that Walmer was extended to include a factory at Chorlton-on-Medlock. Even John was impressed by the turnover.

Then came one of Merseyside's heaviest air-raids.

On May 2nd, 1941, Cecil was on the train coming back from London, where he had been meeting Ministry officials. When he arrived in Liverpool at about 8 p.m., the raid was in full swing, 'a number of buildings being on fire and guns roaring'. He went straight to Hanover Street. The night-shift of about 450 volunteers, mostly girls, was working on making parachutes in spite of the bombing.

'We went up to the roof to watch the fireworks,' Cecil recalled, 'and towards Leeds Street we could see flames raging. We decided to go and see what was happening elsewhere. When we reached Leeds Street, a fire had just started in our building, and the fire-watchers were playing hoses on the flames. They soon went away to get assistance, and it was fortunate that they did for a high-explosive bomb fell plumb on the building next door, hit a gas main, and within seconds that building and ours were just raging furnaces. All we could do was to stand by and watch them burn.

'A bomb also fell at the back of our Old Hall Street head office, flooding the cellars and blowing in parts of the building at the rear . . .

'From there I toured back to Hood Street, and decided that there should be no night-shift at Hanover Street the following night.'

The following night was a Saturday; the factory received a direct hit and was completely destroyed. Three people were killed, but if the usual night-shift had been operating, the number of dead would have been enormous.

John held an emergency meeting first thing on Monday morning at the Littlewoods recreation club in Bold Street, which Ministry officials from London also attended. It was vital that production was somehow maintained. Arrangements were made to start a night-shift at Littlewoods' other parachute factory at Oldham Place; but that same night, before the night-shift had started, this factory also received a direct hit. Part of the rigging section was destroyed, but 'miraculously, there were no casualties'. The building had to be roped off for fear of time bombs, but one of the directors, who had rushed across Liverpool to see what the damage was, took no notice of this. He explored two levels and then decided to have a look at the state of the top storey where, to his surprise, he found a man calmly sweeping the floor.

'What the hell are you doing! Get out of this building! Quick!'

'I've been here all night, and I'm not moving for anyone,' the employee said. And he went on sweeping.

In three nights Oldham Place and Old Hall Street had been damaged, and Hanover Street and Leeds Street had been put out of action. There was still no let-up in the raids. The Irlam Road balloon factory was in the middle of one of the most badly-bombed areas. Buildings all around it were destroyed, but miraculously it managed to escape heavy damage. Incendiary bombs fell on it regularly but the fire-watchers dashed about putting them out and apart from blast damage, it survived unscathed. Canning Street was also showered with incendiaries, also quickly extinguished. A land-mine came down close by, but failed to go off. (Its parachute is still kept as a souvenir.) The narrowest escape Canning Street had was due to the heroism of two railway men. Underneath the building and just above the air-raid shelters was the railway goods yard, where trains ran directly into a loading bay. On the night in question, an ammunition train was in the siding there, in serious danger of catching fire and going up in a giant explosion. The two men, risking their own lives, climbed aboard and drove it to a slightly safer place.

The Alexander Dock stores were not so lucky; they were completely demolished, together with the equipment, furniture and mail-order goods inside; not to mention the tons of paper which had been moved there from Oldham Place, and the pools equipment which had been moved from Canning Street.

The head office at Old Hall Street came into the firing line again, when a 550-pound bomb buried itself twenty-two feet under the foundations. The whole place was evacuated at top speed, and a Royal Engineers bomb disposal squad moved in and defused it. Further damage was averted; the Government was later to requisition the building and use it as a telephone exchange.

Crosby, which was later to become a giant engineering factory and the nerve centre of the entire balloon and dinghy divisions, survived by one of those vicissitudes of war. It was a gigantic building and an obvious target, but was spared when a bomb set fire to a furniture store only half a mile away; the smoke from this was so dense that as it was blown across Crosby, it completely hid the Littlewoods building from aerial view. It was the only one of all Littlewoods' factories and buildings to come through the war undamaged.

There were lulls in the bombing, of course, but raids on Liverpool and on other cities continued until 1945, ending with the last of the V-2 rockets on London. Throughout all this, the firm's production went on increasing and diversifying until the very end of the war.

The parachute division, desperate for more space after the loss of Hanover Street, was looking around for new premises. On May 20th, 1941, just over a fortnight after Hanover Street was bombed, an old shirt factory was taken over at Longford near Warrington, called the Ulster Works. It was quickly converted and by the middle of June, parachute production had started from the initial cutting stage through the entire process. In July, yet another shirt factory, the Eclipse Works, was acquired at Woolton, Liverpool, and parachutes moved in there too. The Eclipse Works was staffed almost entirely by women (185 out of a work-force of 190) and it was run by a works manageress. The next acquisition was a factory in Hart Street, Southport. This belonged to a very successful firm of dress manufacturers, but they were finding it almost impossible to get materials any more and so sold to Littlewoods. By December 1st,

1941, parachutes were on the production line there too. In August of the same year, the Ministry of Aircraft Production suggested to John that the firm should extend operations to Northern Ireland. Cecil took this on, and Barn Mills at Carrickfergus was acquired – a factory which for over a hundred years had been used for flax-spinning. New methods, new ideas and an entirely new industrial system had to be imported to a mill where extraordinarily primitive methods had prevailed. 'Green' labouring girls from the countryside around – girls who had never even seen a sewing-machine, and who had worked in the old flax-spinning days in their bare feet – found themselves employed now under ideal conditions, and earned more money than they had ever visualised. The Carrickfergus factory was re-equipped in seven weeks, parachute production started on October 14th and the first deliveries were made on November 6th, 1941. It was run by a Littlewoods man, 'Scotty' Scott, sent over from Liverpool, and the work-force here alone was to rise to 1,500.

By 1944, the parachute division had taken over the entire production of mine-laying parachutes in Britain, as well as producing supply-dropping parachutes and the 'big fellows', the giant parachutes needed to take the weight of the sixty-foot jeeps, anti-tank guns and howitzers which were dropped to airborne troops. In February, it was offered contracts not only for electrically-heated flying suits and for Mae Wests (the inflatable life-jackets used by airmen if they had to ditch in the sea), but also for parachutes used by airmen to bale out of aircraft. This was the pinnacle; and from now on the girls happily included little notes in the packing – messages such as 'Happy landings, from Sue' and 'Good luck, love Mary'. John was later to receive a letter from the director of aircraft equipment production, saying, 'Past experience has shown that anything from three to six months have elapsed before a firm could produce man-carrying parachutes, and it is a worthy note that your firm commenced delivery in three to four weeks.'

The balloon division was still operating full-stretch at Canning Street, Walton Hall Avenue and Irlam Road, and producing not only barrage balloons, but convoy balloons, hydrogen containers, oxygen bags, lifebelts, rocket-launched projectile kites (designed to enable ditched airmen to put up an aerial for radio transmission), radio transmitter bags, emergency packs and camouflage nets.

Then John took a look round at the acres of unused space in the Crosby factory, and he became even more ambitious. There is no such thing as 'standing still'; you continue to expand or you start to fall behind. Peacetime or wartime, it makes no matter. John wanted to expand.

9

The Machinery of War

'Engineering contracts?'

The Ministry of Supply was extremely dubious. After all, the firm was not an industrial one and it had no previous experience in engineering of any kind. But the North Africa campaign was starting, the British Commander-in-Chief General Wavell had opened an offensive in the desert and a German counter-offensive was expected. And finally Littlewoods' success with parachutes and balloons persuaded them.

The first contract was for the manufacture and assembly of the 119 fuse. This was the detonation for the 25-pound shell which was considered at the time to be the best answer to the German tanks of the Afrika Korps. At Crosby 100,000 square feet was allocated, and the finest precision machinery, costing £80,000, was ordered. A large proportion of it consisted of American machine tools which had never been imported before. They could hardly be delivered immediately, so in the meanwhile Cecil and the firm's buyer, Arthur Williams, 'both good mixers', went to Birmingham for tools, 'and were able to borrow enough to tide us over until our own tool-room was started'. The big engineering firms to whom they had introductions wanted to help with the war effort. They knew Littlewoods would not be in competition with them once hostilities were over, so the two men were given free access to all engineering premises. They were both good snooker players and footballers, often playing with the works teams in their spare time. 'Through this, they were able to find out how the jobs were done and how to obtain the necessary machine parts for the job.'

In the meanwhile, as Littlewoods naturally had no skilled machine setters in its employ, four of the staff were sent to Wolseley Car Works to be trained. Two were 'expert typewriter mechanics, who had been looking after our 5,000-odd typewriters' and two were skilled watch repairers from the mail-order department. They were at Wolseley's on and off for about eight months and when they returned, they instructed the rest of the work-force, both men and women. It was October 1941 before actual work on the fuse was able to start, and the first deliveries were made just before Christmas. 'Well, that's the best present we could give the country,' was Cecil's comment to John.

Cecil himself and the general manager of the section, Eric Sawyer, stayed on the job from 8 a.m. until midnight for months until the project was well under way. And in the next two and a half years, the factory delivered 68,000 fuses, without a single rejection.

No sooner was mass-production of the fuse established than a contract was received for the 20mm oerlikon shell, which had never been made in Britain before. The Battle of the Atlantic was on and convoys of little ships and big liners, as well as Naval vessels, used oerlikon guns to repel not only U-boats but long-range aircraft such as Heinkels and Focke-Wulf Condors. Oerlikon shells were needed to keep open the Western Approaches.

It took six months to install the necessary plant, and again a great deal of machinery was American which caused serious hold-ups. 'Whenever we asked by what ship or date it would arrive, the Ministry would tell us nothing. Suddenly they said, "The machinery is at the docks!" This was an exciting moment. The docks were being heavily bombed, but Cecil went in with his trucks to pick up the crates of machinery and get them out of the danger zone. He was then blandly told, "Oh, those aren't for you. They're for such-and-such a firm." The Ministry did this to us repeatedly, and it became hard work to keep the men contented. But we finally did get our machines, and within three months had doubled our standard target and then doubled it again. Finally we became the blue-eyed boys of the Ministry of Supply, who said, "Keep it up. You are setting the pace for all the other engineering firms; they daren't lag behind you." And we could even get our machinery on time.'

Production was an average of 20,000 shells daily in a seven-day week. By January 1943, the first million was reached, the second three months later, the third in another three months, two million more in September, and so it continued.

Parallel with this, in March 1942, five months after the fuse went into production and while the machinery for the oerlikon was still being sorted out, the aircraft division was established. Balloons made of rubberised fabrics were still produced at Walton Hall Avenue, but some of the staff had been sent for training in sheet-metal work and welding; switch covers, fuse boxes and radar panels were being turned out at Walton Hall again at the same time for firms such as Metropolitan Vickers and Ferranti. John now approached Messrs Rootes of Speke and obtained a contract for making front floors for Halifax bombers. A number of staff led by Cyril Hedges, the works manager, were quickly sent over to Speke to learn how it was done. They had exactly one week to study methods and techniques, and then they were back training the rest. One main-assembly jig and a set of sub-assembly jigs were installed and work was started on those. As more and more operatives were trained, more jigs were installed, until eventually Messrs Rootes handed over the entire process of making Halifax floors to Walton Hall.

Then Vickers Armstrong produced a contract for the Wellington bomber fuselage – the whole fuselage, wings, tail panels and all. Luckily the Edge Lane factory (originally the printing works) had just completed its 'Tilefer' contract – the unboxing of thousands of American Army lorries and other vehicles for the Middle East campaign – so the work on the Halifax floors was transferred there. Production was so fast that Edge Lane was soon doing centre floors and rear floors as well, and finished up supplying the complete floors for Mark III and Mark V Halifax bombers.

In the meanwhile Walton Hall, which had also been turning out balloons, was being transformed for the manufacture of Wellingtons, the aim being assembly within a few weeks. 'The factory had to be completely emptied and equipped with different services, including hydraulic pressure, air pressure, heat treatment, and special water supplies.' In addition to the actual manufacture, sub-contracting had to be arranged for some of the work.

The Wellington was the only aircraft of its class with a fuselage constructed on the geodetic principle. There were more than 10,000 geodetic parts in each aircraft, and the whole thing was rather like a jigsaw. 'We had no experience at all in geodetic production,' John wrote later, 'and so each little item had to be examined, tested, experimented with, and studied separately.' The metal pieces were 'drilled, tested, inspected, cleated and assembled first in sub-assembly, and then in larger proportions as they advanced in orderly fashion down the shop from process to process,' and everything had to be gauged to a fraction of an inch. Duralumin was a used metal, 'slightly heavier than aluminium but twice as strong', and each piece was stamped with a batch and identity number so that should an accident occur, the cause could be traced back to the particular metal part responsible.

One of the characteristics of duralumin is that when once exposed to air, its surface becomes too hard and brittle to be workable, and after two hours, it has to be softened again. Softening (or annealing) was done by heating in baths of sodium nitrate and sodium nitrite solution at a temperature of 375° centigrade. Afterwards all traces of these chemicals had to be washed away. As the rivets employed were of the same metal, at the end of a two-hour period any still unused had to be reheated in the same way and were simply tossed on the floor to await collection. John, who as usual was keenly interested in all the processes, was not at all pleased when

he saw them lying there. Miss Price, who had moved by now to
the aircraft division, remembers him helping sweep them up and
then having to be stopped as he was about to throw them away.
When it was explained to him that they were simply being taken
back to be treated and were going to be used eventually, he was very
pleased and relieved. He hated waste.

He soon learnt the details of all the various stages, and although
he never actually did any spot-welding and oxy-acetylene welding
– as Miss Price and a lot of the other girls were doing – he knew
all about the process. 'He would be out there on the floor with
you,' as Miss Price said. 'There wasn't a part of a job, from pools
onwards, that Mr John himself couldn't do.' He would go round
regularly in all the factories and his usual comments were, 'Now
tell me what you are doing,' and, 'Are you worried about any of
it?' There are photographs of him demonstrating his involvement,
from trying on a parachute pack and testing its fit, to learning how
fabric wiring was done on a Wellington's wings. He had to have his
information first-hand. He had an extraordinary effect on his staff.
'I just can't describe the atmosphere,' one of them said. 'Everybody
was so willing to work.'

The firm was to diversify into several more divisions before the
war was over. The dinghy division, although controlled completely
by the balloon division, was really a specialist unit on its own, and
it was not until 1941 that it went into full-scale production. The
first order was for fifty of the L-type dinghies – the sort used
by Mosquitoes and many other two-seater aircraft. Then came
a much larger contract for the K-type used by fighter pilots.
Several staff members were sent to Dunlop on a three-week course
and returned with prototypes and templates. Production continued
from then until the end of the war, and soon H-type dinghies
were added to the output. These were carried by medium-sized
bombers, which could hold up to five men. Before long, the
division was producing the J-type, used by the big Lancaster,
Halifax and Stirling bombers, which could accommodate eight
airmen in full kit. The D-type was the last of all, a new departure
altogether as it was not made of rubber. A sharp knife was attached
to each dinghy in case an airman's flying suit became waterlogged
and had to be cut off; and there was a variety of other equipment
such as a chemical pack for converting salt water into fresh,
fishing rods and even an extraordinary contraption which would
squeeze any fish caught through a sieve and provide fish juice.

Long-range planners in the Government Ministries were not only
thinking in terms of defensive measures, however; they were looking

further ahead to possible offensives. In North Africa, the Battle of El Alamein started, and Rommel was soon to lose Tobruk and Benghazi. At some point the Allies had to get back into Europe. Littlewoods' entry into the manufacture of front-line equipment came about almost by chance. One evening at Hillside Golf Club, John's cousin, Cyril Hodkinson, was playing bridge with the manager of Harland & Wolff, when he was given a tip to contact a Colonel Benner at the War Office. It was Cyril who together with Charlie Moores had bearded Colonel Disney in Harrogate and obtained the firm's first contract for parachutes, and he was not slow off the mark now. Next day, Littlewoods' representative met Colonel Benner in London, and by the end of the interview he had obtained an order from the Royal Engineers for 250 pontoons.

The new pontoon division was established at Irlam Road, 'starting at one corner with the wood-store racks and going, process by process, down to the water-testing tanks in the far corner'. This time, less training was necessary as there were still several joiners in the firm who had worked pre-war in the contract department of mail order. In addition, several over-sixty-fives came out of retirement and joined the team. Soon there was a staff of 340, with Cyril as general manager and T Rimmer the general foreman. Two days before Christmas 1942, work began on the first pontoon, and eight were completed in the first month. These Mark Vs were produced with modifications until July 1943 when, after two months of experiments, the Mark VI took over. These were assembled on jigs and, apart from metal frames positioned to take the strain of the bridge, were made almost entirely of wood. The girls soon became expert at using narrow-bladed electric handsaws.

The water test entailed lowering each craft into an empty tank by crane, placing heavy steel girders across the decks to pin it down, then pumping water into the tank until a pressure of seventeen tons was reached. The pontoon was kept in this position for an hour to allow detailed observation, and after this were added the 'last fitments, such as rowlocks, a stout canvas wind-and-spray dodger, engine mountings for an outboard motor, a small bollard, another undercoating of paint, and then the final spraying of a top drab colour'.

The pontoons were used to build Bailey Bridges, and it was the invention of this bridge which allowed the spectacular advances of the Allied Armies in Europe. The retreating Axis Armies blew up and destroyed most bridges in their wake to hold up their pursuers, but the Bailey Bridge could be run across the widest river in a matter of hours, and the Allies' progress was hardly slowed. July 10th, 1943, saw the first landing in Sicily and in a few weeks, Palermo was occupied. Not long after, Montgomery was to write from his HQ in Italy, 'We are now encountering demolitions on a scale far above anything we have ever met before. There is never enough Bailey Bridging. This bridging is quite the best thing in that line we have ever had. Even the three-hundred-foot gap over the Trigno, with all the piers blown, was bridged in thirty-six hours after the bridge ceased to be under small-arms fire.' Thirty-eight bridges altogether were erected in Sicily and over 1,600 on the mainland of Italy. Between the D-Day landings in Normandy on June 6th, 1944, and October of the same year, over 400 more were used. 'Hundreds more were necessary before the approaches to the Rhine and the river itself could be successfully negotiated.'

Before that, in October 1943, Littlewoods had received an important new order for storm-boats. These were an advanced type of landing-craft, capable of being driven right up onto the beaches, and able to take even artillery ashore. They were in fact speed-boats which could move over the water at twenty knots, but unlike the usual speed-boat, they were to be mass-produced and not handmade, and they were constructed of wood. Pontoon manufacture must not be slowed down, but at the same time storm-boats were a priority contract. The drawings for them were rushed out in three days. Salerno had seen hard fighting and with the landings for the Second Front planned, the War Office wanted them urgently. By February 1944, forty pontoons and storm-boats were being turned out every week.

Another aid to the campaigns of North Africa, Sicily and Italy was a system known as boxing. This had been originally devised by the Ministry of Supply at the height of the U-boat campaign, to reduce shipping space needed to a minimum. It was also invaluable in providing supplies to Allied overseas troops, and to the Russians in Stalingrad. 'As the word suggests, boxing meant the dismantling of Services vehicles, packing and casing them ready for despatch abroad, with special instructions as to their immediate reassembly at the point of delivery. The major considerations were the reduction of cubic space and the maximum safeguard against damage, but there were problems which involved the development of an entirely new industry.' Littlewoods was one of the leaders in this field. There were only home-grown soft woods available (whereas the Americans had access to hard woods) and even these soft woods were in short supply. But by the end of the war the boxing division had packed over 35,000 vehicles; not only jeeps and motor cycles but three-ton tipping trucks, fourteen-ton mobile cranes and troop-carriers amongst other things.

The firm's contribution to the Far East theatre of war was the Pacific Pack. It was impossible to transport ordinary food the thousands of miles necessary, so a scheme for the provision of concentrated food was formulated. Each pack supplied a day's meals for one man; there were three tins each five inches by five and a half inches by one and a half inches, which separately contained breakfast, lunch, and supper. Together they weighed only just over three pounds, but their contents were staggering, ranging from meat biscuits, fruit bars, cheese blocks and oatmeal blocks for porridge, to such essentials as salt tablets and anti-malaria pills. Cigarettes and matches were not forgotten, while the one constant was 'latrine paper'. It was the former balloon-cutting department at the Crosby factory which handled all this and it managed to turn out 13,000 packs a day.

Looking back now, it is quite extraordinary that a firm such as Littlewoods, specialising in football pools, mail order and chain-stores, all basically paperwork-based, should have been able to switch over to mass-production with such speed, often in extremely technical areas. Sixteen factories and eight different divisions worked flat out, employing over 14,000 workers and producing 12 million shells, 6 million fuses, 5 million parachutes, 50,000 dinghies, 20,000 balloons, over 4,000 pontoons and storm-boats – the list could go on. How did they do it?

According to John, the real secret of Littlewoods' success was 'the facility for the quick training of employees, coupled with the organising ability of the directors and executive staff'. Leadership was vital. John set the example, but it was shown in abundance by other directors and executives too. There was efficient forward planning – John has always been the most far-sighted of men. There was also ingenuity. Lack of experience sometimes produced short-term mistakes, but it also produced new solutions, and people were encouraged to come up with fresh ideas. Tried and tested ways were not just discarded. Very often they were not used because they were unknown to Littlewoods. Problems had to be looked at from new angles, and the 'wrong' way very often got better results than the right way.

The organising of geodetics in the production of the Wellington bomber was a case in point. The famous duralumin rivets were eventually organised into differently-coloured trays to be distributed. 'A large clock in each department – its face divided into corresponding bands of colour – revealed to all workers at a glance what colour rivet trays had to be used during each particular two-hour period' – the time limit of safety before re-annealing.

John's preoccupation with the non-wastage of time found perfect expression here.

The sub-assembly department of the Wellington saw a break-through in systematised time-saving. The geodetic components had originally been laced together only by the system of batch and identity numbering, and operatives had been forced to spend valuable time sorting out the necessary parts, 'just as in doing an ordinary jigsaw, one would have to search through the box for each separate piece'. Now a numbered board was produced for each particular assembly job, and it was constructed with the jig markings and hooks showing where the particular pieces should be hung. The position of the parts on the board corresponded to the positions they were to occupy in the completed job. The board, in fact, was a diagram or picture of what that particular section should look like when assembled. And to speed up the process still further, coloured numbers were used on the actual jig itself, the colour identifying each part used and showing where it should be fitted.

The pontoon division was another innovative area right from its inception. 'They made a pontoon from blueprints, and then from that made the templates needed for further manufacture. Old methods were ignored and the contract work was to be on mass-production, every item being broken down to each separate little process. Previously the makers of pontoons had been satisfied to start on one and finish it before embarking on a second. Our method was to co-ordinate the job so that continuous production proceeded easily and steadily.' It was almost a conveyor-belt system, modelled on production in the car industry. When representatives from other firms called at John's invitation to pool ideas, they usually left converted to Littlewoods' methods. And by the end of the war, apart from one firm of established shipbuilders, the company was turning out more pontoons and storm-boats than anyone else.

In the boxing division, too, many inventive minds were at work. The only instructions it had started out with were 'a handful of inferior photographs and a certain amount of technical data supplied by the Ministry'. The staff, under the management of a former superintendent of chain-stores, 'consisted of six joiners, six girls and two bricklayers'. Then the work-force was increased to thirty, including one actual motor mechanic. By the end of 1942, the division had a staff of 250, and the case-making was done by fifteen sub-contractors to systems developed by Littlewoods.

A vehicle would be 'stripped and experimentally "nested" on a stout wooden base with the aid of stools and cross supports, while each stage of the process was photographed, marked and revised until the perfect packing was obtained'. This was done so scientifically that timber of only a three-quarter-inch thickness was used to box vehicles of four tons and under, and timber of one-inch thickness for vehicles over that weight – which were often as heavy as twelve tons. Such was the success of Littlewoods' experiments that eventually Crosby was selected by the Ministry to replace the Government experimental station at Coles Green. This meant that a new department had to be set up, with a drawing office and staff, so that photographs and written instructions for each of Littlewoods' final solutions could be circulated to all the other boxing contractors. And it also meant that now even more ingenious methods could be developed on the drawing-board and worked out to a fine degree of accuracy.

Right at the very beginning of the war, just before the blitzes became heaviest, the firm's laboratories had invented the chemical KB63, which enabled the manufacture of barrage balloons to be increased with dramatic speed.

Small wonder that John had wanted at the outset to find 'real war work for these capable people of ours'. And by that he meant the whole work-force, not only administrators, executives and inventors. In fact, as he said himself, 'Looking back over the war years, it is the resilience and adaptability of our young women that impresses me most strongly. They were all really keen to pull their weight, and it was surprising how quickly they picked up new and intricate jobs, and having mastered them, turned to new tasks with equal efficiency when the need arose.' One interesting comment he made later: 'It is a curious fact, but I found that it was better to teach our girl supervisors about mechanics than to teach mechanics to become supervisors.' Perhaps leadership is an inborn talent, like mathematical ability or creative flair; it can be cultivated, but it is also inherent. John himself is living proof.

Leadership was also used to keep everyone enthusiastic and giving of their best – the company was not composed of supermen and superwomen, but of 'ordinary' people. The Star Badge system was devised to promote 'friendly rivalry among the workers of the individual factories, besides giving them an incentive to pull out just that little bit extra which makes all the difference'. The badges were made of enamelled metal, and each factory had its own particular design – incorporating a parachute, a balloon or whatever was appropriate – but all with the words Star Operator scrolled underneath. To win one was the nearest equivalent of winning a military medal, and people were encouraged to feel that they were supporting and making common cause with the men and women on active service. Star Badges were awarded to those whose work was outstanding; as well as receiving a cash reward and a certificate, from then on they were given the official title of Star Badge Worker.

Competitiveness was also appealed to in the War Savings campaign. At first there was simply a voluntary deduction from pay each week, but Cecil, who was a member of the Trade Advisory Council of the Liverpool War Savings Committee, encouraged his heads of department to develop the group system in every factory. Silver Shields were introduced to be awarded each month and presented by Cecil to the group which had saved the most, and the inter-factory competition that developed had an astronomical effect on savings.

It was not only the war effort that filled people's minds of course; the ordinary business of life still went on too. It was the fuel that kept them going. A great many girls were going out with soldiers, and the favourite meeting place was under Owen Owen's clock. There used to be a lot of peeping out of the window of the Littlewoods building opposite, to see what somebody's current boyfriend looked like, and the usual sort of giggling and gossip.

John, looking ahead as usual, never forgot the peacetime that was hopefully to come. At the beginning, he had imagined that the chain-stores would continue during the war much as usual, that mail order would be curtailed by at least thirty per cent, and that pools would be drastically reduced or stop altogether. Things did not turn out quite like that. To begin with, the Government was anxious that football pools should be kept going to provide people with some relaxation. The Pools Promoters Association got together, each separate business was wound up and a combined effort called Unity Pools was inaugurated which ran right through the war until 1946. The stores just managed to keep ticking over. Mail order had the toughest time of all; its head office was bombed and having moved to a place on the docks – also bombed – it finished up in two cafés in Southport. Most of Littlewoods' warehouses had switched to war work, and it became more and more difficult to get supplies; added to which Post Offices were bombed, orders held up and often deliveries to customers just did not get through. At one point it looked as though mail order would actually have to close, but John would not hear of it. Mr Hedges, the works manager and troubleshooter, was temporarily seconded back from war work to keep it going. If it was impossible to meet an order from stock, then Littlewoods girls would be sent scouting round all the shops in the area to see what they could find.

It was not only that John did not want to lose one of his businesses; he had promised all those employees now fighting that their jobs would be open for them when they returned. He was going to have those jobs ready to offer them, come hell or high water! The war could not last for ever, and most of the men would have families to provide for. Family life goes on, war or no war. And so did John's.

10

Count Your Blessings

It was the children of the family who had changed the most by the end of the war. And there were plenty of them; as well as his own four, John by now had eighteen nephews and nieces. The war affected everyone, taking five or six years out of people's lives; but that is a larger proportion of a child's life and in a period of that length, a small child can grow into a teenager and a teenager can become a young adult.

John's eldest son, John Junior, was almost eleven when war was declared; even as short a time as two years later, in 1941, he was starting his first term at Eton. He was young for public school, but that after all was the age at which his father had stopped full-time schooling and started part-time work. For once, in the area of his children's education, John's proclivity for looking ahead does not seem to have been employed. Perhaps he left Ruby to deal with this side of things; perhaps the full realisation of how the family's increasing wealth must of necessity change their lives only dawned on him slowly. Certainly there appears to have been no long-term plan; most decisions were comparatively last-minute.

Betty, the eldest child, was sent away to a boarding school in Cliftonville at the age of three and a half – a big wrench for her parents. She had been diagnosed as having bovine tuberculosis, and it was thought that the milder climate of the south coast would be beneficial. In 1934, as soon as her health improved sufficiently, she left her boarding school in Cliftonville at the age of nine, and had then been a day girl at Dagfield High School for Girls in Southport. The decision to send her to Cheltenham Ladies' College was made just before the war, and it was sudden – she left Dagfield without even the customary term's notice being given.

Betty took to Cheltenham immediately. The school's reputation for scholastic excellence was well-earned, and the teaching staff contained a good number of highly intellectual and dedicated women, often unmarried – very much in the tradition of the college's founder, Dorothea Beale who, together with Frances Buss, another member of the Association of Headmistresses, had been one of the pioneers of secondary education for girls in the late nineteenth century. Even in 1939, it could still be difficult for an academic woman to combine a teaching career with marriage and bringing up a family; it was often a question of choosing between the two. In the State sector the choice was obligatory. If a woman teacher married, she was not allowed to continue teaching and had to resign from her post.

> *Miss Buss and Miss Beale*
> *Cupid's darts do not feel.*
> *How different from us,*
> *Miss Beale and Miss Buss.*

Unlike them, the pupils of the Thirties and Forties fully expected to enjoy both marriage and a career. But although they might no longer have shared the same ethos as their teachers, they could still respond to intellectual challenge. Betty was a clever girl and the challenge suited her well.

The whole family began to have different expectations about the education of their children. For John's two sons, it was to be Eton but, again, this was a late decision; it is a school for which a boy's name is usually entered at birth. The best chance of a place was for John Junior to win a scholarship, so his holidays were spent at a crammer's in Liverpool. In the early days of the war, both boys were sent away to Windermere in their school holidays, where they stayed with an elderly retired schoolmaster who gave them extra tuition. Their father believed in pushing his sons, and when John Junior was put in for a scholarship a year younger than was usual, 'that was really being pushed very hard indeed'. He only just missed obtaining one, but he was next on the list and it was wartime, so he got in. The pushing still went on, and John now took a keen interest in his sons' school grades. 'He was always for competition, and if you did well – a distinction – you got a lot of money. First-class, you got less; second-class you got slightly less, and a pass you got frowned on.' He applied the same maxim to his children as to his work-force – credit where it is due and a tangible reward.

The way John treated his two daughters was slightly different. They were encouraged to compete, to develop their talents, but the pushing was not quite as hard as in the boys' case. More importantly, possibly because of the twelve-year gap between their ages, they were not urged to compete against each other as the boys were. This less aggressive approach was in keeping with how he had related to them when they were younger. 'He was wonderful at playing with us,' as one daughter said. 'But he probably played with the boys more because he enjoyed having a rough-house with them.' His ambitions for the girls were expressed in a somewhat gentler way too. 'He never pontificated at you. He never said that you *must* do this or that. He gave you the chance to decide, but he'd lay the points out fairly clearly, in a sensible, practical way.'

One evening during a conversation with her father, Betty happened to mention something about university, and was quite astonished when he immediately responded, 'But *you* can go to university. Why shouldn't you go?' It had never occurred to her that this was even a possibility, and she was delighted. 'When the opportunity arose, he knew when to give you a push.' As a result, she took the Cambridge entrance exam, got a place at Newnham, and went up in 1943 to read History. It was there that she was to meet her future husband.

Kenneth Suenson-Taylor had arrived back from the Army to take an LLB. A first-class mind who indeed already had one First and was to obtain another for his LLB, he was to go on to become a QC and eventually to inherit his father's title, becoming Lord Grantchester. As the important second-year Cambridge exams approached, Betty was in an unusually disturbed frame of mind. Obviously the possibility of marriage was distracting her, and she was also considering a change from reading History to reading Law, like Kenneth. A few weeks before the exams, she wrote a despondent letter to her father, saying that she had lost a lot of energy and enthusiasm for work, and asking for his advice. His reply was long, detailed, full of practical suggestions, and very illuminating as regards his own character and attitudes. To begin with, it was typical of the man that he should take the trouble to give so much time and thought to a twenty-year-old's exam worries during a period that was particularly traumatic, both nationally and internationally. The war seemed to be in its final stages; the British Second Army had crossed the Rhine; the last of the V-2 rockets had fallen on London; the end was in sight. On a personal level, John's five years of broken nights – fire-fighting, sleeping fitfully on site at his munitions factories and waking between shifts; his years of driving himself, of constant efforts to inspire and drive his work-force, of even greater effort to convince the Government Ministries of just how capable his people were; of intense planning, adapting, looking ahead; all this was nearly at an end. Ahead lay the equally gigantic task of converting the huge war work machine he had created back to a peacetime organisation. It meant almost starting again – in pools, mail order and chain-stores. Peace would bring many challenges.

Then the Allies crossed the Elbe. On April 28th, 1945 Mussolini and his mistress were killed by Italian partisans, and their bodies were strung up by the heels from lampposts. On April 29th, the German

Army in Italy surrendered. And on April 30th, Hitler committed suicide, together with his long-time mistress, Eva Braun, whom he had married the day before, and their bodies were burnt. Finally, on May 7th, Germany signed an unconditional surrender.

A week later, on May 14th, John typed a long letter of advice to his daughter, which he broke down into three chapters and in which the main thing he recommended, surprisingly, was enjoyment. It was, however, a conscious enjoyment which he advocated and one which could be attained by mental control and effort. The coming exam which was worrying his daughter was a simple fact.

'One thing is sure, the appointed day for the exam will duly arrive. At the appointed time the examiners will arrive and the students will duly sit for it.'

There was still a choice left to her, however; not as to whether or not she should take the exam – she had already made up her mind about that – but a choice between being happy or being depressed.

'Since you're going through with the exam, you might as well enjoy the experience as be miserable about it.'

And how was this enjoyment to be achieved?

'*Want what you've got whilst you've got it.* For goodness' sake, don't be like those people who are always looking forward to the day of their dreams or looking backward and saying, "We didn't know how happy we were in those good old days . . ." In other words, they always miss happiness 'cos they don't practise getting a day's happiness every day.'

'Practise' is the interesting word, and the operative one; but first he went to great trouble to explain what he meant by happiness.

'A few days ago, General Montgomery thanked his troops for the great efforts they had made and which had resulted in such a great victory. He went on to say that there were many stern tasks ahead of us. Europe had to be restored, resettled, fed and clothed. Further, we had our own post-war problems. He said, "Remembering the glorious victories we have achieved, we will go forward into the future with joyous optimism."'

And this 'joyous optimism', John explained, was nothing more nor less than a state of mind.

'The poorest person in the country can be more joyously optimistic than the richest man in the world.' All that remained was for his daughter to 'see the facts in the right light and to face the exam in a spirit of joyous optimism'. All she needed was a different attitude, and he underlined this particularly because 'there will be a tendency for you to think that there is some other remedy; that you can take a pill; stand on your head; mutter some incantation, or some equal absurdity. *You have all you want now* except the right frame of mind.'

He goes into more detail still.

'The person who is not likely to have the right frame of mind is a person who is dissatisfied, selfish and ungrateful. Conversely, you will have a much better chance if you feel abundantly satisfied; if you are unselfish; and if you are grateful for the many blessings you now have. You must start immediately practising getting into a frame of mind in which you feel very satisfied, unselfish and very grateful.'

This was urgent, because 'the only way to attack a wrong state of consciousness is to *do something immediately*, and to keep doing it'. And the method of practising which he recommended was simple and practical, too.

'You may find it difficult, but time yourself by a watch and for at least fifteen minutes try to fill your mind absolutely full of thoughts around these three points. If it proves rather a strain, then give it up, and if you must be miserable then go away and be miserable and cry and wail and wallow in your misery. If you *must*, then do it for three-quarters of an hour, or even a whole hour. Then come back. Sit down again, and for another quarter of an hour or so, practise being (1) satisfied, (2) unselfish and (3) grateful.

'Last thing at night and first thing in the morning, just before and just after sleep, you *must* fill your mind with thoughts around these three qualities.'

He defined them with down-to-earth examples of how to attain them mentally.

'Satisfaction' could be achieved by going over the pleasant things in one's life. 'Soak your mind in the happiness you have had. Think,' he suggested, 'of the happy times you have had at Loch Grannoch. See yourself in the little boat trying to hoist the sail.' It was a good idea also to make a list of happy remembrances and have them ready 'as an antidote to your black moment'.

'Unselfishness' could be achieved by thinking, too.

'The world wasn't created to revolve especially around you. There are still people starving and suffering the horrors of war. Try not to be too self-centred and see if you can help somebody else's little trouble. Try hard to be kind. As Grannie says, "Throw out love". Think kindly of your friends, of your family, and of little gifts and surprises that you are going to plan for them.'

And 'being grateful' was the most important thing of all. Lists were to the fore again; she should sit down and write a list of things to be grateful for: that she was not suffering from cancer, crippled or ugly; that 'you have your desire of going to Cambridge, which is a devil of a sight better than working at a factory or being in the Services'. And his final advice was, 'It is a long step along the road to happiness to regularly count your blessings.'

One thing that his counselling demonstrated was his own enormous mental control, and how much he lived in his head. Intellectual ability, it had been drummed into him, was his pathway to success and everything was transmuted to the cerebral. His natural reactions and sympathies were strong, but in order to achieve recognition they had to be 'listed' in his mind. He could, and did, sympathise – with feelings, difficulties, troubles which he knew of and could understand from his own experience; but he never made that imaginative leap which can project a man into someone else's experience. Empathy was out. It had not been listed.

The other thing which the letter demonstrates of course is his reading matter. This varied over the years, but philosophy has always been a major part of it. In their youth, when his sons asked him for a good book, he recommended the short stories of O Henry. Bernard Shaw has always occupied an important position in his library – although, interestingly, he could never be bothered with the actual plays; it was the *Prefaces* which he read and re-read. Nothing, however, could ever supplant philosophy, and voracious reading throughout his life took him from Bertrand Russell to Pascal and Descartes, whom he was delightedly discovering in his eighties.

The year in which he wrote the letter of advice to his daughter, he seems to have got as far as Norman Vincent Peale and Dale Carnegie – there is a strong whiff of *The Power of Positive Thinking* and of *How to Win Friends and Influence People*. In fact, he never stopped urging people to read the latter book, which accords with his fascination for all things American – in method and in thought. Perhaps his favourite at the time was a book on psycho-cybernetics by Maxwell Maltz, titled *Acquiring the Habit of Happiness*. And his favourite quote from it? 'I think happiness is not the reward for virtue. It is virtue itself.'

There is one last bit of practical advice – which John was to follow himself, all his life. The best time to practise mind control was, indeed, last thing at night and first thing in the morning.

However, he concludes, 'You can practise any time. Lie flat on your back, preferably in a dark room, relax for a few moments, and then start by getting a satisfied state of mind. Try to do it at least once a day, even for a few moments . . . A little and often is better than a big dose and forgetting it for a week. Try to make the practice a habit, and I can absolutely guarantee that the right state of mind will also become a habit.'

It is the chatty end of the letter which is most revealing, of himself and of his lifestyle.

'It is now 11.30 p.m., which is past my bedtime, and the strain of trying to type accurately is beginning to tell, so shortly I'll go to bed, where your Mummy is quite uncomplainingly reading.

'We have not yet heard from the boys, though they've been back ten days. Peace Day was passed very quietly. A walk on the links and bridge in the evening. On the second day I played golf, and in the evening we went round to Aunt Louise's and had a family chinwag in her bedroom – she had a touch of flu.

'Janatha had a slight touch of scarlatina but is now very fit indeed. She still punches me in the stomach. Either she is growing much stronger or my stomach is growing larger, or both, for I find that I now have to prepare for the blow – and unfortunately sometimes I don't see it coming.

'Will you please write me giving the date of your exam. I shall think of you as confident and successful.

All my love,
Daddy'

He may have preferred a rough-house with his sons, but daughters, when small, were not excluded from horseplay. One of Janatha's fondest childhood memories is of how she and her father would build caves and dens all over the sitting-room floor, using cushions they had stripped from the sofa and armchairs. Ruby was a very tolerant woman. The boys were 'back', presumably, at school – for Peter had now joined John Junior at Eton. They were in the same house, possibly not a wise decision because of the difference in their ages; John Junior was at the top of it and Peter was at the bottom. Before he left, Peter was to become captain of the Oppidans, but at this stage he was the most junior member of his house. And their father was still encouraging competition between them.

Ruby wrote to her sons regularly; John left it to her because he was far too busy. They did not often visit their sons; once a term at the most as petrol was still in short supply and transport was difficult. John and Ruby never attended the big Etonian occasions. It is hardly likely that John ever felt overwhelmed, although Ruby may have done, but he would certainly not have felt at ease or on familiar ground. 'Every time he met other parents, he didn't like them,' John Junior recalls. 'I can only imagine he didn't approve of the sort of people who send their boys to Eton.'

It is interesting, if this was the case, to conjecture why John should have chosen to do so himself. Perhaps it was to give them an advantage which he himself had not had, to make it easier for them to hold their own on a wider stage. He certainly assumed that, while they might acquire new expertise and new experience, at the same time their values would not change, but would still remain identical with his own. He was later to say, 'My sons have had the disadvantage of a good education,' and even more forcefully, 'The trouble with my sons is that they have never known adversity.' The particular sort of hardship which he had known in his earlier years was indeed outside their experience, but their difficulties were equally outside his – and he made little effort to understand them. It is never easy to be the ice-breaker, to forge ahead into unknown waters. And it is the children of self-made men who are the ice-breakers; they have to acclimatise, to learn new rules and customs, to fit into a totally different social scene, and above all to succeed, while at the same time defending and protecting their parents and carrying the weight of parental expectations.

After a slightly shaky start in his first term at Eton – due, no doubt, to being independent of his father's influence and decision-making for the first time – John Junior enjoyed himself. He was an athletic boy – a good cross-country runner who ran for the school, and finally became captain of boxing. John has always been interested in boxing, and he had taken his eldest son to boxing-matches and had him coached from an early age. When the boy was five or six and at one of Lou's family parties, he and two of his small cousins had been togged out in some Christmas present boxing-gloves and pitted against each other in turn as part of the entertainment. The men of the family were very keen on the idea, the women definitely not. Unfortunately Ethel's son, who knew nothing of the finer points of the sport, simply lashed out and made his cousin's nose bleed – the women's viewpoint was definitely vindicated.

At Eton, John Junior's confidence increased by leaps and bounds. Any trace of a Lancashire accent which he might have had was soon a thing of the past and he appeared, superficially at least, a typical product of the place. John still made sure that his son did not lose touch with the nitty-gritty of life, however. Every long holiday, from the age of sixteen, he was sent over to the States to work at Sears Roebuck. And the allowance which he received from his father was by no means lavish. When John was in London on business, staying at the Dorchester, John Junior would sometimes get permission from school to visit him – and this posed a problem. If he arrived and departed by the front entrance of the hotel, he would have to tip someone, even pay for a taxi, neither of which he could afford. He quickly found the back way in for staff and always used that. When this was reported to his father, John simply laughed and said, 'That's my boy!' It would never have occurred to him to put his son's allowance up – not simply in order to learn how to tip and how to go in and out of a fashionable hotel.

John Junior was also at this stage the one amongst his children with whom he always discussed business and company matters. On visits to Eton, instead of having a picnic in the park with all their grand friends which was what most of the other parents indulged in, he would take his wife and two boys out as a foursome, to do whatever appealed to them. He wanted to see his own sons, not other people's, but it was mainly John Junior to whom he talked; Peter was usually left to bring up the rear with his mother. It was a repetition of the world cruise again – Peter was the one who was left behind.

He was always keen to be with his father. There were times before the war when he used to beg to go to football matches with him, and would have to squash into a small car with four men, all of whom smoked heavily and talked over his head; there were the shoots he accompanied John to when he was a little older, hidden in the back of the car with the dogs because it was a business trip. But his own interests never seemed to appeal to his father or to be shared in any way.

Parents exist to be blamed, of course; it is one of their functions. However much we love them, there has to be somebody other than ourselves who is responsible for our shortcomings – emotional and intellectual, not to mention genetic. Certainly John did his best as a father, and he loved all his children; it was simply that he 'listed' them at an early age. John Junior was the heir apparent, who did just what his father told him to do and who was being groomed to run the business – in some very distant future. Peter was the younger son, more of an unknown quantity, clever, argumentative, interested in the arts. Opera was already a passion with him, and it was possibly the one taste he and his father had in common. John in fact had taken him to his first opera in 1942 when he was only ten, and he occasionally took him to concerts at the Liverpool Philharmonic Hall. John himself had a collection of Beethoven symphonies and sonatas on '78' records, which he often played, but Peter's opera records were not popular with the rest of the family. His mother was inclined to say, 'Turn that music down!' all the time. 'There was only one place you could play them in those days, that was in the lounge. Everyone else wanted to read or talk and found the noise irritating.'

Cousins in the same age-group played together a good deal before going away to public school, and even when they grew older they still spent time together in the holidays. The family parties at Christmas and the New Year continued, only now the younger generation took more of a share in the 'turns'. Hilda's children both played the piano well. Several of the girls, who were interested in theatrical careers, would recite poetry; and Ethel's son always sang 'Abdul the Bulbul Emir'. This was a popular item, and so was a performance by Cecil's son. 'Ercules 'e was an 'unter. 'E 'unted 'ares in the 'ampshire 'ills. And when 'e caught an 'are, 'e 'it it on the 'ead with a 'eavy 'ammer, and it 'o–o–owled 'orrible.' Spoken deadpan by a nine-year-old it was surprisingly funny. The song that was the family favourite, however, was one sung by Cecil's wife, 'Outside a Lunatic Asylum', and the great excitement was always that she would include the 'rude' word in the last line:

> *Working for your living! Take my tip,*
> *Act a little funny and become a lunatic!*
> *Oh, you get your meals quite regular,*
> *And a couple of suits beside.*
> *Thirty bob a week! And a couple of kids to keep!*
> *Come on inside, you silly bugger, come inside!*

Not at all politically correct, by today's standards, but typical of a time when working people used humour to help them get through a very hard life.

There was only ever one slight awkwardness, and that was the year after Ethel's husband Bert died. Every Christmas he had always recited a poem called 'Jim' – rather well, as he came from a theatrical family. That year, John decided he would have a go at it himself. In a way it was a compliment, and it would never have occurred to John that this might be rather upsetting for his newly-widowed sister; he would have regarded that as giving in to sentimentality; but for once there were critical looks from some of the family, and he never recited it again.

The competitive element was present even at parties now – there were not just 'turns' but games as well. The most popular was a word game in which the family were divided into two teams. Each team had a room to themselves as HQ, and a representative from each would go to the referee – usually Ruby – and together they would be given a word, which each of them had to go back and draw, without speaking. Their team had to guess what it was; then the next representative would be sent in for the next word. The teams were always men against women. It was great fun and very good-humoured. And there was always the ritual incident of the men 'cheating'. The women, on the whole, were the quicker guessers, not because they necessarily knew more words but because they were better communicators. One of the men would be sent in to infiltrate and listen in, usually hiding behind a curtain. He would always be discovered, and chased out by one or two of the females with mock ferocity. An anthropologist's field-day.

It was not only his sons whom John pushed; his nephews got the same treatment, although to a lesser degree. This was the period in which he decided that they should all learn something about public speaking. The older ones were in their teens now, and Sunday meetings were organised at Lou's where they had to perform. They would be given a subject to prepare earlier in the week and then would have to speak on it for five minutes, in front of John and with their mothers as audience. They would then receive advice from their uncle as to where and how they could improve. 'We used to be terrified,' was a comment made with feeling many years later.

It was not just the family to which John devoted time and attention; there was a lot happening on the national scene. Churchill had stated publicly in 1944 that the defeat of the Germans, when it came, would be the time to end the Coalition Government and go to the country. Parliament, indeed, had not been dissolved since the foundation of the National Government by Stanley Baldwin in 1935, nine years earlier. When the Germans surrendered in May 1945, there was some disagreement between the coalition parties about the suitable moment for a general election – the war against Japan, after all, was still to be won. Churchill precipitated things on May 23rd by resigning. The National Government finally came to an end, and a 'caretaker' government, mainly composed of Conservatives, ran the country until the general election of July 5th. The result was a Labour landslide.

To some people it seemed like a rejection of the man who had rallied the country 'in its darkest hour'; the man who, more than anyone else, had led its people through some very grim years to victory. To others – while they acknowledged his wartime achievements – it was a sign that the country was about to embark on a new phase. The peace now had to be won. Ahead was a brave new world. This feeling of a vast switch to the future was stirring in the world of commerce too. And it was on his businesses that John, as usual, expended most of his energies.

11

Winning the Peace

The wheel had come full circle; football pools were once more being attacked, as they had been pre-war. In 1945 it was the turn of Unity Pools. They had been formed by Littlewoods, Vernons and Zetters at the Government's request, but had never received a paper allocation from the Board of Trade, so had been obliged to publish their coupons in the advertising columns of various daily newspapers. In the winter of that year, a court action was brought against them by a clergyman who accused Unity Pools of breaking the law. Publishing coupons in newspapers was contrary to Section 34 of the Betting and Lottery Act.

In defence, Unity Pools claimed that this had been a last recourse in exceptional circumstances, that the country had been in the middle of a war and that there was no paper obtainable, but the Revd John Bretherton won his case. Unity Pools was no longer allowed to use the newspapers, and it looked for a while as though that was to be the end of pools altogether. The new Labour Government thought otherwise, however. John's explanation for this was simple: 'They must have decided that they valued the millions of pounds we paid in income tax, postage stamps, duties, etc., apart from the fact that we were employing more than 10,000 girls in a depressed area and putting employment stamps on their cards, for we were granted a limited quantity of paper. It was just enough to let us print a coupon slightly less than half the minimum size we had found necessary before the war.'

Cecil and his pools experts designed a coupon of sixty square inches – not much larger than two postcards stuck together.

Then, in the spring of 1946, Unity Pools were closed down and the various promoters went back to building up their own firms again. John and Cecil called a meeting and there was a long and animated discussion as to how Littlewoods Pools were now going to be run. At first it was not legal to send ready money; a postal order had to be purchased and attached to the coupon, and the money was paid a week later. Then this rule was amended and money could be sent after all. John and Cecil were always pushing back the frontiers, always trying to get the restrictions eased, and there were continual alterations in what was allowed and what was not.

Speed was still vital, and however many times directives were changed, it was important to stay ahead of the field. A retired secretary, Bunty Ashton, who was a young girl at the time and working in an office by the Irlam Road factory, remembers being amazed at what was going on. The factory had been making pontoons at the end of the war, and there was now a complete change in production. As the pontoons went out of one door, the men who had been manufacturing them began to make desks; as the desks were completed, they were being placed in position and girls were coming in to sit at them, either to be trained as pools operators, or – if they had come back from war service – to have a quick refresher course; it was like a vast conveyor-belt. Littlewoods was soon to be once again the biggest pools business in the country. Before long, the amount paid in prize money was almost double the amount which had been paid in 1939. The new Treble Chance Pool, started in 1946 at the end of August, was an instant success and has remained the public's favourite ever since.

By 1945 the trickle of fighting men coming back to civilian life and wanting jobs had already started, and the trickle soon became a vast torrent. Those who had worked in mail order pre-war were in for a shock. The business had only just managed to keep going, ticking over very slowly; the allocation of clothing coupons was not lavish and most goods were in short supply. John's policy was to build the division up again as quickly as possible, but it was a hard slog, and to begin with it could not accommodate all its ex-employees. A lot of them were drafted over to the pools side of the company; and there were plenty of them who, once they had got interesting managerial jobs there, never went back to mail order again. 'Mind you, we got on very well with them. They were all Littlewoods people.' A generous comment from Miss Price who during the war had moved from pools to run an entire balloon factory. Pools had been mainly run by girl supervisors and a female work-force before the war; during the war it had been kept going by older women who were exempt from war work. Afterwards the managers were usually male. As Miss Price said, 'A lot of men all got pukka jobs; we were never put in complete charge again. They were expanding the business overseas and people seemed to want to deal with men rather than women.'

With mail order, it was more or less a question of starting from scratch. The main problem was to find enough manufacturers who could produce anything saleable and up to standard. Buyers were sent scouting all over the country, usually by train or bus. There were no buyers' cars in those days. Certain manufacturers, national brand names, were extremely reluctant to deal with mail order at all. They were afraid of an adverse reaction from their usual retail outlets. A lot of the big retailers did in fact stop buying products that were advertised in the Littlewoods catalogues; many carpet manufacturers, for instance, would not supply at all and the company found themselves keenly promoting underfelts and felt stair-pads instead of their pre-war Axminsters and Wiltons. The catalogues themselves, which now came out twice a year, were half the size of the pre-war ones. The first, the 1945 spring/summer catalogue, was restricted to ninety-three pages of fairly basic clothing, shoes and underwear for men, women and children. The 119 very large pages, which in the last pre-war publication had been devoted to household goods, toys, etc., were now replaced by a mere seven pages of 'miscellaneous fancy goods and hardware'. These included such wartime requisites as the 'modern chemical closet for indoor or outdoor use. An absolute necessity in homes without running water or indoor sanitation'; a gas lighter – 'which answers the match-shortage problem'; and the ideal toy – a Spitfire Model Aero outfit.

Prices had gone up considerably too, but gradually, by dint of hard slogging and a lot of legwork on everybody's part, the business began to take off again. Astute manufacturers saw where things were heading and now wanted to get in on the act. 'We were then in a position where we could be selective,' to quote Alec Lindsay, a director who retired in the Seventies. 'We laid down our own terms and those terms were pretty tough.'

One of the tenets of John's philosophy, however, was that suppliers were part of the team. There was no way that Littlewoods could do without them or they without Littlewoods. He was always insistent, nevertheless, that suppliers should not be pushed beyond their capacity. Twenty-five per cent of their requirements had to come from some other firm, in case the time came when a particular manufacturer could not deliver or turned elsewhere. If goodbyes were to be said, they had to be said without ill-feeling. And tough as their terms may have been, Littlewoods got away with it – because they always paid with amazing promptitude. Unlike most mail-order firms, they paid within seven days on the nail, for which, naturally, they exacted a discount; it was not done for nothing. The reason that they were practically alone in being able to offer this speed of payment was the enormous cash flow they had from pools, and to a lesser extent from chain-stores.

The stores themselves, although they had not been as badly hit as mail order, took longer to recover. Minutes of the annual meeting of chain-store managers back in February 1945 give some idea of the difficulties they had been facing, but they conclude: 'Now that the war with Germany will probably be over in three to four months' time, we can expect a big increase in trade . . . It is definitely certain that the Government are making arrangements to increase the supplies of civilian goods as soon as the war is over.'

In the event it was a somewhat misplaced certainty. Not only were there continued difficulties in obtaining suitable stock in all departments, but building restrictions made it even more difficult to do anything about the renovation of the stores themselves. The building of new stores was an impossibility. That word, however, is perhaps one which should never be used in conjunction with the name of John Moores. The same Alec Lindsay made the mistake of using it at his first meeting with the Boss. He was an assistant buyer at the time, and when John asked for something to be done which seemed to him impossible, he stuck his neck out and said so. There was a long pause. 'Mr John just sat there. Then he said, "There is nothing impossible in Littlewoods." I never forgot that, all the time I was with the company. I suppose, for me, that was one of his philosophies: "There is nothing impossible."'

The pools building in Edge Lane, which had been handed over at forty-eight hours' notice in 1939, was not given back to Littlewoods for nearly ten years, although the understanding had been that premises would be returned at the end of hostilities. It was worse in the chain-store division: building restrictions were not lifted until October 1945 and all the sites which had been acquired before the war lay derelict and unusable. Worse still, some properties were compulsorily purchased – at user value. Thus a site ready for development, with drains etc., but being used as a carpark because of building restrictions, would be subject to compulsory purchase by the Government but valued as derelict land. John was prepared to wait it out. Even so, by buying up old properties and shops, he managed to get six new stores going by the end of 1947. Argyle Street, Glasgow, was opened in 1946; and within a year there were five more.

One of John's pre-war preoccupations also surfaced again. In the words of the same retired director, 'The Littlewoods way was certainly that you had to have character, and you certainly had to have morals.' As well as stamping on any possible supplier-to-buyer gifts, John made sure that there could be no back-handers from suppliers to anyone else in the company. In the case of chain-stores, each newly-appointed manager was issued not only with a small pocket manual, *Preparation for Business* – dealing with counter-inspection, merchandising and housekeeping – but also with a rule book. Rule 10 firmly stated that 'the manager must not communicate directly with suppliers unless so authorised by head office'. Rule 19 informed him that 'the manager must not borrow money from store cash. In emergencies, his personal cheques may be cashed to the total extent of £20 in any one week'. Other rules told him that he must maintain strict discipline, but that 'violence, whether of language or otherwise, by the manager, or anyone else, will not be tolerated'; that he must 'ensure the proper treatment of his staff by the supervisor grades'; and that he must do everything in his power to create a good team spirit.

There are twenty-six rules in the book, but possibly the most important are three which reflect John's particular dislikes: drinking – 'Intoxicants may not be consumed on the premises'; and anything which might cause unfair or preferential treatment – 'No relatives, including relatives by marriage, of anyone of or above supervisory level may be employed in this store', and 'Neither the manager nor his male staff must become unduly familiar with the female staff. Non-observance of this rule can result in the instant dismissal of those concerned.' Managers must not take advantage of their position. John now made sure that they did not use their position to obtain goods for themselves that were in short supply.

'With regard to staff purchases and customers' orders, strict instructions have been laid down, but in spite of this we have on occasions found managers selling goods to their friends and themselves, and not keeping to the regulations. The company is quite agreeable to the staff having a small allowance of short-supply goods, about ten per cent, but it must be remembered that first and foremost these lines should be offered to the public.'

'Shrinkage' was another of John's preoccupations. A store manager defined the term simply: 'You buy so much stuff, you sell so much stuff; you know what you've got left in stock, and the difference is what you've lost – that's shrinkage.' The loss could be due to a variety of factors, including soilage, but it was mainly the result of pilfering – by staff, by carriers or by customers – and eliminating it became almost an obsession with John.

This immediate post-war period marked the resurgence of another of his interests: training. At this stage it consisted largely of work experience in the different departments, usually starting at the bottom; when it came to the young of the family, it *always* meant starting there. John Junior had left school at seventeen after taking his final Eton exams, and following a period in the accounts department of mail order, he had worked his way up gradually through stores, spending a short time at each level. Various retired employees remember him from his mail-order days at Crosby, because they were always amazed that Mr John's eldest son had to bicycle in every morning from Freshfield – over eight miles – and clock on by 8.30 a.m. 'He used to bash to and fro on this old black sit-up bike. He'd arrive at the time clock at 8.29 a.m., throw his bag down, stagger against the wall and say, "Made it again!" And he had to queue at the trolley to get his own cup of tea mid-morning. There was no difference to anybody else. He was brought up off the floor. And so was Peter.'

Learning the business was not just confined to his sons; John had always been interested in encouraging talent and in helping people to help themselves. Now he was embarking on a training scheme within his own organisation. It was still in its early days, but there were definite hints of it even as early as 1944.

'Mr John stressed the importance of staff training. He said that some time should be given to this side. The days when we were getting girls of sixteen and seventeen, only to lose them at eighteen, had passed . . . These girls are going to be the foundation of our staff after the war.'

John was to say, 'The question of putting young men trainees in the stockrooms was then discussed. We are quite prepared to do this, provided that we can get lads who will not be liable to call-up. We shall probably have to take for this purpose people of higher age than in pre-war days. But in general, we are prepared in every stockroom to take in promising young men. It is for the managers to see that they are moved into parts of the store when they have passed the stockroom training.'

As usual, it was the managers who were accountable. 'If you live on high hills, you must expect high winds.' The higher up the ladder anyone was, the more responsibility they must be prepared to take – and to John, responsibility meant working harder and it meant carrying the can. Everything was in perspective; if someone were selected as a trainee or engaged for a particular job and they failed to come up to scratch, the fault lay at the door of whoever had selected them. If they were allowed to continue and still had not made good in three or four months, then obviously the manager had been unable to assess the individual's quality, and it was the manager who was not doing his job properly. It was always important to John, if anything went wrong, to find out who was responsible, i.e. whose fault it was. The object was not simply to expose people's defects, but to find ways of ensuring that the mistake was not repeated.

With so much on his mind, even John's phenomenal memory began to need assistance. The Forties saw the birth of his Little Black Book – and once it was perfected, he never moved anywhere without it. He kept it in the breast pocket of his jacket, and anyone seeing his hand moving in that direction knew exactly what to expect. In some ways it was a development of Mr Worrall's epitome, but it contained much more information and it was portable – a small, slim ring-file, something like an early version of a Filofax, but unnamed and unmarketed: his own invention.

'He had everything in this book,' according to his then junior secretary, Miss Richards. 'I used to have to type all his appointments in the front of it, and his forward dates about a month or six weeks ahead. Then he'd have a diary; then, say, the London theatres; everyone's birthday; all the phone numbers. They were all on separate sheets.' His weight was at the back of the book, and every morning he used to weigh himself and write it down. 'If he went somewhere without this Little Black Book, it was pandemonium. He'd be driving along to town and hear something on the radio. He'd stop at the lights and out would come the book and he'd have a little write. It might be something he wanted to send off for, or a tip he'd heard . . . If he visited a store and there was a complaint, out would come the book. And when he got back, he'd have whoever was responsible in front of him. Everyone used to dread this book coming out. If he got to the office and found he'd left the book at home, the gardener would have to bring it down to him; he wouldn't be without it. I think he felt that he might forget things, that they might go out of his mind. He used to write them down and check through it every day, or every other day, and then he would rule through everything he'd done.'

The Little Black Book is particularly revealing because it not only shows the wide scope of his life and tastes from the facts he recorded – addresses and telephone numbers of London bookshops; of restaurants in London, Spain and New York; of museums, galleries and art shops all over the world; it also served to remind him of more personal things. He obviously suffered from a mild grammatical aberration about when to use 'who' and when 'whom'. There is one single succinct entry:

> He is who
> Him is whom.

And just above it is a reminder of a different sort:

Strength in time of sorrow
Courage in time of sickness
Valour in time of hardship

Reading the entries in the last of these books which he made many years later when he was in his eighties, one can learn that his glove size was eight and that he took size nine in socks. He was not a tall man, five feet six inches in his youth, and as he grew older, he lost an inch or two in height as people often do. The number of the company aircraft and how to get to the Portobello Road Market are all written there, along with the mental reminders he found so important – in fact, these occupy the central position in the book.

> PAST: Let the mind dwell only on happy, pleasing incidents; on the achievements and successes; on the loyalty shown to me and the good turns people have done.
> PRESENT: Deliberately turn my attention to desirable elements – shooting, football, holidays, painting – to the appreciation people show.
> *Older employees need me.*
> FUTURE: Think of the pleasant things to come, of the many desirable plans to be made. The many friends I have ready to help me.
> *It's better than being a frog.*

Family affairs continued to occupy him as well as business. As one generation was rapidly growing up, another was ageing. His mother reached her seventieth birthday in 1943, and it had been marked by a large family party at her house in Larkhill Lane. 'Mummy', 'Granny' or 'Mam' – as John continued to call her – was still very much the centre of the family. Now her first grandchild was preparing to get married. John's daughter, Betty, became unofficially engaged to Kenneth Suenson-Taylor in June 1946, just after she had taken her Finals. It was announced officially in July and a grand wedding was being planned to take place early the following year.

John spent part of January 1947 getting to know his daughter's future in-laws a little better. He went back to St Moritz for the first time since the war, taking not only his wife, two sons and youngest daughter Janatha, but his sister Hilda and her children too. Betty and Kenneth were there with Kenneth's parents and his sister, and the two families saw each other frequently. John's party were at the Palace Hotel where he had stayed before the war, but 1947 was still a period of visas and limited foreign currency and the money soon started to run out. With a sensible eye to the future, the hotel management allowed John and his wife to remain in their grand room, but the rest of the party were moved up to much smaller rooms at the top of the building. John, in his organising mode, instituted a nightly financial meeting, at which the family were allowed to put in requests for anything special they needed. A basic allowance was allocated to each person, enough to cover the cost of a skiing lesson plus a cake and a cup of hot chocolate at Hanselmann's when they had skied down to St Moritz at the end of the day. Hilda was given a firm refusal, however, when she said tentatively that her son would like a French dictionary – any extras of that sort and the money would never have lasted.

They were home in Formby again by the middle of January 1947; the children of the two families had to be back at their respective boarding schools, and John was eager to return to work himself. He plunged into his usual long hours straight away; Switzerland with its concentration on skiing, the social round and wedding plans had been the barest of breaks. Ruby and he now had separate bedrooms. She liked to read in bed, which kept him awake; and although they had tried a dividing curtain, or special eyeshades for him to wear, nothing seemed to work. Sleep and a time to recharge were important to him, and a separate room seemed the only answer. It was this which nearly led to disaster.

One day towards the end of January, the maid took him his early morning tea and, finding it difficult to wake him, she put it down on his bedside table and went out again. He was surprisingly late for breakfast, and when Ruby became concerned and called up to him, there was no reply. He was not asleep. He was unconscious.

12

The Message to Garcia

Dr Garry, the family doctor and friend, went to the house very quickly and John was rushed to hospital. He had meningitis. There was consternation in the family, and indeed throughout the business – the Old Man had never been ill before. In fact, nobody was more surprised by the collapse than the Old Man himself, when he finally came round. It took him a month to recover. In retrospect, this was a remarkably short time; and it is even more remarkable that the workload which he had been piling on himself did not have earlier repercussions. Now the family – even brothers and sisters – began to think that he might be mortal after all; and John himself began to wonder what would happen if he were not there to look after everybody.

He delegated for the first time. Some details, like the lease of a field for a clay pigeon shoot – the family were just becoming seriously interested in shooting – he handed over to be dealt with by other people like his brother-in-law, Len, and his solicitor, Holland Hughes; although he still wanted to be informed about what was going on.

His major concern was to organise affairs so that his family would be provided for in the event of his death. Death duties, which would be levied on a business company as part of an estate, were very high at that time; and he had been appalled when a rich industrialist of his acquaintance had died and the man's widow had been forced to sell everything, house and all, in order to meet the tax demand. A wife and family were much more dependent then, and John's children were still only twenty-one, eighteen, fourteen and nine. The first precaution he took was to insure his life for £1m. for the next five years. Then he turned his attention to the business holding.

Instead of all the shares being held by himself and Cecil, a great many of John's were now to be made over to his offspring. (Cecil did not take the same step until considerably later.) The children were hardly to be permitted direct control; as adults they were not to receive interest in their own right until the age of twenty-five, nor final jurisdiction until the age of thirty. Even then there were strings; the shares could not be sold or bequeathed outside the family – family in this case being defined as direct descendants; husbands and wives did not count.

These provisions were fairly normal where sums of such a size were involved; indeed, they could have been much tighter. Where they were, perhaps, unusual was in a further specification: girls were to receive half the amount which boys received. This was partly because in John's eyes, men were the makers of money, and the shares would thus be put to better use. Girls got married, and their husbands provided. It was also a precaution. If a girl married and was then either divorced or died, it would mean some of the shares going to her husband – and outside the family. John's aim was to keep Littlewoods under his control.

Interestingly, the pools side of the business always remained very much a family firm with a family feel. Both Cecil's sons were involved in it, and Cecil had also taken on John's father-in-law, the husbands of two Moores sisters, his wife's brother and brother-in-law, and two nephews; they continued to work for him until they retired. The rest of the organisation – mail order and chain-stores – which was more directly under John's aegis, was always described as a family business and in the sense that it catered for families this was an accurate description, but fewer and fewer family members were to be found in top executive positions. By 1947, the other two brothers, Arthur and Charlie, had already left.

John's youngest brother, Charlie, was now divorced and owned a house and two hotels on the Isle of Wight plus a farm in Wales, but he had been to a large extent eased out of the family firm. The same was true of Arthur, who had divorced before the war and who was now married again to a young Welsh girl, a talented pianist whose playing revolutionised family parties. He also had a farm in Wales and a hotel at Ventnor on the Isle of Wight. Thanks to John, they were both comfortably off and had their own properties to manage, but they were no longer involved in the business. In Arthur's case, this was possibly because although perhaps cleverer than John, he did not always see eye to eye with him; he enjoyed an argument with John which he often won. Charlie, warm-hearted and impulsive, was probably the best-looking of the four brothers, and as daredevil as Cecil – but without his nous; in addition, he had broken two of John's most sacrosanct rules. He drank more than John considered suitable, and he became involved with a member of the staff. Finally, after an exchange of words with his eldest brother, Charlie left and slammed the door. It was never opened again; John did not take kindly to defiance.

'He was always harder on members of the family than anyone else,' as one retired director said. But brothers, and later, sons, probably felt close enough to be able to disagree with him on occasion. This was, however, a mistake. Employees, even high-ranking executives, knew better. 'You don't argue with the Old Man – you argued at your peril.' Or, as the saying went, 'You can always say "No" to the Old Man, as long as you have your resignation in your pocket.' John's sense of humour – or perhaps of irony – was a tool he often used. 'It's my money you're wasting', and 'Always let the Boss have his own way' were two of his frequent comments, made seemingly in joke and with a twinkle in his eye, but with serious intent. He summed up his own attitude in a speech made at a store managers' meeting in February 1949: 'I require unswerving co-operation, complete freedom from preconceived ideas – and a wholehearted determination to carry out to the letter the plans laid down by me.'

This seems in some ways to conflict with his other even more frequent advice to all his executives – the famous *Message to Garcia*. Copies of the message were sent to all of them. Store managers were obliged to keep the printed version in a prominent position on their desks, under glass; it was the first thing that greeted new arrivals. And at the bottom of each copy was a hand-written comment from John: 'There is a moral in this story.' Here it is from one of his own speeches:

'The United States was at war with Spain in Cuba, and the President wanted to get in touch with the rebel leader, named Garcia. That wasn't very easy. The whole of Cuba was in the possession of the Spanish soldiers, who were at war with America. Garcia, the rebel leader, was hiding in the jungles of Cuba, and few Americans had ever seen him.

'The President handed the message to a young man recommended for the task. The young man raised no objection; asked no questions, but simply said, "Yes, Mr President," and nothing more of him was seen until he returned, saying the message had been delivered and the task completed.'

John seems here to be wanting something more than simply strict adherence to his own plans; he seems to be asking for initiative, but his account did not end there; he went on . . .

'Now the messenger didn't raise any objections; didn't ask any questions; he didn't ask why it was necessary for the message to be delivered; whether it was his particular job; whether the job couldn't be given to Brown; whether the whole damn thing was necessary. He didn't ask where Garcia was – in fact he didn't ask any damn fool questions at all. No, he accepted the message, and he didn't return until the message had been delivered and the task completed.'

In other words, initiative must be used – but only to carry out an order – 'the plans laid down by me'. An ability to delegate is often considered to be one of the prime requisites in a leader; in John's case he would seem to have interpreted delegation as 'appointing a representative' rather than as 'entrusting authority to' someone. More responsibility simply meant more work. He liked the input of ideas as long as they did not conflict with his own, and he could glean what he wanted very quickly; for someone who could listen with such concentration, he sometimes surprised people by cutting them short. When asked why, he replied, 'Well, if the first bits disagree with what I know, I don't want to hear the rest.'

What pleased him most of all was dogged determination and perseverance. A case in point was the young lad from head office who was given an important letter to take out to Freshfield and deliver to the Old Man by hand. There was an accident on the Liverpool to Formby line which involved his train. Ignoring the hold-up, he got out and walked the last few miles along the track. His missive was handed over on time and he was highly commended – it was the *Message to Garcia* in action.

'Garcia', in fact, became a password throughout the whole chain. If your immediate superior rang to ask you to do something and started off by saying 'Listen – Garcia – right? Now I want you to . . .', you knew that whatever he wanted was important, and that you were to drop everything else and do it. John once called at a store manager's office and with his eye for detail noticed that although the *Message* was on the man's desk as directed, it was facing the wrong way. It was facing the door. He administered a sharp rebuke; but the manager in question came back smartly, 'I know it by heart, Mr John. It's that way round because I want everyone else to read it.' That man must have gone far.

If 'Garcia' produced an instant reaction, there was one name that was even more electrifying – 'Mr John'. The very mention of it – generally in the form of 'Mr John wants' or 'Mr John would like' – had an amazing effect on every department and on every grade. It was Mr John's business. What he wanted was for the good of the business – and, indirectly, for most of the people in it. His business

THE CANNING STREET
BUILDING IN 1939.

massive undertaking of conversion to war work illustrated John's belief that 'the ordinary man or woman do anything'.

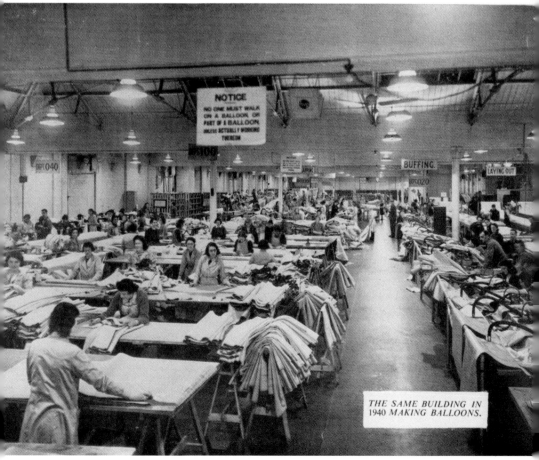

NOTICE
NO ONE MUST WALK
ON A BALLOON, OR
PART OF A BALLOON,
UNLESS ACTUALLY WORKING
THEREIN

BUFFING

LAYING OUT

THE SAME BUILDING IN
1940 MAKING BALLOONS.

Louisa with her four daughters at her seventieth birthday party, Easter 1943. From left to right: Joy, Hilda, Louisa, Ethel (recently widowed) and Lou. It was the women who kept the family together.

Ruby catches the largest salmon and John feels compelled to acknowledge her superiority.

At the British Industries Fair in 1951, John showe[d] himself the ardent monarchist.

had already become, in his mind, an extension of his family. Did it, from somewhere around this time, begin to take over, gradually to replace his family, and finally to become his life?

Outside the business, the family were as close-knit as ever and family gatherings were joyous occasions. Betty's wedding was scheduled for April 12th, 1947, and was to be in London, at St Margaret's, Westminster. The whole family – mother, brothers, sisters, in-laws, nephews and nieces – were transported to London by train, in a positive convoy of first-class carriages. It was a major planning operation by Mr Bagley, who headed the firm's traffic department.

Betty was a beautiful bride in a dress of the most exquisite heavy ivory satin. The material had been given to her by an aunt; it was still impossible to find anything of that description in 1947, even with clothing coupons. Lou had bought the satin before the war and had kept it in readiness for a suitable occasion. There were five bridesmaids, including Betty's nine-year-old sister, Janatha; the reception was at the Dorchester and John had recovered enough from the meningitis to give his daughter away and to make the customary speech. A great many of the family stayed at the Dorchester too, as John's guests. What few of them knew was that the evening before the wedding, Charlie had asked John to call round to his suite for a talk. The two men had gone off into a corner and had a long private conversation, leaving Charlie's three children to amuse themselves. His son, who was only ten at the time, remembers having the feeling that it was about something very important and wanting to know what. It was not until many years later that he discovered it had been about himself and his two sisters. Apparently Charlie had been feeling unwell and was suffering severe pain which had not yet been diagnosed. He was convinced that it was cancer and that he was not going to recover. And he had asked John, if the worst should happen, to look after his three children.

It was just one more worry to add to John's load. Dr Garry and the specialists were far from satisfied with his health, which was still below par. Although he had recovered from meningitis, the war years had taken their toll and he was in a very run-down condition. What they prescribed was a good holiday – a good rest, somewhere with plenty of sunshine and no food rationing, within a sterling currency zone. Bermuda was the place finally chosen, mainly on the recommendation of his old friend and partner from the early days, Colin Askham. 'Col', whom John had now appointed as his personal assistant, happened to be a great radio ham, and in the course of his hobby had been in communication with some people in Bermuda who never stopped singing the island's praises; in fact, they had become friends over the airwaves. Very soon, the two men were on their way to the first really restful holiday John had ever taken. Ruby was left to hold the fort at home.

The start of the trip was not auspicious because they had to travel by boat. (Under the terms of the insurance, which covered his life until the gift of his shares to his children were free from tax liability, John was not allowed to fly.) They travelled in comfort on the *Queen Mary* but even so John suffered agonies with seasickness. However, Bermuda was worth it. They stayed at the Coral Reef Club in luxury. As well as swimming and playing tennis, John indulged in one of his favourite occupations – lengthy walks by the sea. The waters round Bermuda are some of the clearest in the world, translucent greeny-gold; its beaches are not composed of sand but of powdered coral, fine, silky and pale pink in colour. On a longer walk than usual one day, they decided to explore the sand dunes, and there they came across an enormous, disused hotel, the Elbow Beach. John was intrigued. Although gutted of its plumbing and in a badly neglected state, the building had potential and a very good position. John was taken by the whole island. But perhaps what interested him most of all was a possibility he immediately spotted; Elbow Beach might help solve his worry about death duties.

If he were to buy a place like this in Bermuda, where no such tax existed, and build it into a profitable concern, then should anything happen to him, the hotel could be sold and the proceeds used to help pay off his death duties on Littlewoods. His great concern was to preserve the business and keep it intact for his descendants; and, with his customary decisiveness, he set discussions in motion even before he returned to England. The proposal was to purchase the hotel and run it as a partnership with the current owner, a Mr Frith. Negotiations conducted through Sir Henry Tucker of the Bank of Bermuda moved with speed. John bought the place for £350,000 (the equivalent of £6.5m. in current terms), and although he was by then back in England and immersed in work, the partnership was signed and ratified on July 27th.

Less than a week later, his younger brother died.

Charlie's premonition had been surprisingly accurate, although his own diagnosis of his illness was not. Sailing was a favourite pastime and riding was another; he had always been a great outdoor man since his youthful years in Australia and soon after his move to the Isle of Wight, he had bought a small racing yacht. On this particular day at the end of July, he was sailing single-handed in the channel to the south of the island, probably somewhere beyond St Catherine's Point, when he had an acute haemorrhage. He managed somehow to get the boat ashore and to drive himself to hospital before collapsing. It was then discovered that he had a perforated ulcer. He never regained consciousness.

It was soon after the end of the school summer term and his three children were collected and hurried down to the Isle of Wight. His son thinks that his father was probably still alive when they all reached Ventnor and did not die until later that night, but his children were not taken to see him. It was partly a protective attitude towards the young, partly because everyone was upset; the whole thing had been so sudden.

Arthur arrived as soon as possible in a small hired plane, and the children were flown back to their grandmother's house in Larkhill Lane. Charlie's body was brought back to Formby, and there was a sad family funeral at St Peter's Church. Charlie was the first of the eight brothers and sisters to die, and he was only forty-one.

John kept the promise he had made. The children lived with their grandmother, Louisa, but John looked after them as he had said he would. Being John, his idea of looking after someone was not purely financial; he took an active interest in everything they did. He was a frequent visitor at Larkhill Lane in the evenings, and although the three children were not present for most of the conversation, he would sit and talk to his mother while they went in and out, about how they were getting on and how she was managing. It was a happy time for both of them. Louisa still worshipped her eldest son, and he adored his mother. In a way, he was replacing his father and doing what his father had never done – sitting with Louisa, looking after Louisa, and looking after their surrogate children.

The other area in which he supported her was in their religious education. Louisa had always had an enquiring mind and her active interest in comparative religion and theology – even when she had been pressed for both time and money – was remarkable. At one point she had delved into what she called Mazddazzem – presumably Mazdaism, a form of Zoroastrianism. She would describe how she had been walking along in Manchester when she had passed an open door with steps leading to an upper room where there was a 'Mazzdazzem' meeting in progress. Louisa had been unable to resist exploring, both physically and mentally. The concepts of the sect interested her and the idea of a wise and beneficent creator of all things, Ahura Mazda, found echoes in her own belief. 'They worshipped by breathing,' was her simple summing-up of what she had discovered, which sounds more like some form of yoga, involving prana – the breath of life.

In her later years, however, Louisa had discovered the form of religion which suited her best: Christian Science. She attended the First Church of Christ Scientist in Southport every Sunday, and every Sunday in school holidays, John would call for her and drive her and the three children to church. She found great comfort from one particular Christian Science practitioner, a Mrs Holmes, who 'used to give her calming advice'. John himself with his own bent for religion and philosophy, probably inherited from his mother, became interested for a while. It seemed to him a more logical dogma than many, but not logical enough. In later years he was to remark wryly, 'Thank God I'm an atheist.'

Ruby, whose own faith was simple, devout and practical, quietly went on attending her local Anglican church in Freshfield.

One feature of the Christian Science years was a regular call at Hilda's house in Birkdale on the way home; it only required a short detour, and John took his mother and the three children every Sunday. The war had drawn the whole family together again. For a brief period, 1934 to 1940, they had suddenly known money, luxury, travel; even John, with his penchant for the simple life, had employed six staff in his comparatively modest household: nanny, chauffeur, maid, cook, gardener and gardener's boy. It was a paradise gained, and just as suddenly lost again. Air-raids, rationing, shortages and lack of staff hit them just as they did everyone else. Peacetime conditions returned slowly, shortages gradually disappeared, but staff never reappeared – at least, not on the same scale. Even though they were still as affluent (John, indeed, was a multi-millionaire), life was never quite the same. Spending was not in fashion. But wartime difficulties had revived a team spirit between the brothers and sisters which might otherwise have been slowly dissipated, and their ties to each other and to their mother, in particular, were never to slacken.

John's nephew remembers him coming to his prep. school and playing in the parents' cricket match against the boys. And on the first day of every school holiday, he had to go round to Uncle John's with his school report. 'You got a tenner if it was a good one, a fiver if it wasn't quite so good.' Credit where it is due and a tangible reward. Indeed, when the boy after a lot of hard work won a scholarship to Harrow, his uncle presented him with £50, 'in those big white fivers'. John himself called round on the prep. school headmaster and gave the school a fairly substantial donation, and the school gave all the boys a half-holiday. With his customary fairness, John decided that as he could well afford to pay the fees at Harrow, his nephew's scholarship should be an honorary one – so that someone who really needed the money could have it.

John's working hours were now even longer than they had been before his illness – he started going into the office on Sundays as well. One story, from a regular canon of them, recounts how he went down on a particular Sunday and discovered that he had left the key to the building at home. When he banged loud and long on the entrance door, a young girl – a new employee – appeared at the other side of the glass and mouthed at him to go away. He mouthed back, 'I'm John Moores.' But she either could not understand what he was saying or she did not believe him (he was probably wearing his weekend outfit of faded polo-neck and extremely battered jacket), because she refused to open the door. Eventually he had to go home again, in a bad temper. By the time he came in on Monday morning, however, he had had time to reflect. He described the girl; she was located and brought to his office, very nervous and expecting the sack.

'You didn't know who I was?' John asked.

'N–no,' the girl replied.

'You told me to go away.'

'Y–yes.'

'You were absolutely right. You were looking after my property, and I'm going to make you a supervisor.'

John's presence was certainly needed. They were difficult times for business; and it was now that he took the first step along a road that was gradually to lead to a different sort of company. Mr Cooke and Eric Sawyer, who had shown flair and initiative and had proved their worth, were appointed executive directors. They were the first non-family directors in the history of the firm, and John announced their appointment in November at the 1947 executive dinner.

The problems of peacetime were many, but they were compounded in John's opinion by a Labour Government. Whichever Party had been in power, he would no doubt have been critical of some of its decisions – the difficulties he was experiencing in business were as nothing compared with those of getting the whole country back to a satisfactory peacetime economy – but his views were those of a staunch Conservative. In an outspoken conversation with the dockers' leader in Liverpool, John asked why he was always inveighing against 'wicked capitalist bosses' when he knew that there were a lot of very good local employers. He quoted his own employee schemes for holiday pay, benefits and medical treatment, which were way ahead of their time. The reply he got was that the union leader in question wanted people to have all these benefits, but he wanted them provided by the State and not by people like John Moores. The discussion, although animated, was not an unpleasant one. As with his reaction against Catholicism, John's antipathy was towards socialism itself, it did not extend to individual socialists. The Labour MP Bessie Braddock, for example, was always a good friend of his. He had a great regard for her, and they often worked together for the good of Liverpool.

On holiday once, in his seventies, a daughter asked him why someone from a comparatively deprived background, as he was, had favoured the Conservatives rather than the Liberal or the Labour Party. His reply was that people like him never had much chance with Labour. When he had worked for the Post Office, for example, he had job security and was paid a reasonable amount. But when he worked for Commercial Cables he was better paid. 'If I'd done badly, I would have got kicked out; if I did well, I was rewarded. People don't have a chance of getting on and improving themselves with the socialists.'

He put it even more strongly in a speech he made to his executives in 1949:

'The socialists always seem to suggest that the only aim in life is a negative kind of security; security from cold or hunger; or being out in the rain; or having a leaky roof. If this kind of security is all we want from life, we can best obtain it by serving a life sentence in one of His Majesty's prisons. I don't think any of us are opposed to the idea of security. But when we are talking about security, we should be warned against the dangers of thinking that it is the only aim in life; of forgetting that man will be happiest and prosper most in that society which emphasises his need to stretch out and develop himself; to have the opportunity to grow in understanding; the opportunity to develop his personality; and the opportunity and the freedom to shape his own destiny.'

John was busy shaping his business. Peacetime competition was back again by the late 1940s, and although Littlewoods had got off to a good start, there was no time for complacency. 'You must realise you are entering into an era of very competitive selling and to make the grade you'll have to damn well give business all you've got.' That was how he put it to his store managers.

The pools division, although it had its worries – such as further cuts in the paper quota, was the most immediately successful. People were betting in smaller amounts, but there were more of them doing it, in spite of the introduction of a new pools betting duty. This was a levy on the total stakes received which meant that there was less money to be distributed amongst the winners, but the prizes were still astronomical by most people's standards. The tax was first introduced in January 1948 and was ten per cent of the total stakes. Within a few months, by October of the same year, it had gone up to twenty per cent and in October 1948 it went up to thirty per cent. But the boom continued.

It was not only pools that was affected by the paper shortage, as a speech of John's in 1948 illustrates. Mail order as well was suffering from 'a shortage of paper for our catalogue, and the scarcity of packing material'. High on the list of difficulties too were the 'floods of Government regulations, constantly varying purchase tax and coupon values', not to mention 'manufacturers being unable to maintain a regular supply of goods'.

The difficulty of obtaining marketable goods affected the chain-stores as much as mail order. The growth of the stores division was still hamstrung by building controls – although the company did manage to open three new stores in 1949, in Bolton, Worcester and Brighton – but it was stocking them with something to sell that was the problem.

John quickly found a new use for the factories into which he had channelled his energies during the war. As he told his executives:

'It had been our general policy previously not to manufacture where we could purchase supplies, but the war left us with a number of producing units and peace brought us many shortages of goods. By maintaining a number of factories we were saved the embarrassment of dismissing loyal staff, and it also helped to shield mail order and chain-stores from the worst effect of the shortages.'

A year later, in 1949, the factory side of the business had expanded even more: but in many ways, far from being a year of recovery, 1949 was the worst year of all and John was not slow in apportioning the blame.

'In March we had the end of clothes rationing and welcome though this step was, wholesalers and retailers alike were caught unprepared, having not had the slightest warning but being left to untangle the muddle caused by this lack of Government courtesy. In April we had the increase of the pools tax, again without any warning or consultation. In September, without consulting the special committees which were set up for this very purpose, the retail profit margins were reduced by five per cent, and men with a lifetime's knowledge of retail trading were just passed over in a most arbitrary manner . . . Later in the month, by a mere order of the Chancellor, the profits tax was again increased. Just to call it a day, so to speak, September was rounded off by the worst blow of all – the devaluation of the pound.'

His final criticism of a political stance of which he disapproved was reserved for later in the same speech. 'Not content to hinder business, the socialists attack the profit motive. They suggest that the making of a profit is a vice, whereas we, as responsible businessmen, know that the chief vice is making a loss.'

His speeches were made on diverse occasions, at buyers' meetings, chain-store managers' meetings and at the yearly executive dinner, held at the Adelphi Hotel; they were also varied to suit their audiences. Those made to store managers were more detailed; particular managers were singled out for praise or blame, with reference to the percentage of increase or drop in sales in the relevant departments of their store; those made at the executive dinner were distinct from all the others because they included the ladies. It was the only occasion on which wives were invited.

In business, a great many of John's ideas were ahead of his time; his attitude to women, on the other hand, was typical of his time. His regard and care for them was genuine and unfailing; it was simply that wives, mothers, daughters, nieces – family women – inhabited a softer, warmer place in his mind and not the hard, competitive world of the market-place. Women were not in evidence at top executive levels.

As the years went by, more and more women were able to enter the business arena; those who did and rose to executive position, he treated slightly differently. In his seventies, John took on a woman barrister, Theresa Hamilton-Sugden, as adviser. She was young, pretty and extremely able and as she shared an interest in football, he used to take her to Everton matches, but as she said, 'He always treated me like a man.' This was an accolade and it had to be earned.

In common with most of his contemporaries, John respected women as home-makers, as bearers of children, but it was men who were the providers. There was a wartime poster which illustrated the general attitude perfectly. It was one of a series emphasising that 'Careless Talk Costs Lives' and it said simply, in large letters:

BE LIKE DAD
KEEP MUM

In the early 1940s, such a statement seemed perfectly acceptable to many people. It is against this background that some of John's comments need to be set otherwise his references to the 'ladies' in speeches at the executive dinners otherwise appear patronising, his slightly heavy-handed humour seems unfunny and his genuine feeling can go unnoticed. The speech he made at the 1947 dinner was typical:

'I am pleased to welcome you all tonight on the first occasion when all the branches of our organisation have foregathered for a social function. It is the first occasion, certainly, when, in addition to our executives, I have had the pleasure of meeting their wives – and as I look round, I am beginning to understand why our men look so happy, so well fed, so rosy and contented.

'It used to be said in the old days that the men who succeeded in Littlewoods were those who were wedded to their job, and many is the doleful tale I have heard of irate wives who never saw their husbands. Well, ladies, if that state of things still continues, then may I be permitted to say how well that state of things becomes you. Evidently my brightest boys have a flair for other than business matters.

'Speaking personally, I can appreciate how fortunate one is to have the right partner, one who is tolerant and helpful in either trouble or success. My wife has always helped me, although at times in the past it must have been difficult. Success, you know, brings responsibility; which in a true partnership must be shared alike by both husband and wife.'

His tone was still the same in 1949.

'May I say how delighted I am to have you all here this evening – especially as most of us are old friends, and very especially because we are graced by the presence of "the ladies". We are delighted to have them with us tonight; there are so few opportunities in a businessman's daily round when he can introduce his wife to his fellow executives, and have her share in a small portion of his working life . . .

'I think, too, that the good ladies of today have a much wider vision than their sisters of yesterday, and take a very intelligent interest in their lord and master's affairs. Perhaps they don't realise just how much they do towards spurring their menfolk on to greater effort by their interest and enthusiasm, and I believe more than ever in the old saying that a man's wife is his right hand.'

The dinners at the Adelphi Hotel were elegant black-tie affairs, with fine wines and a good cabaret, but as usual, where John was concerned, celebrations were not confined to the top executives. Those first post-war years saw the old comrades' reunion dinners for men coming back from the Forces. The Miss Littlewood competition was started in 1947. More a charm than a beauty competition, it had elimination heats and a selected entrant from each of the Littlewoods buildings (the first Miss Littlewood was Miss Canning Street) and was to grow into a two-night, full-scale organised entertainment. It had the practical advantage of bringing together people from all the different departments of the organisation and fostering group spirit and group loyalty. The Littlewoods girls' choir, known as the Littlewoods Songsters, was started. John had heard some of the girls singing at work as he did his rounds and had been impressed by how good their voices were. Indeed, the original idea for each of these activities came from John himself, although others were deputed to organise and set them up. And in many ways they were only a dress-rehearsal for what was to develop in the next decade.

There were to be two more family milestones before the Forties ended. John's first grandchild was born – Betty's daughter – and the final celebration in December was John Junior's wedding. He had done his training stint at the Brixton and Oxford Street Stores, been assistant manager at Maidstone and manager at Scunthorpe, and in the autumn of 1949 had been sent to Syracuse Business School in the States. Before he left for his first term there, still not quite twenty-one, he had become engaged to Sheila Moore. She was the daughter of Helen Breen who had been a glamorous and popular Principal Boy, and of Sam Appleton Moore, the opera singer, but her parents had been divorced years previously and her mother had married again. Sheila's stepfather was Tom Arnold, the West End impresario, and he and Helen were great friends of Cecil and Doris. Both families were delighted. Sheila was an attractive, apparently malleable girl, a few months younger than her husband-to-be, and John definitely approved. When his first term at Syracuse finished, John Junior came back briefly to England and in December 1949, he and Sheila were married. They were to return to America together for the remainder of John

Junior's business course, but before that there was another grand wedding in London – with the reception this time at the Grosvenor House.

The family seemed more united than ever.

13

The Uncrowned Queen

The year 1950 was a second spring, another growing season. It was a far from easy year; in many ways it seemed almost a return to the Thirties, with Friday nights becoming more and more dreaded for the sackings which they brought. John was building the business up again after the war years and many executives could not stand the pace. Economic conditions were unpredictable, but Littlewoods was a bigger concern altogether this time round, and growth went on, however tough the circumstances.

'We stand on the brink of the second half, I think, of the most momentous century in the history of the world,' was John's verdict on the era. 'A century which has brought about startling changes in the living conditions of the whole of mankind, and during which we have had to stand up to the devastating effects of two World Wars; a century of the most amazing scientific and medical discoveries, which have brought us an easier way of life for the masses instead of for the few; and which has seen the growth of those twin evils – socialism and communism. And we will go forward into the second half of this twentieth century patently aware of our changed way of life, but realising that all the benefits of the age will be lost if we lose our individual liberty, tied hand and foot by regulations and restrictions – bondsmen in our own land. This is the way of communism, and we must fight it now, and we must fight it with all our might.'

It was communism rather than socialism for which John now reserved his particular dislike – not surprisingly; it was the year when Communist China invaded Tibet; when North Korea invaded South Korea, and the United Nations forces became involved; when Fuchs was found guilty of betraying atomic secrets to the USSR – with the discovery a year later that two British diplomats, Burgess and Maclean, had been spying for the Russians; and it was the year when Senator Joseph McCarthy informed President Truman that he knew the names of fifty-seven 'card-carrying' Communists in the State Department and a further 205 Communist sympathisers who worked there. By 1953, he was chairman of the

Senate Subcommittee on Investigations and the McCarthy witch-hunts began.

Political creeds – national or international – had very little effect on the football pools. They became more and more popular, and it was on November 11th of this year that the first prize reached its highest total so far – £104,417. John and Cecil decided that from then on, the amount any single winner could receive should be limited to £75,000, and that stake money in excess of this should be divided and added to the second, third, fourth and fifth prizes. This was also the year when there was no pools betting between the last football matches on May 6th and the beginning of the new season on August 12th; pools staff went on part-time work for six months. Apart from this break, the pools based on flat-racing were not finally dropped until 1970, but their appeal was only minimal. The following year saw the introduction of a new venture – Summer Pools run on Australian football matches – and these proved extremely popular. Equally importantly to John and Cecil, they kept the staff in year-round employment, with no need for any laying off.

The fight was tougher in mail order and chain-stores; but as far as mail order was concerned, the next ten years were probably the most exciting in the whole of its development. It was the division which had been hardest hit by the war years, and in 1950 its shop-window was one rather meagre catalogue. By the end of the decade it had expanded into four mail-order businesses, three of them based on credit. Until now, the idea of credit for the lower-paid was unheard-of – neither banks nor shops would consider it. Mail order gave the opportunity to many. It needed a lot of capital behind it; there not only had to be warehouses stocked with goods, there had to be enough money to enable the business to survive while it waited for the cash to come in; and it had be be able to deal with the problem of bad debt. Nevertheless, John was determined to make mail order 'big', and credit was the obvious solution. His business antennae were always acute and he sensed the coming of the credit-buying society, but he had strong feelings about where credit was good and where it could be damaging. He was evolving the idea in 1951, while at the same time inveighing against the abuse of credit on a national scale.

'This country stands on the brink of the most serious economic crisis, and it gives one a chill feeling at the heart to hear that we are losing dollars and gold at the appalling rate of a thousand million a year. And it's not only dollars and gold – by living on credit, we're rapidly increasing the already large debt within the sterling area.

We've been used too long to being top dogs, but other countries are outstripping us and we're not top dogs any longer.'

There were other areas in which he considered credit pernicious and dangerous; years later, for example, when many chain-stores were offering their customers credit cards, he vetoed for some time any suggestions of a credit card for Littlewoods. Mail order was a different thing altogether. Burlington Credit Mail Order, based in Manchester, was launched in 1952, and a year later was followed by Brian Mills of Sunderland. Customers of these two companies dealt with agents instead of organisers, and their orders were delivered before even one payment had been made.

The development of chain-stores was still held up by building controls, although the division was bursting to expand. As John said, 'They can't create new business by advertising, as in mail order; or take Government contracts, as in the factories; or pay big dividends, as in the pools. They are limited by the number of stores they have in the chain.' Four new ones were opened in 1950; five in the following year and in 1952, there were not only new stores in West Bromwich and Slough, but two very large new stores were acquired in Edinburgh and Leeds. 'We have certainly captured two of the plum sites in the country,' John told his executives. 'But they cost nearly £1m. and all that remains to be done is to sell them to an investment company, and take them back on a long lease.'

The division was still very much feeling its way, looking for its niche or national image – possibly somewhere between Marks & Spencer and British Home Stores. But at the same time John managed, as usual, to inject enormous enthusiasm into everyone involved. There was a feeling that Littlewoods was a growing company, that the chain was going to be something really big and everyone was going to share in its success.

Eric Barker, for instance, remembers coming out of the Navy and joining as a trainee around 1950 in the Blackpool store where he was put in charge of the fruit section. So enthusiastic was he that he got up at five o'clock in the morning to go to the fruit market, and bought far too much. There was still a lot of fruit left at the end of the day, so he opened the doors onto the street and between six o'clock and ten o'clock that evening, he sold his fruit from a stand on the pavement. 'In those days you didn't treat losses lightly; anything to regain credibility and to bring back the money.'

John himself often put in an appearance. Just as during the war he had continually toured his munitions factories and learnt at first-hand, so now he made the rounds of his stores. 'You lock up your office and you keep walking around,' he once told a nephew. 'You don't find out what goes on by sitting at a desk. Keep walking around, that's the only way you'll learn.' Or, as Eric Barker described it, 'I remember Mr John coming round the store in Blackpool. He was the common man, he spoke to everybody, all the little girls behind the counter. He was more concerned with what they had to say, as they were hands-on. He was more concerned with their views of what we were selling; the manager and I just followed on behind.'

Much later, when the chain had already grown to over a hundred stores, John was still doing the same thing. He would often be seen, sitting on a stool in some store snack-bar, having a cup of coffee with his secretary, Miss Mitchell, or eating one of his favourite custard pies. The managers did not particularly interest him on these visits – he could talk to them at other times, at managers' meetings and interviews. When he used to drop in at the Liverpool No. 1 store years later, where the same Eric Barker had been made manager, he would simply stick his head round the office door and say, 'I haven't come to see you, I've come for the custards.'

Another manager, Freddy Oak, had the same story to tell.

'When he visited, apart from saying hello to you, and taking the accounts sheets off you – so he'd got them in his hand, so he knew what he was talking about – he tended to leave you to take a back seat. He wanted to deal with the staff themselves.'

The staff sometimes gave as good as they got, particularly in Liverpool. 'The Liverpool supervisors are a breed on their own; no-nonsense, terse, straight down, a spade's a spade, no trouble.' On one occasion, doing his rounds of the sales floor, John came across a customer trying to return a pair of children's shoes, and complaining that they were faulty because one of them had a worn-out sole, while the other was nearly as good as new. The supervisor in the meanwhile was telling the customer, as politely as she could, to 'get lost'. John, for once accompanied by the manager, said that the shoes must be exchanged. The customer went away happy, but the supervisor, Ivy, rounded on the Old Man in fury.

'You know all that was wrong with those shoes, don't you? You know why there was only one sole worn out?'

'No. Why?'

'Because the kid rides his scooter all day long! He's only worn one sock out as well!'

'I see.'

'And I've just had to give away a brand new pair of shoes! Don't you talk to me again about shrinkage!'

John took the rebuke on the chin and turned to his manager with a smile. 'Mr Oak, next time I come to this store, make sure it's Ivy's day off, would you?'

John was only an adopted scouser, but he and Ivy were on the same wavelength; they understood each other perfectly.

His understanding of people was the key to his success, according to many of his executives. As one of them said, 'He didn't start in the middle or at the top, he started at the bottom. If you start at the bottom, you see a lot more people, you understand what motivates people much better. I think that was his great strength – he was very good at it. He was a very hard man, don't make any mistake about that – you don't get the kind of success that he had without being hard. But I don't think he was unfair.'

With understanding went attention to detail. 'He had his finger on the pulse of the business. He knew all the main ingredients that would make it work or would damage it.' In other words, he had gone on 'listing' things mentally, and he had evolved a set of rules for himself. Better still, he could express them simply and succinctly, so that people could understand them – and remember them. They were homespun philosophies of his own. 'He trots out more sayings than Khrushchev used to do!' said one goaded executive. Another was more approving. 'If you buy any of these big, high-flying management books, they say the same things as Mr John – only they use a thousand more words.'

A cardinal rule of his policy was keeping a low stock and turning it over as many times a year as possible. 'A big stock is a bad stock.' It is a phrase that everyone at Littlewoods still uses.

'I've only got two suits,' was another which he employed as a way of telling executives that they were wasting his money – which was not limitless, or that they were wasting time – and time was money. A newly-appointed executive director, who had heard the saying quite often enough, decided that it would be a good idea to buy the Old Man a third suit, and each director was asked to contribute £50. A little later, a special bespoke new suit was presented to John. He was not amused.

Shrinkage was another area that produced several aphorisms. It was clearly not only pilfering of stock that John objected to, he cared about company property too. 'Every one of my employees has ten of my pencils,' was a particularly deadpan remark.

He wanted popular lines and volume sellers always; 'Eighty per cent of sales are on twenty per cent of your lines.' There was to be very little catering for minority tastes or stocking for extremes of size at either end of the scale. 'We do not sell brown shirts, size eighteen collars'; and 'We cater for the masses, not the messes.' What he wanted was winners. And this was not just in his selling lines. He wanted 'lucky' store managers (i.e. successful ones); he wanted ideas that were winners too. His most often repeated slogan was, 'Every egg a bird, and every bird a whistler.' He had picked it up from the men selling canaries in Lancashire markets, but he applied it to a lot more than canaries.

It was in a speech to his buyers at the beginning of 1950 that he summed up his approach.

'From the bible of good business may I offer you four commandments:

KNOW THY PUBLIC
KNOW THY MERCHANDISE
KNOW THY COMPETITORS
KNOW THY SUPPLIERS

He continued to develop these themes in the years of company expansion ahead; he was always dedicated to growth. He knew that you cannot stand still; you either climb higher or you slip back, and that was something he could not afford to do; there were too many people dependent on him. They were competitive and testing times, but he always used the analogy of the yachtsman: 'An adverse wind is a challenge to him – he doesn't go seasick in his cabin, cursing his luck; he alters his sail and tackle and rises abreast of the storm with his face towards fair weather. By the proper handling of his craft, he turns the weather to his advantage.'

The early Fifties were not all difficulty from John's point of view, however. For one thing, the Conservatives were back. Churchill was returned to power in the general election of October 1951, and although the party's majority was only a small one, John was delighted. What neither he nor the rest of the general public knew was that the Prime Minister's health was not good; Churchill had recently suffered a series of strokes, the first in August 1949. To John and those of his political persuasion, the election result was a deliverance from near ruin: 'The lion hasn't merely had its tail twisted, it's had it damn near torn off!' He propounded again to the firm's executives his strongly-held belief that it is 'businessmen who really run the country'.

'Without capitalism, we'd still be in a state of semi-barbarism. To our own forebears, life was a mere struggle for existence, and for many of them, serfdom. In fact, it's only in those countries which have a capitalistic regime that we find any reasonable standard of civilisation . . . Those of us who believe in private enterprise must make it abundantly evident that not only does it work successfully, but that it benefits the greater majority – that's the point – by giving good quality and a fair deal to all our customers and the best possible working conditions to our staff. It offers the advantage of co-operative effort without compulsion. And by resisting the inroads of bureaucracy, it gives that very important freedom to be free.'

It was not only the change in government that cheered John; there was good news on the family front. Both his sons were coming into the business – indeed, no other option had ever been considered for them – and he had another grandchild. Towards the end of 1950, John Junior and Sheila had returned from America, a little earlier than expected. The year's business course at Syracuse had been a useful one, but Sheila was already expecting their first child and having a difficult pregnancy. The cost of medical treatment in the States had ensured that it was an expensive one too, and the foreign currency allowance was still tight. More importantly, both prospective parents wanted to be back in England for the birth.

When John was given the news of their forthcoming return, he immediately wrote telling them that he had finally decided on their wedding present – it was to be a large house and garden in Freshfield. He offered them a choice between two which he had selected himself; and as Sheila had never really seen either of them, it was her husband who made the choice. So they came back to a place of their own, which they christened Random House. It was not, after all, the house that John Junior had selected – the sale of that had fallen through – but the young couple were very happy with their new home. With it also came the adjacent field, which was being turned into a garden for them. It was an extremely generous gift; and there was one great similarity between the two houses that John had offered them – both were only a few minutes' walk from his own. It was a close family. That was how he wanted it.

That year also saw John Junior appointed as director on the company board along with his father and his uncle, Cecil. Soon after the birth of his daughter, he was sent to the chain-store office in London to learn the ropes. He was still too young and inexperienced to be given total control – he was only twenty-two – but he was knowledgeable enough to be able to inform his father about everything that was going on. For the next three or four years he was sent here, there and everywhere; his function to observe, to report back and to recommend.

He was not the only one feeding his father information; John always wanted to know every detail of what was happening in every corner of his empire, and at this stage everyone involved regarded it as essential too. The Old Man ran the business; he needed to know. He also knew the people he was talking to by their first names, and often an executive or manager would pick up the telephone and find Mr John at the other end. 'Freddy, what's happening about so-and-so . . .?' 'Eric, what are you doing about such-and-such . . .?' It was not resented. People were delighted to feel that they were working with the Boss and happy that he was involved. There was enormous admiration for him throughout his work-force. 'I was very, very fortunate being around at this particular time,' was one retired manager's comment.

As the company gradually grew to its current vast size, the situation changed somewhat. John still needed to know, but he was no longer on first-name terms with all his executives – there were far too many of them for that. His information service became a different thing altogether; in some quarters it was quietly referred to as 'the Mafia'. It was never spying in the sense that a few discontents might have suggested; his network still consisted mainly of those who genuinely cared about him.

His two secretaries, Miss Mitchell and Miss Richards, were protective guardians; 'Mitch' in particular. 'You never got to see Mr John unless you got to him through Miss Mitchell first. She was the five-barred gate to the Old Man; if you got past her, you were OK.' And as a quiet and apparently unassuming secretary, a great many people would say things in front of her which they never would have said to the Boss, and which they had no idea would go straight back to him. It was an efficient and useful information system, but there was one snag to it – according to some. Once John had ingested information about a particular individual or event, he retained it; and it took a great deal to get him to look again with a completely open mind and possibly change his opinion. In other words, he became – for the first time – open to influence.

In the early Fifties, this stage had not yet been reached. John still knew all the individual members of his team; and in 1951 the team was joined by his younger son.

Peter had left Eton after doing the Oxford Entrance Exam and obtaining a place at Christ Church to read Modern Languages. Taking it up was to be deferred for his National Service – there was conscription for young men between the ages of eighteen and twenty-one until 1960 – but when his medical took place, it was discovered that he had perforated ear-drums and he could not get into the Services after all. The University brought his place forward by a year, but there was still an eighteen-month gap to be filled in, so John put him to work in the mail-order department at Crosby. As a treat he was given a car – but only because he had worked in the firm's garage as a mechanic during the previous school holidays. For the final three months before going up to Oxford, he asked John Christie for a job at Glyndebourne – he had been at Eton with Christie's son, George – and was delighted to work there as transport officer. But from Easter 1951 to October 1952, he was living at home and commuting to Crosby.

By 1953, things seemed to be going very much as John wanted. His sons were both close at hand; he had three more grandchildren – five in all now, Betty having produced twin boys in 1951 and John Junior a son, John Moores III, in 1952 – and the business was continuing to grow. He was working harder than ever, but he was also taking holidays. Admittedly, they usually combined business with pleasure, but at least he had some sort of a break – and so did Ruby. She loved Bermuda and the Elbow Beach Hotel, and made many friends on the island. They would travel to New York by boat – on one of the *Queens* – usually accompanied by Colin Askham. John was still not allowed to fly because of his life insurance restrictions. He would have meetings with Sears Roebuck, take in some baseball and then go on to Bermuda.

As well as Ruby and 'Col', he was always accompanied on these trips by his dummy keyboard. He had been learning the piano for several years, a relaxation recommended by his doctor, and it was a good opportunity to practise – he would have found the voyage maddening otherwise. Time always had to be filled. Hilda, his elder sister, remembered a train journey she made with him once when they were both much younger, and how he had insisted that they should use the spare hours to learn their nineteen-times-table. She refused, but he had it off by heart long before they reached their destination. Musicality was not his strong point, however; although he performed occasionally at family parties and although he certainly enjoyed listening to music, his playing never became anything more than automaton-like. He would practise each page, a bar at a time, over and over again, and then fit everything together – so it was certainly accurate. But as soon as his life's real pastime surfaced, piano-playing was dropped for ever.

It was Mr Harrington, artist and interior decorator at the Elbow Beach Hotel in Bermuda, who introduced John to painting. It was a great discovery for John. He had enjoyed looking at other people's paintings for many years, now he realised that painting was something he enjoyed doing himself. To begin with, he learnt by numbers or simply copied, and his greatest pleasure was painting in the company of someone more talented than himself. In Bermuda, he painted with Mr Harrington. At home, he had lessons from Reg Hubbard, the head of Littlewoods' catalogue production department who was also an artist and who used to go out to Fairways to teach him. Another instructor was the then Principal of the Liverpool Art School, Bill Stevenson, who was later employed by Littlewoods to set up and run a design department.

Painting was initially a hobby definitely approved of by John's doctors; piano-playing had not been exactly the relaxation they intended it to be, as he would sit at the piano for three hours' regular practice every night. With painting as a hobby, they imagined that he would be out in the open air with his easel. Again they did not get it quite right; painting, like everything else, received John's intense concentration and an enormous input of his amazing energy. But although it did not prove to be a relaxing hobby, painting certainly provided the second half of John's life with one of its greatest sources of enjoyment. Still hanging outside his office on the eleventh floor of the giant J M Centre is the first painting he ever did, proudly signed 'John Moores 1953'. It is a still life of an apple and two bananas, and he was so surprised and pleased with it at the time that he had it reproduced as his Christmas card.

It was a watershed year in many ways. Amongst other things, 1953 marked the twenty-first anniversary of the founding of mail order, and celebrations were held. For weeks before the actual date, the firm's photographer would go round the Crosby building at regular intervals taking group photographs. Each photograph would be pinned up on the notice-board, with several of the faces in it circled – blindly and at random – and if you were lucky enough to find that one of the faces was yours, 'you got five bob'. When it came to the actual celebration ceremony, wives and husbands were invited as well which was unheard-of, except in the case of the executive dinner. The whole of the Moores family were at Crosby in force, including Louisa. She announced that the entire staff was to have a day's holiday, even telephoning the huge warehouse at Failsworth to say that the staff there were to have one as well. To commemorate the occasion, John planted an oak tree. There is a rumour that the tree actually died a year or two later, but was quickly replaced during the night by another, a little larger, before the Old Man could notice. It was also rumoured that this occurrence was repeated more than once, with a larger tree being hastily shovelled in each time. The celebration on the day was not over with tree-planting; it finished up with a massive coach outing to Blackpool for everyone.

The year also marked Louisa's eightieth birthday. A splendid dinner and dance was given in her honour at the Adelphi and there was a large cake for her to cut. But John's tribute to his mother did not end there; he also recorded his feelings for her in his annual speech at the executive dinner that December. There were national events to be thankful for: the bank rate had been lowered; there was an increase in the gold reserve and a reduction in taxes; there was an armistice in Korea, and – the greatest national celebration of all – it was the year that had seen the coronation of the young Queen Elizabeth II.

John was an admiring and loyal monarchist, but on this occasion his greatest devotion was reserved for someone else.

'Mother chose this year to celebrate her eightieth birthday – in fact, I think she's still celebrating! She even came to Bermuda, "to get some sun", she said, but you know I've an idea that it was to make quite sure that I was running Elbow Beach properly, and to make sure that I was giving everyone enough to eat. Mother's unbounded zest for life is only one of her many qualities . . . I often talk to you about energy and enthusiasm, and here you have a perfect example. I think she can take credit for her share in the growth of the Littlewoods organisation, because her influence has been felt through all our branches since its earliest days. She is the uncrowned queen of the Moores family. God bless her!'

From now on the tempo speeded up even more, and family and business both increased. By 1957, John had four more grandchildren. His work-force had grown even faster; it had not yet reached the 30,000 that it numbers today, but it was on its way.

The big development in pools was the Pools Betting Act passed in 1954. It was high time for legislation controlling pools promoters, and it was welcomed by John and Cecil on two counts: most of the specifications which it insisted on were already incorporated in Littlewoods' rules; and along with these provisions – at long last – ready-money betting was legalised. The accounting system was simplified overnight, which more than made up for any extra paperwork involved in having to make returns to local and other authorities. Two Treble Chance Pools were introduced in the 1954–5 season, each with a 6*d* minimum stake.

Mail order followed its twenty-first birthday by producing such a splendid autumn/winter catalogue in 1954 that it was chosen for inclusion amongst the hundred best in the country; and the following year it survived a rail strike which might have crippled it. The GPO announced that without rail transport, it could not cope with any parcels over eight ounces, but Littlewoods responded by assembling a fleet of vans – many their own, many hired, many even belonging to British Rail – and delivering the parcels themselves to the 400 key sorting offices in the country. With 'sorting clerks and postmen waiting for work', the Post Office was quite happy with this solution. Help came from the pools too. The pools division dealt with so much mail that it had men who knew immediately which districts were served by which sorting offices. 'Flixborough's dealt with in Carlisle', they would say, or 'Nabworth's dealt with in Scunthorpe', without even having to look up the records.

In many ways it was like the war years again, with John enthusing staff to contribute in whatever way they could. 'The control room at Crosby looked like a military HQ, with staff studying huge wall maps and every telephone in the place ringing non-stop.' Every order form was pre-coded and sorted, and accorded not only its area sorting office but its route as well. The forms were sent to Littlewoods' three huge warehouses where the appropriate parcels were packed up, weighed, affixed with the correct stamps and sent in their tens of thousands to one central point to be loaded into the vans. The City Hall in Manchester was hired for this because it had such an enormous floor space that the vans could drive straight in. Unfortunately, 'the first van to drive in pulled the electric lights out of the ceiling before disappearing through the floor into the foundations'. The lights were soon repaired, and luckily the driver was not injured. The vans kept going twenty-four hours a day, seven days a week and at the end of the seventeen-day strike, 350,000 packages had been delivered.

The great news for the chain-stores in 1954 was that building regulations were finally lifted; it was no longer necessary to have a building licence before any work could be done. 'It's the most important thing that has happened in chain-store trading for many a long year,' John announced. 'We can now go full steam ahead, and subject to planning permission, build all the stores we want and develop our splendid sites. We'll open eleven new stores in 1955 – eleven new stores in one year.'

In the event only six were opened, and six the following year, 1956. Planning permission was possibly not as easy to obtain as John had anticipated; perhaps his insistence on exactly what he wanted slowed down the actual building. Certainly he had very firm ideas and very high standards. In the years of waiting for permission to build, John Junior, George Watts, the group director, and John himself had been round America gathering all the newest and most revolutionary ideas in store construction. And it was not only America that they had visited. 'To ensure that these new stores are bang up to date and as good as anything there is, Mr John Junior has become one of our most travelled executives – his wife tells me that his children are always asking when they are going to see Daddy. He and Mr Watts found many outstanding contemporary buildings in Holland and Germany; and later, when I went with them to Rotterdam, Aachen, Paris, Cologne, Bochum and Krefeld, I was tremendously impressed by the vision, ingenuity and courage that had been shown in taking advantage of the opportunity to rebuild.'

The pride of John's heart was the Liverpool No. 1 store, which cost over £1.25m. to build. Various snags were discovered during its construction, including the fact that the city's extremely ancient main sewer, which plans showed as running under the middle of a side street, was actually located almost under the site of the store itself. More money had to be spent strengthening the sewer, but no expense was spared. The place was particularly dear to John as it was only two doors away from 38 Church Street and the small office where the Littlewoods organisation had started over thirty years earlier. When completed, the building was a particularly fine one. His mother was guest of honour at the opening ceremony and she gave him her opinion in one single succinct sentence; 'It's a nice shop, John, but you're selling rubbish.'

It was, indeed, the buying side of the whole operation to which John now turned his attention. At the same time, while pushing ahead with expansion, he began to gently tighten the reins; however vast its growth, he intended the business to remain within his control – and the family as well.

14

'I Want Lucky People'

John's first step was to move the head office of chain-stores from London back up to Liverpool again. Mail order had always remained at Crosby, but about ten years previously the chain's buying office had been relocated in Oxford Street, in the belief that it would be closer to the market in London. Now John wanted it back on home ground. This decision was also very strongly advocated by John Junior, who had been trained in systems management and thought that the whole operation needed reorganising.

The official reasons for the move back north were various. According to John, in his speech to his executives at the end of the year, 'We were not making the most of our buying power; there was much overlapping and waste . . . With central buying, we'll have all the buying sections and stock control under one roof. Most of our buyers will be able to specialise, with the result that the same merchandise for all three sections will be bought by one buyer instead of three.'

The unofficial reason for the move, which most people recognised, was that John wanted his finger on what was happening; or as he put it, slightly more ambiguously, 'With the chain-store buying office and stock control in London and the directors in Liverpool, it became increasingly impossible to maintain general discipline and supervision.'

The two buying offices were not totally amalgamated at the beginning, but having them in the same building still made possible a much broader overall view of the operation.

When full amalgamation was tried at a later stage, it certainly made for economies of scale; and buying in such large amounts meant that buyers were indeed able to specialise in a particular type of merchandise, to tell manufacturers just what they wanted and to examine the goods at source in the factories. On the other hand, it created problems of its own. The range of merchandise offered by each division could not be identical, for a start, because the pricing and mark-up structure was different for each. Also each had its own delivery system – in mail order, the deliveries were to several warehouses; in the chain-stores they were to individual stores. Finally, seasonal merchandise was required by each at a different time of year. If you tried to amalgamate spring buying for the chain-stores with spring buying for mail order, you were out of kilter because the methodical mail-order customer bought much earlier in the season than the more impulsive shopper in the chain-store.

The final problem at Crosby, whether there was complete amalgamation or whether the dual system was left in operation, was the clash of loyalties to which either of these arrangements could lead. The ability to inspire loyalty is one of John's great assets and as the company grew in size, he quickly recognised the need for team loyalty as well as company loyalty. A smaller unit – a department or a buying team – was a group with which you could identify; its size meant that you knew everyone in it, you were important, you could contribute. 'In a team of twelve, say, you're certainly playing a major role, even if you're only making the tea. If you don't make the tea, the other eleven don't get a drink.' Personal achievement was one of the great motivating factors, John always stressed. If the individual achieved for his team, and if the various teams were all geared to the company, then in the end it would be the company which would reap the benefit.

It was not only improvements in the system on which John was intent; he was also interested in increasing the ability of each individual buyer. Training again. Perhaps, given certain other character traits, instruction of the young came naturally to a man with six younger brothers and sisters. It had shown itself in the early pools years, when he had spent considerable time and energy teaching those school-leavers who were his first employees how to work out permutations. Now it surfaced again. Candidates for the buying office faced a tough selection procedure and once accepted, they were put through a form of apprenticeship. A trainee's first position would be as a buyer's assistant; then when he was considered ready for it, he would be moved up to assistant buyer; finally, when he knew his stuff, and not until then, he would be promoted to buyer.

And every year there would be a solid week of buyers' interviews. John took these himself. He was assisted by John Junior, now head buyer, and the group controller, but he did the interviewing personally and he saw each buyer individually. To begin with, there were very few women buyers, but the numbers were increasing. Before long, one senior buyer in the chain-stores was a young woman who had been been picked out of stock control, Jessie Stubbs. And as the women buyers came up to interview time, it was not just a question of knowing chapter and verse with the figures, but of having the right accessories with the right outfit and a hair appointment for the right day.

Eric Furlong, later the building manager, used to sit outside the office with an alarm clock set to go off in twenty minutes for a buyer, and in half an hour for a group controller. He would try to give them advice on their way in – to tell them, for instance, that their shrinkage was above two per cent and that they would be asked about it. As an ex-buyer said, 'You'd have done preparatory work for the interview for weeks beforehand, not just trying to identify exactly what you'd done, but trying to think of the sort of questions Mr John might ask.' He certainly did not spare criticism if he thought it was needed, but he could also be individually caring. On one occasion, when he was about to interview a furniture buyer, Eric Furlong remembers saying to him, 'Mr Rice hasn't been very well lately, so if he doesn't respond as he should today, you'll know the reason why.' John did not reply, but when the interview was over, he suddenly said, 'Mr Rice, I understand you haven't been too good.'

'No, I haven't, Mr John.'

Out came the Little Black Book and John made a note of it. Within two days Mr Rice was in Lourdes Private Hospital for medical care.

Arranging for private treatment for staff and paying for it was something John did with surprising frequency. 'Not many people knew that side of him,' as one man said. Unfortunately, as he got older and the company grew bigger and more impersonal, a specialist's appointment or a course of treatment would be organised for a member of staff as he instructed; but when the time came for payment, it would have slipped the attention of whoever had been deputed to deal with it, and the patient would be faced with paying the bill himself.

Managers of stores had the same sort of interviews as buyers, and they made the journey to Liverpool from wherever in Great Britain their store happened to be. 'Those interviews could make or break your career.' And they had to run like clockwork – timed in fact by alarm clock, just as buyers' interviews were. Managers had to be there two hours before the interview to make sure that John would not be kept waiting and half an hour beforehand they sat outside Miss Mitchell's office.' As each individual went in, Miss Mitchell would set the alarm. It was timed to go off five minutes before the interview was due to finish, so that John could summarise. 'There was a sealed door, but you could hear this damn bell go off in Miss Mitchell's office. Mr John would hear it and know what it was. But *you* didn't.' Not at the first interview perhaps, but after a second or third, the penny dropped.

'Shrinkage' was always a matter on the agenda; a reasonable explanation would be accepted, but woe betide the manager who happened to say that he had been '"unfortunate", because he'd kill you for that'. One manager who made that mistake was given 'absolute hell'; in fact, when he was driving home and saw in his rear mirror that there was a Rolls behind him, he was convinced that he was being followed. 'He thought it was the Old Man chasing him up the M6.' One of John's comments – half in joke, half in earnest – was well known. 'I want lucky people. The luckier my managers are, the better I like it.'

The 'lucky' managers give a slightly different account of the proceedings. According to one of them, Eric Barker, 'Each interview was a résumé of the year's progress of your particular store and profitability was the bottom line. The personal interview with Mr John was very searching; he used to tell you in no uncertain terms if you hadn't done a good job. He would tell you quite simply that he could make more by putting his money into a building society than by giving it to you to run your store. But at the end of the day, he always finished off on a personal note; he wanted to know how you were, how your family was, the conditions in which you lived. You moved from store to store, and in those days there were company houses. He was always interested in the manner in which we lived.'

The constant movement of managers was one of the drawbacks of the position. The company had bought a house in every town where there was a store, and 'by and large, these were better houses than you could have afforded yourself', but moving one's entire family at regular intervals, with all the attendant problems – such as a change of school for the children – was not an easy option. 'Nevertheless, that was the contract that you signed, and that's what you did.' It was usually promotion for the manager that initiated the move – to a better or a bigger store – but that did not always mollify his wife.

There is a very illuminating story of one particular manager's wife – Freddy Oak's in fact – who decided to beard the lion in his den. Every store had a Christmas dance, and John used to attend as many as he could. At the Liverpool No. 1 store, he took the floor with Mrs Oak and during the course of the dance said, 'If you've ever got a problem, Mrs Oak, come to me' which was exactly what she did. Without mentioning it to her husband, she picked up the phone and rang Miss Mitchell. Although Liverpool No. 1 was supposed to be the top store – 'and a right headache of a store, because you were sitting under head office' – the house that went with it was inadequate and in need of repairs. When the complaint reached the sales manager, he simply dismissed it, but by then it had got to John's ears. Before long there was a convoy of cars going through the Mersey Tunnel and on its way to Meols, where the house in question was situated. The convoy contained not only Mr Oak, but the sales manager of the whole chain-store division, several more of the top brass and John himself.

Once there, John instructed the rest of his team to 'go and have a look round the house, get lost, and leave Mr and Mrs Oak to me'. In the conducted tour that followed, he listened to all Mrs Oak's complaints, agreed with her about them, and said that each would be attended to and put right. There was only one at which he jibbed. Mrs Oak did not like the old Aga in the kitchen, but he was quite firm about that. 'My wife has one of those and she swears by it.' The Aga stayed.

At the end of a very helpful and satisfactory tour, Mrs Oak was encouraged enough to ask whether it would not have been better had they been allowed to buy their own house. 'Your husband can buy his own house whenever he likes, Mrs Oak,' was John's response. 'But he won't be working for me.' At least the Oaks got their repairs done; although how much good it did Mr Oak with the sales manager is a matter for conjecture.

The yearly interviews had one other advantage for John. As well as forming part of the training scheme, they allowed him, in one week, to get a tremendous overview of the whole chain-store operation. It was impossible for him to visit all the stores himself, but by interviewing both junior and senior managers, as well as area managers – which was the term for superintendents – by examining the figures for each particular store over a three-year period, and by close attention to the manager's gradings, he was able to get a potted history of each store.

The grading system was introduced by John and the managing director, George Watts. He had been a Wing Commander in the RAF and had used a similar sort of system there. It was an important part of the training scheme, and consisted of about ten different gradings: use of footage, merchandise knowledge, café operation, shrinkage control, wage cost control, approach to and control of staff, approach to and effectiveness of training, quality of all-round performance, and personal capacity for a larger job. Each manager's grading was done by his area superintendent, not just once a year but every three months; and at the end of every quarter, the superintendent would sit down with each man individually, go through his gradings with him, commend his strengths and try to suggest ways of eradicating his weaknesses. It was in fact an early example of an appraisal system, which is now standard business practice.

The marking for each grade was out of ten, and this permeated John's thinking to such an extent that he tended to mark everybody and everything out of ten in most other areas of life as well. 'Fair – I'd give him six,' was a typical remark of his, whether applied to a footballer or to an artist. Counting, indeed, became almost an obsession with him; and years later, when someone commented to his younger son how like his father he was, Peter's reply was immediate. 'Yes, I realised that when I suddenly noticed that I was counting the number of pats I was giving the dog.'

Group tests set up by the National Institute of Industrial Psychology were introduced, and the training scheme was refined and improved over the years; it was an area in which John was always breaking new ground. His direct involvement and his personal interviewing continued until he was well into his seventies, when there were probably sixty or so stores to deal with. By the time the number had grown to over 120, he was getting older and he delegated, but he always remained interested.

The targeting of younger men for managerial positions, which started in the early 1950s, was due entirely to a decision of John's, made as soon as he had fully recognised the very demanding nature of chain-store management. 'OK, they hadn't the experience, other than this training programme, but they had the legs and the energy to learn,' as one retired main board director, Stanley Page, commented. At that time there were a lot of young men about who had proved themselves, albeit in a different situation – the war. A tremendous number of those taken on were ex-Forces – including Stanley Page himself. John was explicit in the measures he proposed to his executives in his 1954 speech:

'In the normal course of things in most organisations, the average executive doesn't come to the top until he is about forty-five to fifty. Within ten years or so, he begins to think of retirement and gardening. We'd do much better if we could produce executives at an earlier age – say, thirty-five . . . For a while, we have been experimenting and developing the technique of recruiting promising young men for special training. Of course we must recruit the right men; we can't afford a high percentage of failures

– not so much because we don't want to waste money, but we can't afford the time . . .'

As usual John had made sure that one of his executives had done research on the subject in the States.

'He found their methods basically the same as our own, but they lay more responsibility on the shoulders of the executives in whose departments the trainees are working . . . Most of their schemes have a carefully considered programme of job rotation; that is, a trainee is given a selected job to do for which he is held responsible; when he can do it efficiently, he's moved to the next selected job. And so on. All the schemes emphasised that the only successful way to produce executives early is to give promising men responsibility whilst they're still young – not when they're ninety-nine; and if they carry it well, to promote them and give them added responsibility.

'Executive capacity is mainly the ability to carry responsibility successfully. And just as the best way of learning to do the job is to actually do it, so the best way to learn to carry responsibility is to actually carry it.'

This became a credo of John's. The only area where perhaps he did not put it into practice was in the handling of his sons. When both of them were mature men in their forties, and they asked him to consider taking a slight step sideways and giving them more to do, his answer was a definite 'No'. In fact, he gave the impression that he thought this was a move to oust him.

In other ways his psychological handling of people was acute. The managers' and the buyers' dinners were a case in point; after the interviews and the meetings came the fun. As one manager said, 'We always finished with a dinner at the Adelphi, where he would say, "Well, the business is finished; now we can enjoy ourselves." So the following day, everyone goes back to their store feeling a lift from his wisdom – the wisdom of the interview, the wisdom of his speech and Mr Cecil's speech. Mr Cecil always put on the funny side, whereas Mr John was the business side, so there was a tremendous balance between the two brothers.'

The managers' order of seniority was clear, as each particular manager's status was dependent on the size and importance of his particular store. The buyers' positions were not so clearly defined; and when it came to the buyers' dinner, there was always a rush to look at the seating plan which was invariably displayed on a large board in the foyer of the Adelphi. The first thing every buyer did on arrival was check to make sure that he had not slipped a place or two. The pecking order was very important. That apart, buyers enjoyed the evenings as much as managers.

Perhaps Freddy Oak summed them up best: 'They were absolutely cracking dinners; and while we always enjoyed the food, the wine and the cabarets – the stars he used to get were very, very good – there was that picture above the top table in the Adelphi, a picture of two hands being shaken – the Happy Circle. I always thought this was a message – apart from the generosity of the dinner – it was a bit of a message from him: "All right, you've had a tough year, I kicked you to death last week at the interview, now forget it, enjoy yourself and start again." Not actually said in words, but that's the kind of message you'd get.'

Messages not actually said in words were something John was expert at. He was a great demonstrator, an ability perhaps learnt or inherited from his mother. There is something very reminiscent of her china-smashing episode in some of the stories recounted about him. On one occasion, still very concerned about the quality of his merchandise, he called a buyers' meeting at the State Restaurant in Dale Street, which the company owned. One end of the room was curtained off; and when all the buyers were assembled, the curtains were drawn aside to reveal all the returned items for that week – rows and rows of them, on hangers or laid out on tables – with the accompanying returns notes. One look at that enormous collection of failed merchandise, packed together in a confined space, was enough to make his point. And he worked the same technique on businesses other than his own. Mail order used British Rail for a great many of their deliveries, so he once invited the Liverpool manager of British Rail to a meeting. When the manager had arrived and was comfortably seated in John's office, one of the mail-order wardrobes was carried in, plus a large axe. John rose to his feet, seized the axe and in front of the astonished BR man, proceeded to demolish the wardrobe. When he had finished smashing it to pieces, he returned to his seat and said, perfectly pleasantly, 'That is how your company is treating my furniture. Do something about it, please.'

It was not only buyer and manager training that John was setting up; he was also instigating a major restructure in other areas – but all with the same end in view. 'My mother says, "Let's get decent merchandise",' he told Stanley Page. Now he instituted a quality control department. At that time there were no official British standard measurements; each manufacturer of a brand name had their own block, i.e. their own set of measurements for each size.

: the Hungarian uprising of 1956, Peter, then a
:nt in Vienna, assisted in distributing aid from
:woods to the refugees.

John receives his knighthood in 1980. With him are
three of his children; from left to right: Betty, Janatha
and Peter.

chairman joins in enthusiastically on a Motorists' Outing for Handicapped Children in 1962.

John congratulates David Hockney on winning first prize in the 1967 'John Moores'. (*photo courtesy of John M*
Photography)

John's ninetieth birthday in 1986. He was happiest
painting in his studio. (*photo by Don McPhee, courtesy of
the Guardian*)

John in his nineties at a football match,
wearing his famous hand-knitted Everton
scarf. (*photo courtesy of the News of the World*)

Clothes coupons were only just coming to an end and goods were still difficult to obtain, so getting any sort of standardisation was out of the question. As the next best thing, John decided that Littlewoods would draw up its own specifications list and create its own quality control rules. These would apply not only to cutters and general machinists; the components of the merchandise would be scrutinised as well as the finished product. Clothing was given particular attention. The material to be used, whether provided by the supplier or purchased by Littlewoods, was first subjected to rigorous tests, even including a check on the number of threads per inch.

The Littlewoods laboratories were enlarged and improved to cope with the enormous amount of extra work involved. Boys' blazers, for example, were tested to see how many times the elbow could withstand a rubbing movement before it went into holes. Toys were checked to make sure that they did not have razor-sharp edges. Cap-firing pistols were safety-tested; an order for one particular type had to be cancelled when it was discovered that it was actually fitted to fire cartridges! And to maintain the required standards, spot checks were made on ten per cent of every delivery. If the goods from a particular supplier proved in any way unsatisfactory, then the check was extended to the entire consignment.

Computers, still in their early days, were John's next innovation. The first was installed in 1957. It was enormous, consisting of an entire room full of equipment. To illustrate how much computers have developed, the same sort of power would now be supplied by something the size of a small box.

The computer system was introduced specifically to assist with mail-order stock control, and it was certainly effective. Before its advent, the procedure had been complex and time-consuming, everything being done on a manual basis. A battery of clerks was required and it could still take a week before the stock controller knew what the position was. With a computer, the balance could be drawn on a Friday, and by Monday there would be a complete output for all sales and stock by colour and option.

By the end of the Sixties, all agency information had been computerised in the same way. Previously, agents and organisers had sent in their own record cards every week. There was a card for every single customer with what each customer had ordered being marked in a vertical column on the left, and what each was paying per week reading horizontally. The cards were checked by Littlewoods girls and sent back to the respective agents and organisers within days. There were over a million cards to be dealt with weekly and they were not exactly small in size, so neither was the bill for postage.

The computerisation of chain-stores was started soon after it had been introduced into mail order, and development proceeded at much the same pace in each division. Chain-stores had no agency data to be recorded, but the calculating and recording of sales figures for each store was speeded up enormously by computers. Littlewoods was certainly one of the first chains to have point-of-sale equipment. This was tried out in various pilot stores in the late Sixties, and by 1972 was a fully-fledged system operating throughout the chain. It meant that each individual sale was recorded, the information transmitted straight to the relevant department and stock at the store in question was replenished. If, for example, a size fifteen and a half collar white shirt had been sold, that information was keyed in and relayed back, and another white shirt, size fifteen and a half collar, would be delivered to the store in its place. It made for much more accurate provisioning, it stopped any possibility of fiddling or of manipulating stocks and it saved everybody a great deal of time.

The introduction of computers was resisted at first, in spite of seminars planned to instruct people. 'Everybody was in fear and trepidation. We were going to be like kids going back to school.' After a certain amount of preliminary discussion, however, John had had enough; the computers were installed and the specialist instructors arrived, but it still took some time for staff to get used to them.

Owen Musther, then a buying controller, remembered the first buyers' interviews after their advent. When it was the turn of his group and the first buyer had been called in, John opened his briefcase and took out 'a complete set of sales figures of my division on the computer sheets. Everybody's hair rose in horror, but he flipped through those sheets and he read all those figures out to the individual concerned, as though he had been opening his own ledgers. When the buyer had gone, he looked at me – and he could twinkle, you know – and he said, "Yes, you couldn't do that, could you?"' John could soak up information like a sponge, and he was always difficult to keep up with, even at seventy.

John's most original idea for improving merchandise was possibly 'the panel system', as he called it. Certainly none of the staff had ever come across a similar scheme. His first move was to call his buying office executives together and tell them, point-blank, that they were not doing a good enough job, that there were far too many mark-downs and returns and that he now intended to try an experiment. The buyers would select in the usual way, but before the merchandise was offered to the public, it would be viewed and graded by panels of ordinary working women. Each panel would include two store supervisors brought to Liverpool specifically for the task from two different stores anywhere in Great Britain; plus six girls drawn from different sections of the organisation, who had shown themselves to have good dress sense and good common sense. No buyers or executives would be represented. It would be the panel's gradings which decided which samples were to be included amongst Littlewoods' selling lines (sometimes as many as nine out of ten samples would make the grade, sometimes none at all) and anything rejected by the panel was either to be replaced or simply thrown out of the range.

The idea was not exactly well received. 'Of course it created absolute hell as you can imagine' was one comment. It certainly had its drawbacks. Fashion always has a forward trend, and even a fashion-conscious woman may not be able to envisage the coming line. To some extent, it also limited creativity and made it more difficult for the buying office to put together a whole new season's merchandise to create the new look. But it certainly weeded out the rubbish. The all-women panels had discrimination, practicality and appreciation of value, learnt from their own personal shopping. They knew what they wanted and if they did not want something, they knew why. From time to time, it was necessary to co-opt men as well. On one occasion in 1956, when it came to selecting men's shoes, an emergency call was sent out round the Crosby building for men who took size eight to report for a trying-on session. Harry Thomas, who was then a junior executive, was pressed into service and to this day remembers his embarrassment. He had holes in his socks.

The first panel was put into operation just as the seasonal range of merchandise had been selected and was virtually being 'put to bed'. John stopped it dead and insisted that every item went through the panel first. Starting from scratch again (which was more or less what it entailed) was a tremendous operation, but it was typical of his drive for quality, for customer service and for customer satisfaction. Also typical was his refusal to give up his idea in the face of an apparent impossibility. Everyone buckled to, and in spite of the hiatus, the mail-order catalogue was out on time.

The pools division continued to grow. There were various changes: in March 1957, the sixpenny Seven Match Treble Chance Pool was replaced by two Eight Match Treble Chance Pools, one of *6d* and one of *2d*. The total stakes were between £33m. and £35m. each week during this period, returning betting duty of £10m. to £11m. a week. Then, in September 1957, both treble chance pools were consolidated into one with a *2d* stake and the dividends were increased from three to four. At the same time, the limit of £75,000 to any one winner was removed. Already there had been three winners of this amount on one match played in 1954 on November 13th – not such an unlucky number, after all. Now it remained to be seen what sort of sum a single winner could reach. The punters did not have long to wait; less than two months later, on November 2nd, a Mrs N MacGrail won £205,235, equivalent to £2.4m. in today's terms.

Six-figure winners started to come in regularly, and John's immediate response was to set up an advisory service to help people deal with such vast sums. This still continues today. Each big winner can consult a group of professional people – a solicitor, a stockbroker, a banker, etc. – who are able to give advice on how best to handle the money and invest wisely. Use of the service is not compulsory, but it is obviously welcome as ninety-nine per cent of winners do use it.

Thanks to John's insistence on better merchandise, the chain-stores were now improving their image, and their numbers continued to increase. There was a temporary pause in 1957 and 1958, the only years when no new stores were opened, due partly to the credit squeeze and partly to the Suez crisis.

The Middle East was like a powder keg, with explosion possible at any time. As soon as a peace initiative was accepted in one area, trouble would flare somewhere else. There were border raids between Jordan and Israel; in 1956, both countries accepted the UN truce proposals. Israeli troops invaded the Sinai peninsula; Britain and France called for a cease-fire. Then Britain and France were themselves embroiled when Nasser seized the Suez Canal, of which they were the major shareholders: in retaliation, they bombed Egyptian airfields. The UN fleet cleared the Canal, and British and French troops were withdrawn. There were still problems – martial law in Jordan, and recurrent US aid to Israel – but the skirmishing did not escalate into full-scale war as it might have done.

From John's point of view, the worst effect the Suez crisis had on Littlewoods was that his factories lost their market for selling 2,000 oil heaters a week to the Middle East. 'Seems pretty incongruous, anyway, selling oil heaters to the burning deserts,' as he observed. His business was much more affected by the credit squeeze caused by the rise in interest rates.

In 1956, interest rates in Britain were raised to five and a half per cent, their highest since 1932, and although this had very little impact on pools, the credit mail-order firm, Brian Mills, and the chain-stores were badly affected. 'Both these sections had been expanding very rapidly – an expansion based on a free economy with plenty of credit available,' John commented. 'The credit squeeze radically changed the situation and almost overnight we had to completely reverse our policy and stop all our expansion.'

It was the stores, his current baby, that he was most concerned about.

'We had got over most of our teething troubles, and with the end of building controls I felt at long last I could see my way to planning a really first-class chain. We were building right and left on sites we had been holding for years, as well as acquiring new sites for future expansion. As fast as we built one store and started trading, we were able to sell it to a finance house, take the store back on a long lease and get on with building the next with the proceeds.'

The credit squeeze put an end to all this. But as John said, 'Major developments, planned for years and under way, can't be stopped at the drop of a hat. Once a building has been started, with raw materials on the site, you're almost bound to go on.'

He was determined that the stores at Watford, Slough and Worcester should be completed, but work on the fourteen-storey building planned for Glasgow had to be put on hold, just as the excavations were finished. 'All we can see for the years of preparation behind the whole thing is a big hole in the ground. And by Scottish law, you have to pay half-rates for such a hole.'

John's policy of pushing on with the expansion as fast as possible when he could, had certainly paid off. There were already sixty stores in the chain and when one considers that during its entire nineteen-year history, building had only been allowed for four of those years, the rate of growth is even more amazing.

But the business acumen which John had demonstrated was more remarkable still. He had created a formula which could withstand almost any economic conditions. Of his three major divisions, two were nearly always in a position to support a third through difficulties. The cash flow from the pools was more or less continuous; in good times – when things were going well on the High Street – the stores thrived; and when times were hard and there was recession, then mail order got the benefit. It was an ideal diversification. And he had the whole organisation back in Liverpool again, under his wing or, as some might have said, under his thumb.

His handling of the family was equally protective and equally authoritarian. While hardly comparable with the international crisis, in the 1950s there had been a family crisis to surmount as well. In the spring of 1955, Cecil's daughter Patricia married. On the face of it, the engagement had seemed a very suitable one. Her husband-to-be was the son of a distinguished Liverpool architect; intelligent and presentable, he was himself in his fourth year of a five-year course in architecture. But he came of a staunchly Catholic family. Patricia was a beneficiary of a family trust which owned a proportion of shares in the business and would one day own shares in her own right. John believed that a wife's loyalty was always to her husband and although a Catholic influence which was purely religious gave him no cause for concern, one which might give rise to divided loyalties *did* worry him.

When his attempts to dissuade Patricia from the marriage failed, he then banned the rest of the family from attending the wedding. With great tact, Cecil and Doris refrained from even sending them invitations. In protest, one young cousin did creep into the back of St Patrick's Church, Soho Square, for the service but, needless to say, did not dare to be seen at the reception afterwards. That was attended by the bride and bridegroom's immediate families, and friends who did not work for John. As far as the John Moores cousins were concerned, Patricia was to be incommunicado, officially at least, until her marriage ended in divorce in the late Sixties. Until then, the couple lived in a comfortable and pleasant house which Cecil had specially built for them in his own grounds. John spoke to their children amicably enough when they met at Cecil's house or at the family shoot, although he never overtly acknowledged the relationship; but at a family party years later when he was in his eighties, he suddenly went up to their eldest son and said, 'Shall we let bygones be bygones?'

The family was still important to John and it was still one of his most reliable sources of support. Now he had to tread the fine line between keeping that support and enlarging the business beyond it. In 1955, Eric Sawyer was made a full director of Littlewoods. As John reminded his executives in his Christmas speech, 'Littlewoods is a private company and we've not previously appointed a full director outside the family.' But he went on to give a hint of his plans for the next ten years, by the end of which time he would be seventy.

'With the growth of the organisation in the future, we may wish to extend our directorships. We're growing fast, and leadership is going to play a big part in the scheme of things. Mr Cecil and I are your leaders – but with the growth of the organisation, more and more will have to be delegated to you. Most of you have grown with the organisation and so you are the men best fitted to search for potential talent lower down the ranks and having found it, develop it and lead it. You! You are the men who must lead the way, and on whom I know I can confidently rely.'

But not quite as confidently as he could on his own family. John Junior was fully committed to the organisation, but by 1957, Peter appeared to be moving towards an independent career of his own. Now John drew his younger son back into the Happy Circle.

15

The Old Victorian Principles

Peter was in Vienna, the opera capital of Europe. In 1954, after reading Modern Languages for two years, he had decided not to finish the course but to leave Oxford before his final year and before taking his degree. This was not because he found the life uncongenial. He had enjoyed himself at Christ Church and had made some lifelong friends, but his Italian and German were fluent, he found the Oxford tradition of teaching both literatures mainly in English slightly irritating and, above all, he thought he had discovered his real vocation. He wanted to be involved in opera.

Whether his talents fitted him for directing or producing, or whether they were more entrepreneurial, he was still unsure; he needed practical experience in order to find out. David Webster, the Director of the Royal Opera House and a Liverpool connection, gave him advice and help. It was arranged that the Vienna State Opera, which did not take students, would employ Peter in the position of *voluntär*, or unpaid producer's assistant. This involved attendance at morning rehearsals and usually at the performance in the evening as well, but it left his afternoons free. Like his father, Peter did not believe in wasting time, so every afternoon he attended the Viennese Academy of Music and Dramatic Art. As this training would take about four years, Peter rented a small flat in Vienna.

The operatic world was a milieu which suited him well and he learnt a great deal. Before the end of his third year, he had staged at the Academy the first Viennese production of Britten's *Rape of Lucretia* in German, and although his singers were only students, it had been well received and was a success. As 1957 approached, he was already beginning to plan ahead and to look around for possible future jobs. Then he received a letter from his father.

John was writing to ask whether his younger son would consider coming back into the business. If he did not wish to return, then John would like to buy the Littlewoods shares that Peter owned – for £100,000. Like father, like son. Peter realised that if his father was offering that amount of money for the shares, then they must in fact be worth a great deal more. He declined the offer. But there was something in the letter that he could not resist. At the same time as asking whether Peter would consider coming back into the business, John also told his son that he could do with his help. Just as he had called his younger brothers, Arthur and Charlie, back from Australia almost thirty years earlier, now he called his son. Peter gave up his own career at once and went back to Liverpool. His father needed him.

The help consisted in learning the business from the bottom up, as his elder brother had done, and as Peter himself had started to do before embarking on a career of his own. So he went into chain-stores to learn the ropes.

Everything seemed to be going exactly as John wanted. The colossal effort of the war years and the equal effort involved in post-war reconstruction had produced a very positive result: a Littlewoods way of doing things had evolved, a Littlewoods way of thinking and approach. It was classless; it demanded loyalty and commitment to common aims; it believed in system and attention to detail; and it never looked back – it was always looking ahead. Stopping to consolidate was not something that John believed in: that was simply stagnation. You consolidated as you went along; if you paused – for whatever reason – you could be overtaken. John was preparing for further expansion. And packed though the Fifties were in business terms, it was not in business only that John deployed his extraordinary energies. He found time for other interests too.

Shooting and fishing were still great family pursuits. John regularly attended a shooting school in London throughout the decade. But whereas the family's shoots were all more or less local – at Halsall and Ince Blundell – they fished mainly in Scotland. The lease on Loch Grannoch which expired at the end of the Forties had not been renewed. Instead, another loch had been acquired, in Wigtown as it was then called. It was considerably less isolated and less rugged than Loch Grannoch, and the lodge itself was more like a small and comfortable hotel. Whether because of this or for other reasons, it never held quite the same place in John's affections; it was Cecil who found the place most congenial. John did continue to holiday there, however, usually in August with the family; and as there were plenty of midges around at that time of year, Ruby made him a special fishing hat draped with net. He found his visits perfectly pleasant but he did not consider the fishing to be as good, and although the surrounding countryside was picturesque, it did not provide the same walking opportunities as Loch Grannoch. John's main fishing jaunts were on the stretch of the Spey which he still owned. Records going back to 1955 show that the party usually included John himself, Cecil and Arthur, their wives, and later on Betty's husband, Kenneth

– also a keen fisherman. Typically, the fishing was run on business lines; those salmon not allocated to family or friends were sold on the market.

The new loch is still used by a great many of the family. As it is owned by the firm, they pay Littlewoods when they take holidays there; but in true Moores tradition, groups of Littlewoods employees are also sent up to the loch, either for a break or if they have been ill, to convalesce in idyllic surroundings.

The situation was much the same with the hotels which the company owned in Harrogate – 'The Prospect' and 'The Prince of Wales' – and which had been bought at about the same time. While providing pleasant, indeed luxurious, accommodation for the family (which, again, they paid for) on their visits to York Races, Littlewoods executives and employees were also invited there, particularly in the low season when the hotels were not so busy. As more and more of the British started to go abroad for their holidays, business dwindled even in the high season and both hotels were finally sold. John had decided that the hotel business was too uncertain, and it was not one in which he wanted to be permanently involved. The exception was the Elbow Beach Hotel in Bermuda which he himself had bought, and which was only disposed of recently.

The two brothers were equally generous to staff, but each gave in his own way. John enjoyed acquiring new skills, learning and developing any latent talent, so he provided the same opportunities for his 'girls'.

Potential singers continued to be encouraged and given training; the Littlewoods girls' choir or songsters went from strength to strength in the Fifties. Each building had its own choir, but the Littlewoods Songsters were the pick of the bunch. They played a major part in an annual Christmas show, put on at the giant Odeon cinema in Liverpool to raise money and gifts for the orphaned and the disabled children of Merseyside. And they did not only perform in Liverpool. In 1952, for example, dressed in Elizabethan costume, they took part in *Castle in the Air*, held at the Palladium in Llandudno, along with professionals such as Margaret Rutherford and David Tomlinson. The Songsters went on to be filmed by Pathé Pictorial doing a Shakespearian pageant in Bodnant Gardens in the Conway Valley, accompanied by the Liverpool Philharmonic Orchestra. One of their London appearances was at the Coliseum in *Salute to Ivor Novello* – this time with what was described as 'the greatest gathering of actors and actresses ever to appear in one performance', and which included Noël Coward, John Gielgud, Edith Evans, Sybil

Thorndike, Gracie Fields, Jack Buchanan and countless others. They were also regular performers on Radio Luxembourg.

Budding amateur actors and actresses were encouraged in the same way. Each building had its own drama group and there were competitions between them. There was an annual drama festival which was judged by a professional and for which John presented a trophy. There was a company pantomime every Christmas, reviewed by professional critics. And last but not least, there were the arts and crafts competitions and exhibitions. Group activity encouraged achievement, and there were always prizes to be won. The wide range of classes for which employees could enter varied from dressmaking and model-making to painting and drawing.

Painting and drawing were John's own interests. He had not stopped painting, in spite of pressure of work, since the first still life he had produced in 1953. His other passion, languages, developed soon afterwards – for purely practical reasons. He painted on holidays in Bermuda and at the loch, but he wanted to paint in Italy. It was nearer than Bermuda and although not as near as Scotland, the light was better and also lasted longer.

His approach to learning Italian was like most of his other activities: informal, through friends and acquaintances, and to suit his own convenience. Working for the independent accounting firm Roberts Legge, which was used by Littlewoods, was an accountant who had an Italian wife. His name also happened to be Roberts and his wife, Rosetta, taught Italian at the Liverpool College of Commerce. As soon as Miss Mitchell got to know of this, she went into action. Rosetta Roberts was approached and asked if she could fit in some lessons for Mr John. She worked at the college in the morning and the evening, so lessons were arranged for the early afternoon. Straight after lunch, she would go over to John's office in Bootle, wait until whatever meeting he was in was finished, and then give him about an hour's lesson in Italian.

She started with the grammar, which is the standard introduction to a language; but to her surprise John insisted on learning by numbers – just as he did with his painting and piano playing. *Io sono*, for example – 'I am' – was number one; *tu sei* – 'you are' – number two; *egli/ella e* – 'he/she is' was three and so forth. Rosetta did not think this at all a good idea. As she said, 'It is very difficult to make a sentence by thinking twenty-four, twenty-six, ninety-four, forty-six; you have to learn grammar the proper way.' John, however, insisted, and while he was writing everything down, Miss Mitchell was keenly typing it all out for him as well. This went on for some time, but eventually even John had had enough and capitulated to Rosetta's method.

The lessons continued, on and off, well into the Sixties; and although each admired the other's character, they continued to cross swords. When Rosetta decided one year to take September and October off and return to Italy with her small son, John was extremely put out. He informed her immediately that he would not be continuing his lessons with her when she came back; he would have them with her husband instead. After that, whenever he could fit in a lesson at the weekend, one of his secretaries would telephone Len Roberts, who would immediately have to take a train out to Formby to instruct John in the intricacies of Italian grammar. Later, when John decided that he would like Italian conversation as well, Rosetta was useful again. By this time she was working at the Italian Consulate in Liverpool. When she finished at six o'clock, there would sometimes be a message for her to go out to Formby, as Mr John was ready for his practice. After the lesson, of course, Rosetta had to return home and cook the evening meal for her husband and her son.

It would never have occurred to John that he was using people – he felt they could always say 'No'. Naturally, he paid, but that apart, most people were somehow pleased and flattered to be involved, to be treated as friends, to be needed by him. He was, in spite of his determined 'ordinariness' and lack of pretension, a very rich and very powerful man.

The same sort of thing occurred when he decided to try out his Italian in Italy. He went to stay with Rosetta's brother and sister-in-law who had a house in Venice, but was very quickly on the telephone to Liverpool to say that he could not understand everything, that he wished to continue his lessons at the same time, and that he needed his teacher on the spot. Len Roberts flew to Venice without demur, but found himself staying in a hotel instead of with his relatives because John was ensconced in the only spare bedroom which their house possessed. When the two men were leaving to return to England at the end of the week and Len suggested that John might like to send his hostess flowers, John appeared surprised.

'What for?'

'Well – as a thank you. It's normal behaviour.'

'*You* will never be rich!' was the crushing response.

He did send the flowers, however, and his attitude may have been something of an act, to emphasise his dislike of elaborate social convention. Anything with a 'snob' element was anathema to him. On one occasion, when dining out with his elder son, John Junior, they had a particularly fine wine; although always a light drinker, John enjoyed wine with a meal, and he was reasonably knowledgeable about it.

'This is a very nice wine,' he commented. And then added deliberately, 'Who's the brewer?'

He was never, ever, going to be involved in 'claptrap' about wine. As a contrast, when no display was involved, his manners could be impeccable. The early Miss Littlewood shows used to take place at the Liverpool Stadium, with top show business personalities appearing and a great deal of razzmatazz. An early employee, George Farrar, who worked in stock control, remembers sitting with his wife watching one of the acts during a show, when John arrived a little late. 'He stood at the door, even though people were waiting to show him to his seat. Anybody else would have come in and sat down, but the Old Man just stood waiting; he wouldn't take his seat until the act had finished. It was the old Victorian principles.' They were demonstrated in other ways, too. Tom Jones appeared in one show, and although he was extremely popular with a large section of the audience, John was not so sure. 'He never booked him again, because of all the gyrations. He had very strict morals.'

As his knowledge of Italian increased, so did his painting trips to Italy. Sometimes they would be made with Reg Hubbard or Bill Stevenson, while Ruby stayed at home, busy with her own interests. On his April visits, however, he nearly always took his wife and his youngest child, Janatha with him, and while he was off painting, they would sit on the beach wearing thick sweaters and reading. It was not exactly sunbathing weather at that time of year.

Not all John's painting took place out-of-doors. He painted in the conservatory – or the sun-room, as it was called – at Fairways, until Ruby was finally provoked into complaining about the terrible mess he made; so he had a studio built in the garden. Before very long, there was a studio opening off his Littlewoods office in Irlam Road as well. Painting for John may not have been exactly relaxation but at least it gave him a break from work. As it demanded his full concentration, it took his mind off any business worries or problems he might have had – for a brief period, at least. When he painted, he was totally engrossed. And as painting was something which he never mastered to his own satisfaction, it remained a challenge and almost a lifelong obsession. 'I'm not a good painter, but I'm getting better,' was his comment as an old man to one interviewer. And to a painting friend, more ruefully still, 'I've got all the equipment – but not the talent.' He was being overly modest. But it is typical of his often contradictory character that while believing that his decisions were always right and that he always knew best, at the same time he possessed a deep and genuine humility. Both aspects were on a larger-than-life scale. Or as a grandson said of him, in a different context, 'He could be a charmer ninety-five per cent of the time, and for five per cent he could be a swine. It's just that he could be "more so" than most people at anything.'

As his technique improved, he progressed from painting by numbers to copying. His favourite artists were Cézanne in particular; Gauguin, Van Gogh and Miró. It may seem a surprising selection to those who consider that John was only interested in a painter's technique and not in what the painter was attempting to convey. True, he was trying to master perspective. His approach was an intellectual one, and Cézanne's remark that 'one must detect in Nature the sphere, the cone, and the cylinder' must have appealed to him. What appealed even more was the fact that every one of Cézanne's paintings dealt with a fresh problem – what was it that the artist was actually seeing? (A gifted art teacher once explained that her job was not to teach people to draw, but to teach them to look.)

By copying, John was in a sense employing the artist to do his looking for him. Cézanne lamented that he himself did not have 'the magnificent richness of colour that animates Nature'. John, as a fellow-painter observed in some surprise, was a 'colour man'. Cézanne admitted, 'With me, the realisation of my sensations is always painful.' John was perhaps not allowing himself sensations at first-hand any more, not as he had on that German tour long ago in the Thirties. Time was what mattered; he was taking short cuts. Indeed, it was possibly not simply painting that John was trying to master: through painting he was trying to make sense of the world around him, of the nature of things themselves. Putting them on canvas was his equivalent to 'listing' them, and it gave him a feeling of control. He was always a good listener; he could pick people's brains and take the exact piece of information or idea that he needed. Subconsciously he was using the great artists whose work he copied in exactly the same way.

Copying was very useful when working for short periods inside one of his studios, but he sometimes attempted still-life compositions of his own. There is a story that the chef at Irlam Road once received a message that Mr John would like a cauliflower. One was duly cooked and served for his lunch, and it was then discovered that he had wanted a cauliflower to *paint*.

His major contribution to painting is the John Moores Liverpool Art Exhibition, which has now become known in art circles simply as 'the John Moores'. It dates from 1957, but its inception was triggered by something that happened in 1955. Hugh Scrutton, the director of the Walker Art Gallery, instituted an open section in the Liverpool Academy's annual Exhibition. Painters other than Academicians were to be allowed to compete as well, and the works selected hung in the same show. Only a small percentage were accepted, as the judging was rigorous, and amongst the many that were rejected was a small still life signed 'John Moores'. 'Of course, we all knew who it was,' as one of the judging panel commented, 'but it made no difference.' John was not going to get his painting hung just because of who he was. On the other hand, the fact of who he was might have contributed to its rejection. Power must clearly be seen not to influence artistic judgement.

One of the paintings which were accepted was by another Liverpool amateur, George Kennerley, who had taken up painting at about the same time as John, and whose work had already appeared in the Royal Academy Summer Exhibition in London for three years running. The two men were acquainted, although only slightly. They had met when the various pools companies had formed Unity Pools at the beginning of the war; Kennerley was the managing director of Vernons Pools. According to one opinion, it was the fact that they were also rivals in business which rubbed salt in the wound of John's rejection; he could not bear to be beaten.

Within two years he had founded the John Moores Liverpool Art Exhibition, a biennial competition with a top prize of £20,000. There have been seventeen of these exhibitions so far, and they attract a large field. Artists they have helped to launch include David Hockney, Richard Hamilton, Peter Blake and R B Kitaj, and the exhibition has acquired an international reputation; it has been called the British Biennale. What is more, it has remained at the Walker Art Gallery in Liverpool, and its founder has resisted all persuasion to have it moved to London, or even to let it travel there later. Every two years, important and influential art critics make the journey north, and it may be Liverpool's resulting prominence on the contemporary art scene that was one of the reasons for its choice as the site of the Tate in the North.

It is true that John does not like to be beaten, that he does not like to fail at anything. 'Whatever you start, you've got to take it past the posts' is one of his maxims. More importantly, his lack of success in that 1955 competition showed him what it felt like, as a painter, to be rejected. He inaugurated 'the John Moores' to give painters opportunity – to have their work seen, to have it judged by the best, and possibly to have it displayed with the best; to give the artists the opportunity to acquire the confidence that recognition brings. And the prize money was to give the opportunity to study, to travel, to experiment, which might not otherwise have been possible. If an artist lives in the South and does not have the time or the money to make the journey, there are collection points in London and in Bristol where a painting can be handed in, and it will be transported free of charge to the Walker Art Gallery.

John sat on the selection committee himself for some years, and not just as a figure-head. According to a fellow member, 'He had very strong views and would always speak out,' definitely squashing the suggestion that conceptual art should be allowed in the competition. On the other hand, those who considered that he put his opinions forcefully had probably never seen how autocratic he could be. His younger son, Peter, considered that the periods when he sat on the art juries were the only times when he was not 'very bossy'. 'He was out of his depth, and he didn't want to be seen to be out of his depth.' He was there to stop horse-trading between the different judges; i.e. 'If I back you on your choice of second, will you have my first?' Friends and colleagues, whom he took occasionally to look at the winning paintings, concur with this view. 'Good job I didn't do the choosing' was one of his comments. He left it to the experts.

His reputed rivalry with George Kennerley may have existed, but if so it was an extremely friendly one. The two men did, in fact, become good friends. They met again when Unity Pools was being disbanded and got to know each other through the discussions that the break-up involved. In the years that followed, they often went on painting holidays together, to Wales, to Italy, and to Bermuda and Barbados; and John made a special trip to Florence when his fellow painter had an exhibition on there. Unfortunately, this coincided with a staff strike at the hotel where he was staying, and the visitors had to look after themselves. He had taken his secretaries (Miss Mitchell and Miss Richards) along with him, which was lucky because, as one of them said, 'He couldn't even boil a kettle.' John's lack of practicality was well known in his immediate family circle. He knew how things worked in theory but left the application to others. Perhaps it was because there had always been someone to look after the practical details of life for him: first his mother, then his wife. John had been brought up to believe that his job was a different one; his job was to concentrate his energies on important mental effort.

The Fifties also saw his energy and dynamism channelled into various charitable enterprises. The paternal responsibility which he had felt first for his entire family, including brothers and sisters, and then for his work-force, now spread to include the city he loved. He has always given quietly and with as little publicity as possible.

Nor has his charitable giving consisted solely of money; he has also given his time and his detailed attention. He has always been personally involved.

His strong anti-Communist stance found expression at the time of the Hungarian uprising in 1956, but his giving then was more on humanitarian than political grounds. His younger son, Peter, was still a student in Vienna when the first flood of Hungarian refugees hit the city. Many families had walked all the way from Budapest, well over a hundred miles, skirting minefields or even picking their way through the middle of them on the journey. 'Some people lost a leg, or even one of their children,' as Peter explained. But the alternative – staying behind – was even more dangerous; martial law had been declared and mass arrests were taking place. There were refugee camps all along the Austro-Hungarian border; and countless more refugees (the lucky ones who had friends or relatives there) made for Vienna itself. If you had a sofa, you let a refugee sleep on it; if you had a second winter coat, you gave it to someone who needed it more. Peter was on the telephone to his father without delay, and met with an immediate response. Medical supplies and any surplus blankets or warm clothing that the mail order department had in stock were loaded onto planes and flown out; Peter met them at the airport and handed them over to the Red Cross.

Most of John's other charitable giving was in Liverpool. It was nearly always connected with the young and was aimed particularly at providing opportunity. The longest-running of all his charities is probably the Liverpool Motorists' Annual Outing for Handicapped Children – which was originally for the physically handicapped. The idea did not come from John himself, however, but from a Liverpool businessman, James Reece, who soon after the First World War took some physically handicapped children to his farm in North Wales for an outing. This became a yearly excursion. The venue was changed to Southport, more and more children were included, and more motorists volunteered their services. It stopped during the Second World War, but in 1951 James Reece's son organised a commemorative outing which involved nearly a thousand children. John took over and became chairman of the event in 1956. There was a petrol shortage for the following two years, due to the Suez crisis, but the outings started again in 1958 and before long included eight Liverpool special schools and about 1,200 children. A mail-order stock controller, Frank Hoare, who was also on the board of the Alice Elliott School for Deaf and Dumb Children, described how all the schools would meet up with the chairman in Southport. 'Mr John was there every time. Each school would have a different coloured ribbon, and Mr John had a rosette on the front of his Rolls which incorporated all the colours of the schools. He really looked as if he enjoyed himself. He was available, he'd go up and chat – one of his favourite subjects was football. He mixed with the children and he walked around. He'd go off with Mr John Junior and some of the directors for lunch and come back in the afternoon. At the end of it all, by four o'clock, there would be tea in the marquee. And when they were leaving, there was a present for every child. He and Mr John Junior used to stand at the end of the road, giving them out personally. Until he got too old . . .'

'Too old' was certainly well into his eighties, and John still attended even when he was in a wheelchair. The first year that he was in a chair, some people were concerned that he might feel embarrassed. They need not have worried; that happened to be the year when a great many of the children attending were in wheelchairs as well, and John whizzed around, talking to them all on a level and discussing the pros and cons of the wheelchair situation.

When he did finally step down from the committee, John Junior took over; and in 1990 the brief for the outing was widened to include all children with special needs. The number of schools for the physically handicapped had been falling; with the change in approach to the education of such children, many are now happily absorbed into mainstream schools, and due to the advances in medical science they are actually fewer in number. There are still a great many children, however, who for a variety of reasons never get an outing of any sort; and the scheme has now been extended to include youngsters nationwide and not just those from Liverpool. The Littlewoods Organisation opened talks with Rotary International of Great Britain, and the outings are now organised by the Rotary Club and supported by Littlewoods.

John was still very far from a wheelchair and retirement in the late Fifties, however. Road traffic was increasing considerably at this time – 1959, for instance, was the year that a section of the first motorway, the M1, was opened – and he was very keen to make children more aware of road safety. First he started a nationwide programme of inter-school road-safety competitions, and he provided a shield for the winners in every town where there was a Littlewoods store – there were about sixty by then. He also gave shields and organised safe-driving competitions for lorry drivers in most of the major cities – Manchester, Birmingham, Newcastle, etc. There have been internal safe-driving awards for Littlewoods' own lorry drivers for even longer.

Taking advantage of his mail-order network, he introduced the Little Woody Club for the children of all agents and organisers. Its main theme was again road safety, but the children were encouraged to contribute to activities through the club magazine. Two issues appeared every year and each child was sent a birthday card, a great many of them signed by John himself. The children also had the chance to take part in a number of outings organised for members in different parts of the country.

Traffic was not only proliferating on the roads; there was also considerably more traffic in the air. Man was on the brink of venturing into space; in 1958, NASA was established and the first moon rocket was launched. Although it failed to reach its target, it did travel 79,000 miles from Earth. A whole new era was beginning.

Littlewoods did not yet have its own plane, as it was to do in the late Sixties, but by 1956 the allotted length of time had elapsed, and John's gift of shares to his children would no longer be heavily taxed if he were to die. The enormous life insurance was not needed any more, and John was at last allowed to fly again. It was the form of travel he preferred, either first-class on one of the big airlines or by charter plane. Flying saved him from the acute discomfort he suffered on boats, but better still – and even on internal journeys – it saved time. The pace of life was speeding up everywhere, but John's life was still faster and more action-packed than most people's.

Before the end of the Fifties, John and Ruby already had nine grandchildren. Their two younger children were not yet married, but in November 1959 Janatha's wedding took place. Like her elder sister, she had also read History at university, but at Bedford College, London. She had met her husband, Patrick Stubbs, while on holiday in Bermuda. The two were to restore Medmenham Abbey in Buckinghamshire as their first home and to own and run 'The White Hart Hotel' at Sonning for a time. However, the wedding took place in Formby and the bride was married from her parents' house in Shireburn Road. An enormous marquee was erected in the garden – carpeted, heated against the November chill, and filled with flowers. When the reception was in full swing and the speeches were over, John quietly slipped out, found the gardener, Hinde, who had been directing the guests' cars, and said, 'Put my warm boots in the car, and my big sweater, and open up the garage for me, will you?' Then he got in and drove off. A little later, Ruby came out to look for him. When she approached Hinde and asked if he had seen her husband, he was slightly embarrassed to have to reply, 'Well, yes, I have, Madam – he's gone to the football match.' It was Saturday afternoon, Everton were playing at Goodison Park and he was determined to make the second half. John had not yet taken over as director of the club, but he had recently become a large shareholder; and, incidentally, a significant shareholder on the board of Liverpool as well. He was very close to his younger daughter, but he had his own priorities.

His mother, Louisa, was still a major priority and she continued to be very important in his life. A few years earlier, when she was eighty-three and had been finding stairs a little difficult, John had a bungalow built for her. He had refused to employ an architect and the design was changed several times during building, growing larger as work progressed. Charlie's two daughters were now married, with homes of their own, but his son, who still lived with Louisa, was in the Army doing his National Service, and she wanted him to be comfortable when he came back home. The bungalow was placed more centrally in the village than her old house in Larkhill Lane had been, only round the corner from Cecil and Lou and their families, and just across the road from her daughter Ethel who was married again by now. She also had a devoted housekeeper named Blodwen to look after her.

Louisa enjoyed life, and the 'energy and enthusiasm' which John had praised were still in evidence; but Janatha's wedding was to be her last family party. Earlier that year, soon after her eighty-sixth birthday in March, she had started to feel unwell and was suffering a certain amount of pain; it was diagnosed as cancer of the bladder. John and the whole family were extremely concerned, but the doctors thought that it could be contained. Louisa went through the discomfort of radiation treatment and seemed improved; she was a strong woman and the prognosis was good.

What few people knew, even within the family, was that Ruby herself had already been through a similar ordeal; nearly two years earlier, she had developed cancer of the breast. Various treatments had been prescribed, including a mastectomy. Ruby had insisted that very few people should be told, not even her own children. She wanted as little fuss as possible. The secrecy was such that she went into hospital under an assumed name. And she planned the date of the operation carefully; there was another family party coming up, and she intended to be present. If she had not been there, questions would have been asked as to where she was. The operation was carried out; two weeks later she was home and that very evening she was present at the family event. Ruby had come through it, so there was every reason to hope that Louisa would too. John was persuaded to take a slight risk and to take a trip abroad.

For some time, Ruby had very much wanted to visit her brother in New Zealand again. He and his family had visited England in the Fifties, but that was the only time they had met since Ruby and John's trip to New Zealand in 1935. John's timetable was always full, but Ruby had carefully planned a holiday well in advance. They would be going via Bermuda and then the States, so that John could conduct some business on the way. For a time it looked as though Louisa's illness meant that the trip would have to be cancelled. However, aware of Ruby's deep disappointment, John gave in on this occasion. The two of them flew off on the first leg of their journey.

They got as far as Bermuda. There, four days after leaving Liverpool, they received a telegram telling them that Louisa's condition had deteriorated and that she was in Lourdes Private Hospital. John's reaction was instantaneous, and within a few hours they were embarked on the 4,000-mile dash back to England. Detailed plans were made to get them there as quickly as possible: an airliner to New York, then a jet airliner to London, a fast car to Gatwick, and a charter plane from there to Speke, the airport at Liverpool. Seats were booked; specially chartered aircraft were ready, not only at Gatwick but at Prestwick as well, in case London Airport should be closed by fog and the jet diverted there. A fast car was waiting for them at Speke. John may not have been too well acquainted with the many ways there are of spending on personal luxuries but spending money to save time – that he knew all about. And he would have spent everything for his mother. He did get back in time, and he was by Louisa's bedside when she died.

16

Nothing But the Best

Far from distracting John from business and other interests, his mother's death seemed to have exactly the reverse effect; he threw himself into all his activities with even more energy and dedication. He is not a sentimental man: it is an attribute which he dislikes and which he tries consciously to avoid, although it must be said that what he would consider to be 'sentimentality', many people would describe as sentiment – a very different thing. The woman who had had such a profound effect on his life was dead – the woman to whom he had once written, 'Whatever success I shall have, yours will be the bigger share in it.' The extra zeal with which he now turned to his pursuits may have been a refusal to be affected by the event; it was also his tribute to her memory.

Life went on. Little more than a month after his mother's funeral, John was flying out to Vienna to the wedding of his younger son. Peter was marrying Luciana Pinto, a young Italian girl. Her family lived in Naples, but she had a cousin of the same age in Vienna and frequently spent holidays there. Her uncle was the managing director of Olivetti in Austria; he and her aunt had a large house in the capital and a wide circle of friends. Peter and Luciana had decided to get married in the city where they first met, and were offered the use of her aunt and uncle's house for the reception.

Peter had already been to Naples to meet Luciana's parents; she had visited England several times to be introduced to Peter's relatives, and had even met Louisa. 'We hardly talked, but there was something about her that was quite striking,' was how Luciana described the encounter. 'There was an aura about her.' The two families, however, did not meet until the wedding day.

The English party was a small one which was just as well as the English Church in Vienna is very small. Even so, the groom's side of the church was half-empty. The bride's side was still completely empty five minutes after the wedding was due to start. Minutes before the bride actually arrived, there was a sudden influx of Italians and Viennese, to the point where they practically overflowed the pews. They had been busy greeting each other and talking outside the church, and went on gossiping inside as well. Then there was music from Mozart's *Idomeneo*, and Luciana was walking up the aisle on her father's arm. It was all very different from an English wedding.

The rest of the family found Luciana something of an unknown quantity when the couple returned to Lancashire. Her English was still almost non-existent, and she was 'foreign' – to everyone, that is, except Peter and his father. Peter was a European as much as a Lancastrian; John knew Naples and other parts of Italy from his travels and his painting trips; and if his command of the language was not yet as good as his son's, it was certainly good enough for him to make a speech in Italian at the wedding reception – with apparent ease.

It took a little while for the family to get used to someone as 'different' as Luciana: it also took her some time to acclimatise to a very different culture. The couple were living in Lancashire. Some time before the marriage, Peter had bought a large, derelict, early eighteenth-century house on a hillside in the country outside Wigan; and Luciana had been taken to see it on one of her earlier visits, while it was still a ruin. It was there that Peter proposed. By the time he brought his bride home, the restoration work was well under way, although it was not yet quite the elegant mansion that it is today. Luciana had a good sense of humour, and she was not in the least intimidated by the family. Above all, John took to her, and that was enough to guarantee her acceptance.

A new daughter-in-law may have taken up some of his attention, but family matters were not the only thing on his mind in the months following Louisa's death. His major preoccupation was football.

In the June of 1960, John became chairman of Everton. Surprise has been expressed over the years that he should have chosen what some regard as a Catholic team, in preference to the Protestant team, Liverpool, in which he also held shares. In fact, there has never been a religious divide between the two teams – not in the way that there is, for instance, between Rangers and Celtic. After the war, in the late Forties and early Fifties, there was a large influx of Southern Irish players – great footballers such as Jimmy O'Neal, Don Donovan and Tommy Eglington – and the Southern Irish or half-Irish section of the Liverpool population, many of them Catholic, may have gone to watch them play. There was always a number of Church of England members in the Everton team. 'The religious side has never been as fervent in Liverpool as it has in Scotland. Not in football.' This comment came from an ex-captain; but he could also remember a time when the Orange Lodge had stones thrown at them as they paraded past his old school, Liverpool Collegiate; right across the road was Saint Francis Xavier's. Every Christmas there used to be regular snowball fights between the two schools and the snowballs often had stones inside them. 'But the way you are when you're kids, you don't realise. It's just your school against theirs.'

The Orange Lodge, dressed in orange in memory of the Protestant king, William of Orange, celebrated the Battle of the Boyne; the Catholics celebrated St Patrick's Day. The divide between Catholics and Protestants has always remained stronger in the North of England: on Merseyside, particularly, as a result of the influx of Irish Catholics after the potato famine of 150 years ago. The rest of Lancashire remained a stronghold of English Catholicism after the Civil War, 200 years earlier still; earlier even, in 1536, many Lancashire families were involved in the Pilgrimage of Grace, a protest against the dissolution of the monasteries. In rural Lancashire, although Methodists may now 'walk', or parade, on the same day as Church of England members, the Catholics still walk on a different day. Even as little as twenty years ago, the Protestant mother of a boy marrying into a Catholic family refused to go to her son's wedding, or to see his children – her own grandchildren. Times have changed and there is less animosity now, but even in the Twenties it did not extend to football, certainly not in John's eyes.

When he was first married, he lived in Walton, where Everton was the local team. He supported the team then – no particular religion seemed to be influencing its composition – and being John, he did not change his allegiance. He made other changes, however. And he started making them almost as soon as he arrived.

The manager at that time was John Carey. 'A cheerful, easygoing Irishman,' according to Derek Whale, a well-known local journalist. Carey was 'a delightful man who smoked a pipe through each and every crisis, major or minor'. He had also been a great footballer in his day, an Irish international. Everton were a First Division team, but they were at the bottom of the division. At one time, they had been heavily in debt and John had helped them financially. When he had first joined the board and examined the balance sheets, he had felt that money was being wasted and made reforms there so that by the time he became chairman Everton were not doing so badly. Not well enough for John, however; he felt they were not moving up quickly enough. He seemed to have a speed demon behind him all through the Sixties; he was always hustling, always pushing. And the first thing he did was to give the push to John Carey.

The story of the sacking has gone into legend; and the almost brutal directness of it is reminiscent of the way many a Littlewoods buyer was given the chop on those Friday nights before the war.

The two men got into a taxi together in London, and by the time they arrived at their destination, the annual meeting of the Football League, John Carey was no longer boss of Everton; he had been peremptorily sacked. His contract still had some time to run and he quite rightly demanded compensation. Apparently he was paid £17,000 – worth a great deal more in the early Sixties than it is today, and a large sum for a football club to have to find. On the balance sheet at the end of that season, the figures showed a loan to the club for exactly the same amount. 'A shareholder asked John, who was chairing the annual meeting, who had made the loan. Club secretary Bill Dickinson replied, after consultation, "A friend of the club".' The chairman remained silent.

The next manager to be appointed was Harry Catterick, from Sheffield Wednesday. He was an ex-Everton centre forward as well; a keen disciplinarian, determined and dedicated – like John himself, and in fact he had been picked by John. New players were signed on but the buying was left to Harry. As John said, 'I never interfere with managers. Directors should not do so, they are really just amateurs in the football world.' The first to join the team was Bobby Collins from Celtic (the Catholic team, and another sure sign that John would allow no bias in football). 'Collins was the foundation that the team was built on,' according to ex-captain, Brian Labone. Before long there were more additions – Alex Parker, George Thompson, Alex Scott. The club was paying £25,000 and £30,000 a time for such players – vast sums in those days, and it was obvious where the money was coming from. The club began to be known as the Millionaroes. Harry was a shrewd operator; no rumour ever got around when he was after a particular player – if it had, a lot more would have been quickly added to the transfer fee. There would simply be a report in a morning paper, after the contract had been signed, 'and that's the first you'd hear about it', as Brian Labone said. Not all the old team members were dropped, by any means. Brian himself – an eighteen-year-old straight from school – had joined the side just before John took over, and he went on to captain Everton when they won the FA Cup.

Although the handling of the team was left to Harry, John was always involved; he never missed a match if he could help it – away games as well as those at Goodison Park. He did not travel with the team, but he was there before, during and after the match, and he always said what he thought – 'no nonsense, terse, straight down, a spade's a spade'. The great Alec Young, still talked about by Evertonians thirty-five years later, was a temperamental player; at his best a near-genius. John would go up to him before the match and simply say, 'Alec, you *are* going to try today, aren't you?' Not quite the remark to make to a professional football player; as Brian Labone commented, 'A bit like saying to a chap, "Have you stopped beating your wife yet?"' Somehow it was never resented; people respected John, and there was 'a bit of fear there, too'. 'Nothing but the best' was the club motto, and he was going to see that they got it – from star players to improved spectator accommodation for the World Cup.

And John was not above doing a spot of coaching himself; he had been a good amateur footballer until his forties. Winger Derek Temple was right-footed and his left was not as strong as it might have been. John wore what he called 'flying boots' and he would tuck his trousers into them and try to show Derek how to cross the ball with the left foot, on the run. Twice a week he would put in an appearance at Bellfield, where the team did their training. 'I can remember him having his trilby on, and his black crombie or whatever it was. His trouser used to get inadvertently stuck in the back of his boot. He didn't look like a millionaire.'

The only time the team were ever disappointed was when they visited Fairways. Harry Catterick was a keen golfer, along with several other team members, and John would get them a game at Formby occasionally. When it was over, they would all go back to Fairways for tea. 'It was a bit of a let-down'; pleasant and comfortable enough, but not like a millionaire's house. As one of them said, 'I thought it should have had gold taps and hot-and-cold running champagne.' And with the scones and cakes, the drinks offered were tea or coffee. 'It was mid-week, so he didn't allow us any alcohol; that was a bit disappointing as well.' His attitude was the same when he went round to the dressing-room after a match. 'He tried to be one of the boys, but I don't think he was a great drinker. He'd come in and have the odd glass if we were celebrating, but there was always that aura of "the Boss".'

'One of the boys' – something he always longed to be, but rarely achieved. Perhaps he always tried a little too hard; perhaps the effort was always too conscious – whereas with someone like his brother, Cecil, it came quite naturally. A daughter-in-law whom he used to take to matches said, 'I saw another side to him there that I never saw before. He met some football people from the old time and they said, "Hello, John." He was over the moon! They were people with no connection with his business, men he'd met all over England from different football clubs, so he reckoned they were his chums – to do with football.' If someone called him 'Jack', then you knew that they were *really* old friends. Many years later, during a television interview, he commented that had he been a carpenter or an electrician, he might not have got on and made as much money, but he might have been happier.

But it was because he *had* got on that he was able to help; it was his money, his drive, his choice of manager – all these things – to which Everton owed its resurgence. The club went from strength to strength in the Sixties; Everton were twice League Champions and twice FA Cup Finalists and were the winners in 1966. When John resigned the chairmanship in 1965, because Ruby was seriously ill, it was taken on by none other than Littlewoods' legal adviser, Holland Hughes (nicknamed Dutchy by the players). Two Littlewoods directors have been chairman since. Cecil's younger son is presently chairman of Liverpool. When John gave up the chairmanship, he still remained on the board, but as he said, 'After two or three years I thought it was wrong that one man should go on being a dictator like that.' Equally, he considered that every director should have the experience of being chairman for a period, as the experience gained would make for a more efficient board and would benefit the club. At one point, he returned briefly to the chairmanship for a year, when Everton seemed to be in difficulties again, and he never ceased to take an interest. 'He was always there behind the scenes.' He was present at nearly every match, even when he was in a wheelchair and so frail that he had to be carried up and down the steps. (The directors' box is down at the front of the stand; home team directors and the directors of the visiting team sit there, to take public praise or blame for the success or failure of their particular team.) And he always wore his famous scarf.

His adviser, Theresa Hamilton-Sugden, who was also an Everton supporter, remembers its first appearance.

'We used to go to the home matches every Saturday. We were walking down the steps of the directors' box and a big chunky fellow leant over and gave him a parcel, and said, "Here you are – the Missus has knitted this for you." It was an Everton scarf, hand-knitted by this lady, and it had got "Sir John" and "Everton" knitted into it. He wore that scarf each time he went after that, and each time when he walked past this man he'd say, "There you are! Got it on!" The fans of Everton loved him very much, they'd always be grinning and waving and smiling. The Littlewoods directors would be there in their fine clothes, but he'd come down in his scarf. "Why should I get all dressed up to go to a match? I'm coming because I'm a fan, not because I've done some things for Everton." People made comments about the match to him, as he was walking up the steps. I think he felt that was the best time of his week.'

This was when he was in his eighties. For the same reason, while still in his seventies, he insisted on being dropped some distance from the main entrance, so that he could 'chat to the lads' on his way in and out, and get their reactions. Often, if he had to stop at traffic-lights while driving in Liverpool, there would be a tap on his car window and an Everton supporter would be smiling and saying, 'Hello, John!' If the match was the best time of his week, it is hardly surprising; it was one of the rare times when he could really feel 'one of the boys'.

In order to become chairman of Everton, John felt obliged to give up all direct involvement with pools; retaining both positions could have been regarded as giving rise to a conflict of interests, and everything not only had to be fair, it had to be seen to be fair. Just before taking up his new post, he and Cecil had commissioned a team of experts to study data processing equipment and mechanisation for the whole pools operation; with John's removal from the scene, it was Cecil who made all decisions concerning the major developments in that area. There were various technological advances; a machine was installed, which optically read and sorted five coupons a second and could deal with 18,000 coupons per hour. The competitions themselves changed slightly too; in January 1961, the minimum stake was reduced to a penny, and one month later to ¼d. Littlewoods was following various other pools firms in this; indeed, it was obliged to as it had been losing clients to the same firms as a result of their reduced stake.

In January 1963, even the problem of the British weather was overcome. Prior to this date, if enough matches had to be cancelled due to bad weather, then the pools could not be run that week. The pools companies solved the problem by setting up panels of experts – ex-footballers and ex-referees – whose job it was to decide what the result of each match would have been if it had gone ahead. Their decisions were counted, along with the results of those matches actually played. The system is still used, and is activated whenever twenty-five or more matches are postponed. In March 1964, the 2d and the ¼d Treble Chance Pools were amalgamated as the 1d Treble Chance Pool, and that very month there was a new record dividend of £225,134. The amounts that Littlewoods were paying annually in pool betting duty, and had been doing since the Pool Betting Act of 1954, were considerably larger than the dividends; in 1962, for instance, the sum paid for that year was £15,972,000.

Mail order and chain-stores, with which John was still directly concerned, continued to expand. A fourth mail-order company – a third credit business – Littlewoods Warehouses, were launched in 1960. Littlewoods Mail Order had been rechristened John Moores Home Shopping, in order to free the name of Littlewoods for use on the new credit business. In 1964, a fifth company, Janet Frazer, was added to the division. The chain-store division saw three new stores opened in 1960, two in 1961, three in 1962, five in 1963 – the rate kept up not only through the Sixties, but into the Eighties.

John's funding of the arts and his charitable giving increased, too. The 'John Moores' with its first prize of £20,000 is still held every two years. In 1963, he funded a school of business management studies at Liverpool University. He became involved, together with the City Council and the Government, in the funding and building of boys' clubs and youth clubs, covenanting £20,000 a year for seven years. Edge Hill Boys' Club was the first in 1961 and there were seven more in 1963. There was always a Littlewoods director or a family member of the company conscripted onto the management committee of each. John Junior has always been active in this area. Years earlier, on leaving Eton where he was captain of boxing, he started teaching boxing in the boys' clubs in Bootle.

For the past forty years, his father had been ahead of his time with views that were extremely socially progressive – medical welfare, pension schemes, part-time work – long before most employers even considered such things. As John grew older, he mellowed in many ways, but his attitudes became more entrenched. John Junior's ideas were as progressive as his father's had once been, particularly in combating any form of discrimination – racist, sexist, ageist or economic. Like his father, he wants to help the underprivileged and his influence has been profound. His area is local, his giving mainly in Lancashire, centred in Liverpool and the family firm itself. He has been a leading spirit in ensuring that Littlewoods' equal opportunities policy is one of the most enlightened in the country.

His younger brother, Peter, is also concerned with racial issues and he funds projects aimed at giving opportunity and ending prejudice or discrimination. His other interest is the fine arts: like his father before him, he wants others to be able to share his enjoyment of them, and to make them more available to everyone. He has had seven Peter Moores projects at the Walker Art Gallery. Through the charitable foundation he has endowed, he brings opera to Liverpool and underwrites the cost of tickets for first-time visitors; he also finances opera recordings and productions sung in English. Before setting up his foundation, he personally gave help – while they were still comparatively unknown – to artists of the calibre of Joan Sutherland, Geraint Evans and Colin Davis. The foundation awards scholarships to young musicians and singers, and he continues to provide knowledgeable assistance throughout their careers. Both brothers give not only money, but also time and personal involvement. Like father, like sons. In other ways, they do not always see eye to eye with him.

It was possibly in the Sixties that John began to sense stirrings in the ranks of the next generation; even some of his grandchildren seemed to be developing minds of their own. There was nothing as overt as defiance to begin with, but the signs were there.

John had always disapproved of divorce: in 1962, John Junior and Sheila were divorced. He disapproved of remarriage after divorce: in 1963 John Junior married again. To make matters worse, John's new daughter-in-law, Jane Stavely-Dick, had connections with the firm, breaking yet another taboo: 'no family relationships with employees'. The connection would have appeared very tenuous to anyone but John; it was simply that Jane's sister had once been John Junior's PA and had introduced the two – although by the time the engagement was announced, the sister had already left Littlewoods and was working for the BBC. Too late; the line had already been crossed – as far as John was concerned. At first, whenever Jane called at the house, he refused to speak to her; but Ruby asserted her rarely-used authority. 'Aren't you going to say hello to Puffin?' (Jane's nickname.) Usually John did but few further words were forthcoming. He refused an invitation to the wedding. Endearingly, when asked afterwards if he would like any of the wedding photographs, he completely forgot his non-attendance and replied that he would like all those in which he appeared himself. (Being John, it is always possible that he knew exactly what he was saying.)

His attitude towards the marriage was probably compounded by the fact that Jane was a socialist. She was also a clever woman who came from a family where discussion and argument with the older generation were acceptable; she was used to speaking her mind. One particular incident showed clearly that John's household was very different. Positano had become one of the places where John and the family holidayed together, staying in a house which John rented. On one occasion when John, Ruby, John Junior and his new family were in residence, there was a disagreement. John was trying to persuade John Junior and his wife to sell him the shooting rights over their farm land, while they were insisting that the people who worked on the farm should be allowed to shoot there as well. In a burst of surprise and irritation, John exclaimed, 'You might as well give guns to the Chinese and let them shoot each other!' Jane just laughed and said 'Rubbish!' The explosion that followed has never been forgotten.

'You were allowed to say anything to *my* father – as long as you didn't say it in anger,' Jane explained. 'It didn't occur to me that you couldn't say that to his.'

She was banished from the table, and retired to her room and the comforting presence of her baby son who was in his cot. When she returned a little later, contrite and tear-stained, to her immense surprise John apologised. Ruby had insisted on it. 'She could be very tough just occasionally, and he actually did what she told him to.'

Although the relationship was always a slightly wary one, John did come round to his son's second wife eventually. 'We decided we'd love him into submission,' Jane explained.

Another Littlewoods executive who had been through a divorce, received a memo at the time telling him that he would continue to be employed, but only as long as there was no adverse publicity about the case. He had also been John Junior's PA for a period and, meeting the Boss's son in the lift at work, commented, 'When are you getting the sack? Because I was told when I got a divorce, that if there was any publicity I'd be sacked.'

'This is ridiculous!' was John Junior's reply. 'I'll have a word with Daddy about it.'

Next it was Peter who placed his father in a slightly awkward situation, although with the best of intentions. In 1963, John and Ruby celebrated their fortieth wedding anniversary, and the four offspring had decided that there should be a suitable celebration. Peter was deputed to organise both a dinner dance at the Adelphi and an anniversary present from them all. As he said, 'It was no good giving the two of them one present between them; there was nothing they'd both like equally.' Their tastes were indeed very dissimilar. So Peter found a modern painting by one of John's favourite artists for their father, and proposed a diamond necklace for their mother. Five necklaces, in a variety of styles, were laid out for her to choose from, and she picked one in a chunky Thirties style. She was absolutely thrilled with it, 'like a little girl'. John was slightly shamefaced. He himself had never given Ruby anything of that sort. 'You've shown me up! You've shown me up!' was his muttered comment. But in a short time, he had recovered enough to say firmly that in any case their mother did not like jewellery. 'Which is what she *would* have told him,' Peter remarked, 'so that he never had to pay for any.'

It was not that John was mean – he could be extraordinarily generous in many ways – but he was a frugal man, a result of the hard times he had known in his youth. John Moores was a millionaire many times over, but he had said that he did not want yachts and racehorses; all he wanted was a suit and a pen. His favourite artists were the Impressionists, but he refused even to contemplate the purchase of such expensive pictures, although he could well have afforded them. He preferred to spend his money giving opportunity to young and unknown painters. When, at the urging of his younger son, he did eventually buy one or two pictures by respected British artists, even these were eventually sold. He did not like spending money on himself, and spending on Ruby was the same thing. She was his wife, his right hand; she was a part of him. But Ruby was 'out of this world' over her necklace. She told everyone she met at the party that her children had given it to her, and there was a real glow about her as she danced. She looked radiant, and cherished.

Later that year, her cancer recurred. Still she insisted that things must carry on as normally as possible. John had just started Spanish lessons, and had been going to Spain without her. Now Peter bought a house in Positano and revived the family holidays there that Ruby enjoyed so much. John switched back to learning Italian. There were Italian conversation sessions with Rosetta Roberts again, several times a week after work. When the following year Rosetta's husband had a bad heart attack and was discovered to have angina, John was as generous as ever, insisting that he go into Lourdes Private Hospital to be looked after. As ever, he also demonstrated the strange dichotomy in his character. He continued to expect lessons from Rosetta every evening as usual as if nothing had happened, and he very rarely even asked about her husband's progress; he was concentrating on his Italian.

Business, of course, went on as usual. The new headquarters of the company was being built, the giant J M Centre in Old Hall Street. At the same time, John was looking for a means of expanding the business into continental Europe. Littlewoods' opening of two shops in St Petersburg in 1991 was simply an extension of the policy John was then originating. He wanted his company in the really big time, on the international scene. He never managed it himself, but he sowed the seed.

Ruby's fight against cancer went on, but it continued to invade her cells. She began to lose weight; before, she had been a well-built woman, but gradually she became almost skeletal. There was still very little said about it in the family; she refused to discuss, or even to recognise, the losing battle. She wanted no fuss, and she wanted to carry on as normally as possible.

In 1964, John Junior was involved in a serious accident – a head-on collision between his car and a lorry – and was rushed into hospital in great pain to have a shattered knee-cap removed. Ruby responded immediately. Peter had hurried from the Oswestry store, which he was visiting as area superintendent, and was sitting at his brother's bedside two hours later, when the door opened and their mother walked in, looking very old and 'absolutely green'. John was at home, having taken a tranquilliser and gone to bed. He did, of course, visit shortly afterwards; but Ruby had immediately set off on her own to be with her son. Nothing would have kept her away.

Later, in October, as her seventieth birthday approached, another party at the Adelphi was suggested. Ruby was touched, but she turned the idea down. A grand hotel was not the setting in which her old friends, 'the people I love', would feel comfortable; they would not have the right sort of clothes to be at ease. She had never lost touch with the good friends of her earlier days – people like Wynne and Jess, who had been waitresses with her once; people like Dora Gledhill and Elsie Phillips – and it was these friends and relatives whom she entertained quietly at Fairways, during John's absences in Barbados or Spain, and whose houses she enjoyed visiting. When she did visit them, she went by train; she would never go by car, in case it put them out of countenance – although the car she drove was always, on her own insistence, a small one. Many years later, John's senior financial adviser, Mr Fisher, said with pride and admiration, 'I knew Ruby. She was not tainted by money whatsoever. She was a very nice woman.'

John Junior was in Berlin with Eric Sawyer, where on John's behalf the two had been looking for possible ways that Littlewoods might infiltrate the German market, but he hurried home when he heard that his mother's condition was deteriorating. She was in a coma by the time he reached her, but he was there with his brother and his younger sister, and John's two younger sisters, Lou and Ethel, when she died. John himself was at her side until almost the end; just before it came, he went into another room with his elder daughter, Betty, and he cried.

She died in 1965, on September 8th, less than two months before her seventy-first birthday, and there was not enough room in St Peter's Church in Formby for all the people who came to her funeral.

John seemed stunned. It was like an amputation. He had lost someone who had always been there when wanted, someone he could always rely on, a part of himself. They had been married for almost forty-two years. After the funeral, Peter took John to Vienna for a break. He needed quiet and privacy; a place where they would not always be meeting people that they knew, people who would ask after Ruby, people who would refer to her death. His younger daughter, Janatha, had flown up to Liverpool to be with her mother two weeks before she died, taking her third child, a small baby, in a carry-cot. On John's return, she came back to stay with her father and look after him until a housekeeper could be organised. 'I wanted to clean up and cook for him,' she explained. There was the very real complication of arranging for the care of her children and her husband; and there was the exhausting business of serving every meal on the dot. Dinner was at seven o'clock: no earlier, no later. When her husband got up to Formby – as often as he could – he and Janatha liked to watch *The Muppets* together on television. Special dispensation had to be asked for and granted on those evenings, in order for dinner to be served at ten past seven. Even a man of George Kennerley's standing was not excused from John's obsession with punctuality. On a drawing weekend at Blandford Forum, many years later, the two men arranged to meet in the hotel bar at 6 p.m. and Kennerley was a minute and a half late. He still remembers, with a smile, the trouble which that caused.

Time still mattered to John. And he could not waste too long on a grieving period. Very soon – or 'in two shakes of a lamb's tail', as Ruby would have put it – he was forcing himself back to work again; if anything, the pace was hotting up. His rooted dislike of sentimentality would not even allow him to avoid reminders of his wife. Ruby had always enjoyed Bermuda, far more than John himself did. After her death, he forced himself – for a time at least – to continue going there in October, just as they had always done. The Elbow Beach Hotel was a work project, and he continued with it until he handed over to Peter. John still went up to the loch in August with his children and his grandchildren, although the atmosphere was very different without Ruby there to contain him.

Moores family holidays seem to have been tricky times in the Sixties, and holidays at the loch were no exception. John had had a bad fall in November 1965 and was still in some pain with his hip, so he could not walk in the surrounding hills; the fishing was not good enough for him; there was not enough to do. He was restless and on edge; everyone in the family seemed frightened of him – except for his teenage grandchildren who seemed to like challenging him. John has always been good with small children, particularly the sort who enjoy a little ragging and a little rough-and-tumble. Mrs Walther, a housekeeper who looked after him some years later, always said how kind he was to her young grandchildren when they visited her. He would let them swim in the pool, feed them grapes (his favourite fruit) and talk to them. 'The first thing he did was to get on the floor and get to their level; he used to get on his knees. He'd say, "You must be on eye-level with children."' He had got on well with his own grandchildren when they were younger. They remember him reading to them and telling them bedtime stories; the expensive presents he used to give them on their birthdays and at Christmas; the excitement of travelling in his Rolls-Royce with him; and the way everyone they met seemed to like and to respect him. 'He was always alert, energetic, inquisitive. I really looked up to him,' as one grandson said.

Teenagers were a different thing altogether, particularly by the Sixties. They were no longer the obedient youngsters of John's boyhood, not like his brothers and sisters who went to bed at half-past nine, as soon as their father got up to wind the clock. 'The Times They Are A-changing' was a Bob Dylan song of the period, and it was very apposite. It was the Beatles era too. 'She's Leaving Home' described a daughter walking out on her parents and their way of life, with its sad lament, 'What did we do wrong?' 'When I'm Sixty-Four' was another.

John Moores was seventy the year that song came out and although *he* was certainly not worried as to whether he was still needed, he was not entirely sure how his teenage grandchildren thought of him. They seemed to enjoy disagreeing with him and those holiday arguments, although purely theoretical, often turned into quarrels. One such discussion was about the best way to help people. A grandson said that if someone were in a hole and you were on top, it was your duty to give them a hand out. John's reply was that you had to be careful that they did not pull *you* in as well. The grandson came back with a metaphorical comment about finding a ladder. John insisted that the point be conceded to him. The grandson refused. John said that he would never talk to him again.

For a man of his calibre, it all seems surprisingly petty, almost neurotic. But he was not used to having his authority questioned. He felt threatened; his hip was painful; he missed his wife; no doubt there were continual worries and problems, and decisions to be made concerning the company. He was still trying for expansion into the German markets. 'He was in his prime, from a business point of view,' as one ex-main board director remarked. But he was driving himself almost too hard.

17

Doctor's Orders

'I could feel Mr John's presence in every corner of this company. Even after I'd been here for a year. It really shook me.' This was the reaction of a new main board director when he joined the company in 1966. Archie Hutchison had been a very senior executive with two big American companies, one of them a large family concern like Littlewoods, but 'you never sensed an individual in any of the offices there'. He had never met anything like it before. 'I never went into any of the company buildings in the first ten or twelve years I was with the company without somebody, somewhere, making reference to Mr John. Terror could be created round the place by dropping "Mr John said this" and "Mr John said that". Fifty per cent of the things that were then threatened, the Old Man knew nothing about but it created this fear.' And one or two senior people knew how to use it.

John's grandchildren may have been brave enough to argue with him, but it was more than any of his executives dared. The same Archie Hutchison remembers, before his first board meeting, asking another director, 'What happens if you challenge him on anything? After all, it is his business.' The man went white. 'You be very careful how you go about challenging Mr John. You'd be on a hiding to nothing.' John did not like being challenged, particularly on a matter about which he had already made up his mind, and particularly in public at a board meeting. It was better to have a word with him in private, and it was imperative to know what you were talking about as well as proof to back it up. Then, very occasionally, he might change his opinion. Peter was now on the board – he had been made a director in November 1965, soon after Ruby died – and he knew what was required of him. His father had made that clear when he had persuaded him to come back to Littlewoods in 1957: 'I want you to be like a soldier. Just do as you're told.'

The main board was still a small one in 1966; apart from family members – John himself, Cecil, John Junior and Peter – there were only four other directors: Mr Sawyer, Mr Hedges, Mr Watts and Mr Hutchison. From now on, it was to grow in size.

The J M Centre was also growing apace. The back section was

completed in 1966, and everybody moved into that; then work started on the front section. It cannot have been exactly quiet or comfortable, trying to continue the daily routine literally next door to a building site. Nobody could object, however; John had moved his office in too. It had been at Irlam Road until he resigned his pools directorship on becoming chairman of Everton. At that point, he had moved to Waterloo Buildings as it had to be clearly seen that he was severing his connection with pools; like Caesar's wife, he must be above suspicion.

Interestingly, until the J M Centre was built, he had always kept his own particular eyrie *outside* head office. And he had always insisted on a room somewhere nearby with a bed in it. During the war, at Irlam Road, there was a divan on which he had taken catnaps in between keeping his eye on both the day- and the night-shifts. There was a separate room at Waterloo Buildings too, and at the new J M Centre a specially designed bedroom and bathroom were built behind his office. Now, as he entered his seventies, he followed Churchill's example and had a rest every afternoon. When he was at home he used to get undressed and into his pyjamas, and get into bed; when he had his lie-down at work, the room had to be in complete darkness and he gave instructions that nobody was to disturb him. Miss Mitchell and Miss Richards were admirable guardians, and any visitor would have had to pass through their office to reach him. The break always seemed to recharge him, and he could still keep going for a thirteen- or fourteen-hour day.

The only snag was that he expected other people to be equally full of energy, and available whenever he wanted them. The stories are legion of high-powered executives receiving telephone calls from him in the middle of the night. While he was still general manager, George Watts was rung at one o'clock in the morning. John had been sitting up, checking through the gradings of the recent managers' interviews, and had decided that there were one or two which he wanted to query. George was kept up for over an hour, going over the ten different gradings under the ten different headings for the ten different managers. As his telephone was in his hall, it was night-time, his central heating was off and it was freezing cold, he was 'a bit cross'. But not with John, of course.

On another occasion, an executive who always looked after John's travel arrangements for him, Dick Ashton, was telephoned at five o'clock in the morning. He yawned his way down to the hall and picked up the receiver.

'This is Stockholm calling.'

'You've got the wrong number!' Dick was still half asleep and somewhat annoyed; but his wife, Bunty, described how he suddenly became wide awake.

'I heard him say, "Hello, Mr John," and I was out of bed like a flash,' she remembered.

John was on his way back from the Commonwealth Games in New Zealand, the last leg of the journey being from Bangkok to Copenhagen.

'We've overflown Copenhagen because of the fog. Now bloody well get me out of here!' was his irate command.

Dick asked what hotel he was in and what room. Then he got dressed, immediately, and went down to the J M Centre to look up all the requisite travel information and start making bookings. He did get John home, as soon as was humanly possible, and was sent for immediately. The Old Man was in his office.

'I didn't realise, Dick, that it was five o'clock in the morning. Sorry about that, so – here's some perfume for your wife.'

'That was the nice, kind touch he had,' said Dick. 'But he didn't give *me* anything.'

As usual, the extra effort put in was treated almost as doing John a favour. And John himself would often make the same sort of effort for other people. Years later, aged ninety, when he had flown down to London for an important meeting and was flying back that night for another engagement in Liverpool next day, he broke his journey for two or three hours because he had promised a niece he would attend her birthday party. It was important to him that any extra effort was made out of goodwill and not for money.

Coping with the Boss's travel arrangements was not, in fact, part of Dick Ashton's official job. He was not paid for it, he got no overtime, he never claimed expenses; it was personal. And, like many others whom John approached in the same way, he loved doing it. It was flattering when something you did for your boss was treated as an act of friendship; and John could be very generous in response if there were any real need involved. He could also be terrifying if things went wrong and it appeared that you might be to blame. 'He really threw the book at you.'

One of his secretaries, either Miss Mitchell or Miss Richards, would ring through to someone and say, 'He wants you.' The employee would arrive, suspecting nothing, 'but *they* knew that you were going to be told off. When you walked into the outer office, they wouldn't talk to you. And *you* knew then, as soon as you walked through the door.' After one particularly fierce dressing-down over a cancelled air ticket – which was entirely the fault of the particular airline – Dick Ashton came out looking extremely shaken and bumped into the personnel manager whom he had known for some time. 'He's told me off *again!*' was his forlorn comment. The man simply put his arm round Dick's shoulders, 'Don't worry about it,' he said. 'He thinks you're one of his sons.'

The sons in question were working practically as hard as their father. They were both in responsible positions and on many occasions having to use their own initiative, but when it came to the big decisions, they were 'behaving like soldiers and doing what they were told'. And John was making plenty of big decisions.

In 1966, an IBM 360 computer system was installed. It was specially designed in consultation with the company's own experts, making the Littlewoods computer system unique throughout the world, and certainly well in advance of most other companies at the time.

In 1967, Sherman's Pools of Cardiff were taken over.

In the chain-store division, new stores were being built or bought every year; there were eighty-four by the end of the Sixties, and three years later the number had grown to over a hundred.

In 1967, John launched a sixth credit mail-order company, Peter Craig. Archie Hutchison, the main board director, remembers being called into his office and told to 'locate the site and get started'.

A clapped-out old cotton-mill was found in Preston, full of out-of-date machinery. 'It was bought for a song; now it's worth a million or two.' Before long, it was employing 2,000 and turning over £20,000,000 a year for a three-year period. 'I never found him scared of taking big risks in business; he was quite unique in that respect.'

The next risk he took in 1968 was the biggest yet, and it was to get something which he had wanted for quite a while, something which John Junior and Mr Sawyer had been searching for on his behalf: a German company. Medaillon Mode was a fashion mail-order business in Germany run by Spiegel of America and catering mainly for the middle classes. Although it was outside their usual range, Littlewoods had enormous mail-order expertise, and it was a foothold into Continental Europe. It cost, but John thought it was worth it. As a retired director commented; 'I've heard people say he could be tight, but I never found that – ever. If you put over a case to Mr John about spending money to improve the business, you had to convince him that it would be money well spent, but there was no messing about. In the early days, in the Sixties and the Seventies, this company used to roll on really rapidly. He would give you a quick nod to get things done, rather than mess around for months and months.'

As a privately-owned company, Littlewoods is not answerable to its shareholders in quite the same way as a public company. Littlewoods' shareholders are all John's and Cecil's children and grandchildren, and expected to behave as such; indeed, it is only recently that they have started to receive anything like a suitable return on their respective holdings. For many years the money was ploughed straight back into the business, although as the shares were originally gifts, they no doubt felt they could hardly complain.

One even greater advantage of private ownership was that it enabled John to make decisions quickly, without consultation. 'That may get criticism from sophisticated professionals,' but John's decisions had usually proved right. And 'he was a really tough fellow – he never looked it, but he was really tough underneath; and he was really hard on *himself*; that's quite an important part of his make-up.' Now he made the decision to buy Medaillon Mode.

Peter was called to John's office, and informed that his father had picked him to go out to Germany and run the new company. In many ways Peter was an ideal choice. His business expertise was now considerable, after the training he had been put through; he knew Europe and his German was fluent. The main snag, from Peter's point of view, was that it would have meant uprooting his family, just as his Italian wife had become fully acclimatised to England – both its language and its way of life. His response to his father's offer of the job was quite firm. 'Thank you very much, but I don't think I want it. It's taken my wife eight years to learn *English*.'

As far as Peter was concerned, the matter was closed – amicably. To his surprise, at the board meeting half an hour later, John informed the assembled directors that Medaillon Mode had been acquired and that Peter would be going out to Germany to run it. John's younger son was just as stubborn as his father, and he was just as decisive. Within six months, he had moved to London and got a job at Sotheby's. Although he kept his seat on the board and continued to oversee the running of the Elbow Beach Hotel in Bermuda for his father (for some time the two of them had been going out there together on a twice-yearly business trip) by 1969 Peter was a director of a merchant bank in London.

John turned next to his elder son. John Junior was enthusiastic. He had been instrumental in finding the business for his father, and as head buyer he had started offices in Germany and Italy, and so had some knowledge of the scene; and he was just as keen as his father to break into Europe. He had been deputy chairman since 1967, taking over occasionally when his father was away having his hip treatments, but John wanted him to go, and John Junior took on the job with relish.

Although he was still driving the business at a pace, John himself was almost crippled as a result of the fall in 1965. Nothing seemed to produce a cure, but for one week in every four, he had taken to flying up to Glasgow to visit an osteopath twice a day. The treatments were extremely painful. 'He used to be grey,' his secretary Miss Richards remembers. 'At the time, he was walking very badly with a stick.' Miss Richards as well as Miss Mitchell would fly up to Glasgow with him, and all three would stay at the Central Hotel, virtually next to the station. John always took a taxi to the consulting rooms, and on one occasion was cutting through the station to get to the taxi rank as usual when half-way there, he decided that he wanted to go to the loo. To his horror, he discovered that it cost 3d to use the station 'Gents', so he turned on his heel and hobbled all the way back to the hotel and up to his suite, which was a good distance. 'I wasn't going to pay 3d to have a pee!' was his outraged comment.

Typically, he was happy to pay both the hotel and practitioner's bills for one of the firm's buyers, Owen Musther, who was also in Glasgow for treatment. He had a bone problem, and on John's recommendation was visiting the same osteopath. 'I should think the number of medical bills that have been picked up by that man could never be counted,' he said of his boss. 'And no one ever knew anything about it.' Owen did some business in the city as well, and he stayed at a less expensive hotel, but he was invited to dinner at the Central Hotel every night. It was a meal the two secretaries looked forward to, because lunch would usually consist of sandwiches made with the chewy Cambridge Formula bread which John insisted on, and which they ate sitting in the park. This was one of his dietary hobby-horses, along with cabbage juice for breakfast every morning. His obsession with good health followed on from Louisa's interest in healthy eating which was in advance of her time; she advocated vitamins long before they became fashionable. He was also so fanatical about his weight (following a doctor's warning) that he would not allow himself to gain more than a pound before immediately taking steps to lose it again. 'I'll have one chop for my lunch, with nothing,' he would say. And he felt it necessary to have a full medical check-up every week with Dr Irving, the company doctor.

As well as fitting trips to Glasgow into his very tightly-packed business schedule, John was now also taking holidays. When he was seventy in 1966, the company doctor, Dr Irving, had told him firmly that as well as having a rest every afternoon, he was also to take a holiday every three months. John was the sort of man who did what his doctor told him, so he was having more holidays than ever before in his life. Very often during this period, they were taken in the company of his younger daughter, Janatha; and they would go either to Positano or to Las Palmas. She remembers that there would be about three days of lying around the swimming-pool, sunbathing and reading; then he would be bored. A trip somewhere would be organised. Once it was to the Spanish Sahara in a small moth-eaten plane which had to be propped up when on the ground. There were painting trips too, to Ischia and Lucca with Kennerley or Hubbard; visits to Italy to polish up his Italian, often staying with Peter's mother-in-law, Vittoria, in Naples.

The trip he made in 1969 for her son Roberto's wedding nearly ended in disaster. As he was well looked after while there by someone he regarded as family, he went without his faithful secretaries; but both Miss Mitchell and Miss Richards were in London, staying as usual at the Grosvenor Hotel to meet him when he got back. On this occasion, it was simply intended to be an overnight stop in London before flying up to Liverpool the next morning. When John had retired for his two-hour afternoon rest, his two secretaries decided on a quick shopping trip to Harrods. By the time they got back, John was calling out for them, saying that he felt ill. He was, indeed, seriously ill. It was dysentery, contracted from eating mussels in Naples the night before he left. He was so ill that he could not be moved. When a London doctor did not produce an immediate cure, Dr Irving was flown from Liverpool. Miss Mitchell and Miss Richards, with Peter in constant attendance, nursed him night and day for a week – probably saving his life. At the end of the week, it was considered safe enough to fly him to Liverpool where, by now severely dehydrated, he was taken straight into Lourdes Nursing Home.

In some ways the illness was a blessing in disguise, for while he was in Lourdes his hip was X-rayed. It was then recognised that the treatment in Glasgow was having little effect; what was required was a hip replacement operation. 'It came as a great shock,' as one of his directors said. Artificial hip joints were still a recent development, but medical science was racing ahead. Two years earlier, the first human heart transplant operation had been performed; in 1970, the first nuclear-powered heart pacemakers were implanted. The pioneer in the field of hip joint replacement was Professor Charnley, who was working at Wrightington Hospital near Wigan, and it was there in July 1969 that John was taken. The operation was a great success, and John made sure of showing his appreciation, not this time with flowers, but by donating £10,000 to the hospital for special equipment.

He was invited back to watch the operation being performed on another patient at a later date, and to be shown what advances had been made. He was extremely interested – he has always been full of curiosity as to how things work – but also slightly stunned. 'If I'd seen that before, I don't think I'd ever have had it done,' he said, half in joke. 'It was like a joiner's shop!'

But the operation had a revolutionary effect, and he was always grateful. He was told that he would not be able to ski again, or to water-ski – a sport which he had taken up at the age of sixty-nine; otherwise, he was back to normal.

Life opened up again for John. He was now seventy-three but he was still as determined. Miss Richards remembers the constant activity at Fairways. 'He had physiotherapists teaching him how to walk again. He had the Everton physio, too. He had mirrors put up so that he could make sure his shoulders were straight . . .' And he had been told that swimming was the best therapy, so he made sure that he swam every day. At first he was driven round to John Junior's house and he swam in the pool there. Then he had his own pool built. The squash-court in the garden at Fairways was seldom used any more, so he decided that he would take over part of the specially-erected building which housed it. The pool was not to be a large one, however; it was not to have a special tile surround or steps leading down into the water like a proper swimming-pool. That would have cost far too much money for John's liking, particularly as he was spending it on himself.

One end of the squash-court was sectioned off with sliding partitions and the pool was sited there. Its length was only the width of the court and there were steps up to get into it, 'like a big bath'. It was actually made of canvas. In vain, everyone tried to persuade him to have an extension added to the house and a decent-sized pool built in that. Nothing would budge him: 'He just went his own sweet way.' And every day, for the next twenty years, rain or shine, even in the depths of winter, he would put on his old towelling robe and trudge half-way down the garden for his swim.

His dedication paid off, as usual. 'I used to see him walk backward and forward heavily, on two sticks. Then on one stick.' Then he was walking perfectly normally again. 'It never failed to amaze me how quickly he mastered it,' was Archie Hutchison's comment. Before long John was fully mobile again and just in time.

On February 25th, 1970, the City Council of Liverpool resolved unanimously, 'that in pursuance of the Local Government Act, 1933, the Honorary Freedom of the City be conferred upon Mr John Moores, in recognition of the eminent service rendered by him to the City through commercial development and by his support and encouragement of the arts and recreation'.

And at the ceremony in the Philharmonic Hall on April 30th, John was able to walk forward unaided to receive the silver casket containing the illuminated scroll which made him a Freeman of the City, to sign it, and to make a speech of thanks. He had prepared this with great care, but forgot his words in the middle and had to cut it short; he had been surprised and overwhelmed by the warmth and affection he could feel from his audience.

There were six Freedoms conferred that day, one of them on John's old friend, Bessie Braddock. Sadly, on doctor's orders, she was not able to attend the ceremony herself, and the scroll and casket were received on her behalf by a sister. But John made it, and without sticks.

It was at this point in his life that he began, for the first time, to give himself occasional small luxuries. The Freedom of the City ceremony started it. He suddenly realised that he ought perhaps to give a little thought to his appearance and to what he was going to wear. Owen Musther, considered an expert on menswear, was sent for. John was as direct as ever.

'I've never bothered with clothes, as long as they fit me. Now I realise I want to improve my image. Will you take me over?'

'I don't think I succeeded in changing his image,' said Owen. 'But at least I made him take more clothes with him when he went abroad. I made him wear colours he would never have worn – like brown or grey. Before that, it was always navy. I made him wear slightly better shirts and ties. He had tiny feet for a man, size six and a half, and I bought very expensive shoes for him. He nearly went berserk when I told him the price, but he liked them and wore them.'

More and more, Owen took over the choosing of John's clothes and would even go out to Fairways, if a special occasion was coming up, and lay out what he thought John ought to wear. Eventually, like a great many other things in John's life, all his clothes had to be numbered, so that he could see at a glance which tie and which shirt to wear with which suit. It saved time. Miss Mitchell and Miss Richards packed for him when he went anywhere, but strictly in accordance with his 'lists'; John was still 'listing'. There was a list for Italy, a list for Bermuda, a list for Scotland, a list for painting . . . 'Over the years we added things or things were crossed off,'

Miss Richards explained. 'If he went somewhere and found he hadn't used something, he'd cross it off the list and add something else. These lists were like bibles. I used to pack from them, and he never checked to see if everything was there. I used to think he was so trusting.'

That was another talent of John's – the ability to choose people on whom he could rely. He had always relied on Ruby. She had chosen a lot of his clothes and done his packing, but Ruby was no longer there. Now he left it all to his friends and relied on *them*. They were, of course, also his employees, but there has always been this strange mix of the two functions in all John's relationships.

Dressing up was still something he did not care for. Cecil and Doris's golden wedding a few years later is a typical example. 'He turned up in a dirty old yellow polo-necked sweater with coffee stains down the front.' The housekeeper, Mrs Walther, was caring and non-dictatorial and she did her best. 'His younger daughter, Mrs Stubbs, was staying at the house. She went upstairs and came down in her party dress, and we had the diamonds out of the safe, that sort of thing. Sir John was sitting there and I went in and said, "Don't you think it's time you went to get dressed, Mr John? You have to be there at seven." He said, "I look all right in this, don't I?" I said, "I imagine they might be getting dressed up, Mr John." "Well, hard luck!" he says. And he went to the party like that, with everybody else in black ties. I thought – only someone of his standing could do that.'

He was always impeccably dressed when he went to Wimbledon; his helpers made sure of that. Now that he was getting a little too old to take quite the active part in sports which he once had, watching tennis was another of his treats. He became a Wimbledon Debenture Holder in 1970, and from then on was always present at the last three days of the championships, accompanied by one or other member of the family, usually his elder daughter.

The oldest of John's grandchildren was now twenty-one, and the youngest, John Junior and Jane's third child, a daughter only twelve months. The year that she was born, they also adopted another son, a young man of seventeen; so John now had nineteen grandchildren. But 1970 was also the year in which there was a major break in the family.

Buying Medaillon Mode, the German mail-order firm, had been something of a gamble, and it was one which did not come off. Various reasons are given for its failure – different versions by different people – but on one point there is unanimity: Medaillon dealt in high fashion and it catered for the upper middle classes, and both were areas in which Littlewoods was not so experienced. Fashion is unpredictable in any case, and the safe part of mail-order – household goods, things such as blankets and sheets – was missing. There was no solid core; the catalogue was all fashion, all risk. The company also had enormous overstock and understock problems, as Spiegel had discovered to their cost. To add to the difficulties, exchange controls were still in force in Britain, and only so much cash could be exported. The whole thing was run from Britain, but the German end protected German interests and wanted goods from German factories. When a British page was introduced into the catalogue, there were difficulties because the sizing system was different.

One of John Junior's functions when he had been based in Liverpool was to guard his father's back; now he was in Germany a great deal, and there was possibly no one to perform the same office for John Junior himself. A number of high-powered Littlewoods executives went out to Germany at different times, but it was John Junior who was in charge, and it was John Junior who took responsibility. John made another of his quick decisions. Any progress Medaillon was making seemed either too slow or non-existent, and too much money was being lost; he was going to sell. Certainly if the purchase price of Medaillon were to be added to its running costs, the resulting loss could be calculated in millions of pounds rather than in thousands. But John Junior was still optimistic about the final outcome, still enthusiastic, and also very worried about entrée into Europe being lost.

The result of the argument was a major clash between John and his elder son. At the next board meeting, there was a violent row. A great deal of shouting and table-banging could be heard from inside the boardroom. A trusted secretary who had been buzzed to bring more coffee in was met at the door by a member of the meeting. The tray was taken from her very quickly and she was told that Mr John did not want her even to come into the room, 'because he can't swear in front of you!'

John won the argument; hardly surprisingly, as his word was still law. Medaillon was sold. John Junior was angry enough to resign his executive position. He still remained on the board, and has always had a great deal to do with Littlewoods' staff policies and charities. Yet in a way, by giving up a more active involvement, he had also forfeited any possibility there might have been of succeeding his father. There was now a large gap in his working life, which for over thirty years had been concentrated on the family firm. He missed the business a great deal, but he became even more actively involved in charities of his own, particularly with Liverpool youth clubs; he also started breeding cattle and building up a prize herd. John Junior's second wife, Jane, was a great support. 'Puffin helped me to get a life of my own, and to do things and to run things – the first time I'd ever run things myself. You realise that you can make mistakes – your *own* mistakes which is fantastic.' He described his self-discovery at this stage as one of the most wonderful bits of his life, but at the same time felt, 'My God, I wish I hadn't left, because I adored it.'

John was now without either of his sons at his side; but he had a larger board, a probability he had hinted at back in the mid-Fifties. George Watts was the managing director; Cecil was still a partner and still running pools; John had seven nephews and two brothers-in-law working for him, as well as several more distant relatives, and he had his own 'information service' within the company. Although he had lost the two women who had meant most to him in his life – a loyal wife and a mother who had been in many ways his inspiration – there was still family to fall back on.

Hilda, his eldest sister, had died in 1967, but he would ask himself and a fellow painter to Sunday lunch with Lou and her family; he played bridge round at Cecil's; he regularly dined and made up a bridge four at the house of his ex-daughter-in-law, Sheila. John Junior's first wife still lived a few minutes' walk from Fairways, and John and Ruby had always remained fond of her. He saw a fair amount of his grandchildren; and even though the older ones might argue with him, there was still a strong relationship.

One grandson remembers, at the age of twenty, organising a fish and chip van, brightly painted with cartoon characters, which he positioned daily in the summer holidays on Formby beach, so that 'Liverpool kids could have a day out at the beach and get something to eat', and he had a team of some of the same 'Liverpool kids' helping. When he asked his grandfather if he could park the van in the drive at Fairways overnight, John readily gave permission. Even when his granddaughter-in-law drove into and demolished a gate-post one evening, he did not seem to mind. And the Liverpool children who were helping were asked into his home. 'He was very kind to them; they thought the world of him afterwards.'

His faithful secretaries continued to be in attendance. Although they were still called 'Miss Mitchell' and 'Miss Richards' – their maiden names when they had first joined the company over thirty years earlier – they were in fact married women and had been for a long time; but in spite of husbands and families and full lives of their own, they were always there to look after John when he needed them. John may have been seventy-five, but he was still captain of the ship.

18

Do Not Disturb

'An adverse wind is a challenge.' It was twenty years since John had told his executives that, but his analogy of the yachtsman still applied, and particularly to John himself. His drive and his expansion of the business still continued, whatever sorrows he had to face in his personal life and whatever difficulties presented themselves on the national scene.

The first blow to the economy fell in that same year. The postal strike in 1971 lasted forty-seven days and caused disruption to a great many firms. Littlewoods might have been thought particularly vulnerable, with two of its divisions – mail order and football pools – both postal businesses. In the event, they survived comparatively unscathed. Pools even improved its takings. As early as 1957, a collector system had been introduced; coupons were collected from people's homes and workplaces, saving them not only the bother of mailing the coupon but also the expense of buying a stamp. During the strike, the collectors made extra efforts and brought in more coupons than ever before. It was in the middle of this dispute, too, that Littlewoods paid out, on one coupon, what was then a world-record win of £355,329.

Mail order could have been much more badly affected, but everyone rallied round as they had during the rail strike in 1955. And John had as usual shown remarkable foresight. In the words of the divisional controller, Frank Hoare, who was there on the spot:

'It'll show you the sort of company we had. We could overcome any problem – and I say that with pride – because we had a management here at the time who didn't *wait* for things to happen: they could see things that were *going* to happen. Before the postal strike actually came off, we had people here earmarked to go out to different parts of the country, all head office staff would be given different towns, and would be sent out and booked into hotels. The main thing was to collect orders. We took this place where all the parcels went for our transport staff. We spent weekends over there, loading the vans. The strike lasted six weeks. You can imagine – with *mail* order – for a postal strike to be on. It could have been a killer. I suppose it did make a mess of our finances, but at least we were ticking over – because of the organisation that was planned beforehand. That's one of the things I've often admired about Littlewoods. We weren't caught with our pants down. Most things were ready; we were always ahead of the game.'

Another hurdle to clear in 1971 was the conversion to decimal currency, but Littlewoods, along with many other businesses, managed this more smoothly and easily than most private individuals.

Although the company had coped well with the two main crises it had to meet that year, in other ways John was not too pleased. And he made that quite clear to his executives at another of the Adelphi gatherings in March 1972.

'Since I started this business, I have never changed my basic policy. It is very simple:

'First,' to give all our customers real value for money, consistently; so that they return again and again as customers and friends.

'Second,' to give all our employees the opportunity to contribute to the growth and development of the company; and to develop their own abilities to the full, with every prospect of promotion and financial recognition.

'And then – by the grace of God – to make a profit for the company.'

He was clearly not convinced that his aims were being met.

'You are the senior managers of the organisation. I want you to look very carefully at the way in which you manage money. Spend it as if it were your own. Every penny you save will help Littlewoods regain its reputation for giving value for money. *Which at the moment we are not doing.*'

There was also something else on his mind. As his eightieth birthday drew near, John was looking for a successor.

'I know that you are all vitally interested in the question of the new chairman,' were his parting words. 'Unfortunately, everyone we have seen so far has failed what, to me, is a relatively simple test. Not one of them can walk across the bloody Mersey.'

That year was much more to his liking. In spite of 'the miners' strike, builders' strike, minibudget, unseasonable weather – which we always get – warehouse unrest, the freeze, etc.', John was able to welcome his executives at the beginning of the next year's dinner with much more cheerful words.

'It's very nice to see you all, particularly to see you after a very good trading year. It's a wonderful feeling, isn't it, when everything is going well?'

After a bad year in 1971, a shopping boom had started, and Littlewoods had record sales. John was delighted.

It was also the year in which he was awarded the CBE. This coincided with the fortieth anniversary of the start of mail order.

'We celebrated Mr John's forty years in the business, and we had a collection amongst the old-stagers,' George Farrar remembered. 'We bought him a stainless steel floral trough and a painting. I never saw anybody so proud. He had his CBE scroll, and we all had a sherry with him – all the old people who started with him. Generally he thought a great deal of people who had been with the company for any length of time.' As Frank Hoare said, 'We used to be called "the good old Littlewoodies".'

John made sure that he showed his appreciation of his Littlewoodies in tangible form too. The twenty-five- and forty-year awards which he inaugurated are still continued. The family directors still present a cheque to each long-serving member of staff – whether office cleaner or director – along with a handsome gift. John made the presentations personally for as long as he was able. Eventually he had to cut down his commitments and hand the job over on occasion to one of his children; but the lower in the hierarchy someone was, the more likely they were to receive the award from Mr John himself.

Nowadays there is a list of gifts to choose from, instead of the obligatory watch or silver tea service. Very often in fact, a man due to receive a long service award will pick something from the women's list – a ring or a piece of jewellery – and give it to his wife as a thank you for her support. John would understand that perfectly. In a true partnership the reward is shared – just as he once said that responsibility and success were shared – by both husband and wife alike.

For many years, there was an annual dinner at the Adelphi for those who had reached the forty-year award before retiring, and all retired employees of over twenty-five years' service continued to receive the Littlewoods magazine. Both these courtesies have been discontinued now, and are badly missed. Company pensions are still well above average and there are regular visits to pensioners to check on their well-being, but a certain amount of the old family feel has gone. It went when John went.

Back in 1972, aged seventy-six, he was still very much present. He returned to shoulder the chairmanship of the Everton board for another year. He took an active interest in the Winter Olympics held in Japan, sponsoring the high altitude training for the British team. He saw the biggest pools win so far, when a Hampshire man, Mr C Grimes, received a dividend of £512,683, and before very long he was witnessing the half million eclipsed by a million pound winner. Then, in October 1973, he presided over a change of name for the whole company. The object was 'to bring mail order, chain-stores and pools activities together under a shorter and what is considered to be a more appropriate name'.

All personnel were to be informed of this with a full explanation of the reasons, before it was made public. It is interesting to see from the briefing group preparation note, how much care was taken to keep staff not only fully informed, but also involved. Full and open communication had been developing since the early Fifties. Managers were given guidance on the sort of questions which they might be asked, along with appropriate answers. Two are particularly interesting. 'Will Mr John continue as chairman?' and 'Having announced his intention to retire, why is Mr John staying?' There is no company record of such an announcement having been made, but clearly the staff knew; there is always a core of fairly acute perception present in any well-run and united organisation. And the answer which the managers were to give was that 'a suitable successor has not yet been found'. Was anyone really looking? John's energy and application seemed as phenomenal as ever.

It was in chain-stores that John's qualities were demonstrated most. 'There used to be a lot of criticism in those days from the people in head office that Mr John favoured the stores, and I guess that was true,' as Harry Thomas, who is now PR Director, commented. 'He conquered mail order and he conquered pools, but he never quite conquered retailing in the High Street, and to that extent it was always a challenge to him.' In a way it was akin to his passion for painting – another thing he never quite mastered to his own satisfaction – or to his regard for people. They were always more interesting while they were still independent and not totally subject to him. 'Everything to the Old Man was a challenge,' as Harry Thomas recognised.

'The chain-store was almost like a magnet to him, and he used to love going on store visits. You had to turn up on a Sunday to go with him; what he wanted, he had. And wherever he went, he was acclaimed: not only by the staff, who knew he was coming in advance. I've seen him walk onto a sales floor – I've seen him in

Scotland, in Newcastle – and people have recognised him and said "Hiya, John!" He didn't know them from Adam, but the customers knew *him*. He used to love it. He'd stop and chat. "What's wrong with my merchandise? Why don't you buy such-and-such?" He never stopped working.'

And he went on visiting until he retired, even when he was in a wheelchair. Before he reached that stage, the store visits were 'quite exacting', and many of them were flying visits – literally: via the company plane. Men may by then have survived out in space for a month and spent over seventy-four hours on the surface of the moon, but light aircraft on domestic flights could still be very uncomfortable.

Harry Thomas particularly remembers one trip that John made.

'He flew up to Aberdeen with Stanley Page on a Sunday. There was no catering on the plane; it was one of those damn little Aztecs we had in those days, a four-seater job and two pilots in the front. It used to buffet you all over the place. Mr John came with his flask of hot coffee. He insisted on pouring some for himself and Mr Page, the plane lurched, and of course he scalded his hand. He was in a terrible state when he got off the plane at Aberdeen airport.' Luckily Harry himself was on the spot; he knew that Boots, the chemists, were doing their inventory that Sunday, and he also knew the manager. John got his hand properly dressed.

One unalterable part of the routine, whether a Sunday or a weekday, was always the afternoon rest. 'He used to lie down in the stores. We always had to reserve the first-aid room for him; wherever he went, he would always sleep after lunch. We used to have to provide him with ear-muffs and things for his eyes, as the first-aid rooms had natural light. Anything would do – I've seen him with socks over his eyes. We used to put a *Do Not Disturb* notice on the door, but occasionally someone would go in and get a terrible fright.' He always recommended the same routine to his store managers too, until one of them finally said, 'Mr John, if you came into my store and saw me lying down on the first-aid room bed, what would you say to me?' John laughed; but he always had his twenty minutes or half-hour himself, 'and by God, it recharged the batteries!'

'He'd go to Aberdeen and say, "We'll do a few on the way back." So we'd go to Dundee or somewhere like that, and then he'd pop into Leeds – as you go over the Pennines. He didn't waste any time.'

Time was not wasted during the holidays that he had been prescribed either. He was now learning Spanish again, to stop his brain slowing down, as he told his elder daughter. As well as attending the Berlitz School in London in 1973 at the age of seventy-seven, he enrolled for a course at a college in Salamanca; in 1974, it was a course at Santander. 'He used to stay in quite grotty little hotels,' according to Miss Richards. But as usual, although he was loth to spend on himself, he would spend to save time. 'He never quibbled about paying to use the company plane, and he always insisted on paying if it was not on company business. He had permission to use the RAF station at Woodvale, on the outskirts of Formby. The plane would be waiting for him there, and he would go to Heathrow. Mac would meet him with the car, take him to the terminal, book him in, stay with him and see him off.' Mac would then ring the office and report that Mr John was on his way. 'He worries the life out of me,' he used to say. 'This little chappie going off by himself, this billionaire – just toddling off on his own. He could be kidnapped!' John always travelled first-class. But as Miss Richards explained, 'I don't think people would expect to see a little millionaire wandering around on his own – certainly not the way he was dressed. On the plane he would have spilt food down his front, and he wouldn't look anything by the time he got there, so no one would give him a second glance. I suppose he thought he was quite safe.'

Security had been carefully considered for most members of the family, and the correct procedures to follow with regard to police action, payment of ransom, etc., should any emergency occur, had been carefully explained to them. John was quite clear on the subject. If he himself were ever to be kidnapped and a ransom demanded, his instructions were explicit. 'Don't pay it.'

His instructions with regard to the appointment of a successor were still awaited, but events now began to push him into making a decision. In some ways, 1973 was the last of the 'good years'. July 1974 saw a fuel crisis. Then, in October, a Labour Government was returned to power with a small majority, and the familiar anti-socialist tone began to appear again in John's speeches. 'We have a Government which is very anti-capitalistic, extremely socialistic . . . whose policy is to soak the rich and nationalise industry. A Government which proposes equality, but instead of equalising upwards seem only to have the idea of equalising downwards, reducing us all to a very drab level.'

In November, Cecil's son, Nigel, resigned his directorship. He had been on the board since 1969 and was regarded by many as an astute businessman – indeed, as a possible contender for the position of chairman; but after a disagreement with his father, he left. Now he turned more of his attention to motor-racing, a long-standing interest, and to building up his collection of vintage racing cars.

The following eighteen months saw no improvement in the economy. On April 5th, 1976, Harold Wilson resigned as Prime Minister and was succeeded by James Callaghan. Ten days later at the executives' dinner, John had little good to say about either of them, or about their policies.

'We are greatly concerned with the future, which doesn't look good. Recently there was another business forecast predicting gloom and despondency . . . To get through this slump we shall need all our wisdom, all our energy. It has always been my policy to turn adverse circumstances to our advantage. It's no use belly-aching about a profligate Government wasting our assets. We won't do any good predicting the ruin of our economy. Rather we must show ourselves as men who can perform in face of all the odds. And in spite of Sunny Jim, we'll do it.'

John's eighty-first birthday was approaching. He may have decided that to deal with the tough times ahead, more energy and more stamina were needed than he himself now possessed. He began to think about reshaping the board.

In September of that year his younger son, Peter, was made vice-chairman.

Then, in the following spring, came bad news. On April 9th, 1977, Nigel was killed in a car crash in the South of France. His parents were devastated and the whole family was in shock. John was triggered into speedier action. Less than three weeks later there was a new main board director – his elder daughter, Betty. In some ways, it was a surprising appointment.

If John's business ideas were still in advance of his time, his attitude to women was not. There may have been a woman at the head of the Conservative Party (Margaret Thatcher had been elected leader two years earlier) and Betty may have had a good brain, a Cambridge degree and have only recently finished a course in accountancy and statistics; but John still needed convincing of the suitability of any woman for high office or for top responsibility. It took a certain amount of persuasion from Peter before he would even allow Betty to be shown the company accounts. Her ability and grasp, however, were quickly apparent.

Within three months, there was a new managing director. Philip Carter had been with the company since joining as a management trainee in 1944. He had started in the home shopping division, but then switched to chain-stores, worked his way up the business and was made a main board director in 1965. John had always thought very highly of him – in some ways regarding him almost as a third son. John Junior's wife, Jane, remembered that as far back as 1961, when they were first engaged and they happened to pass Philip Carter on the stairs, John Junior had commented to her, 'That's someone who might get the chairmanship one day.'

In July, another main board director was appointed; Arthur George. And finally, on October 17th, 1977, John made his decision: he resigned from the chairmanship and Peter was appointed chairman in his place, for a term of three years.

It was still John who made the speech at the executive dinner in April of the following year, which began, 'I am welcoming you not as chairman, but as Mr John . . .'

He gave a brief résumé of the company's history, a reference or two to its current position, and went on:

'So much for the past and the present – what of the future? My feeling is *confidence* – confidence in the future of this dynamic business of ours. In particular, I feel confident in handing over the responsibilities of chairmanship to Mr Peter, backed up by the knowledge and experience of Mr Carter and a very strong board of directors, all of whom will safeguard the history and traditions of the company.

'But equally, much depends on you, the senior management group – your standards and the example you set and, not least of all, the development of those coming on in the business and to whom, one day, you too will hand over.'

Handing over was something that John himself found very difficult to do. Within three years he was back again.

19

In My Beginning is My End

The fact that his younger son was chairman had made very little difference to John's daily routine. He still continued his flying visits to stores all over the country. He still went into the J M Centre three days a week, on Monday, Wednesday and Friday; his pet aversions were Bank Holiday Mondays, because they kept him out of the office for four days. His time-keeping was still as accurate; he would leave Fairways at nine o'clock, the housekeeper would ring to say that he was on his way, and he would be at the J M Centre on the dot of half-past nine. On one occasion, he got into the lift with an employee who should have been there at half-past eight; it happened a second time and John could not let it pass.

'Late again!' he exclaimed.

'So am *I*, Mr John!' the man panted guiltily.

'The Old Man told us the story himself; he thought it was very funny,' one director commented.

Honours continued to come his way. In 1978, it was the first Liverpool Gold Medal for Achievement. In 1980, it was a knighthood. A great many of his employees thought that this was long overdue, and not only for his efforts during the war. One of them, Eric Furlong, felt so strongly that he had even written to the Prime Minister about it as far back as 1972.

'Dear Mr Heath, My object in writing to you today is not only to express my appreciation and support for your efforts [entry into the Common Market] but primarily to make a plea for national recognition of a man who has done so much for his fellow men, and whom I have known as a just employer for thirty-four years. I feel the country owes him a great debt. I refer to Mr John Moores . . . I know I speak for many thousands of my fellow men and women, not only employees of Littlewoods Mail Order Stores Ltd and its subsidiary companies, when I state that we in the North-West look at the Honours List each year and cannot understand why a man who is so socially minded, who has given so much, and is so loyal to Lancashire, and to Liverpool in particular, who has aided the arts, supported welfare for youth and the aged, medical research and business management research, and who has given anonymous help to many charities and individuals, why such a man remains unrecognised.'

The reply he received was gracious, and promised that Mr Moores' name would be fully considered. It was over eight years and a Conservative Government later that the knighthood followed. This was possibly because John himself made no efforts in that direction. He continued to donate to the causes which he himself wished to support, which were not necessarily those which would have brought instant recognition. An action performed because it was 'gong-worthy' would have been anathema to him. It would have looked like buying a title; and if anything were to be conferred on him it had to be simply because of who he was – plain John Moores.

When the knighthood was finally offered in 1980, it came almost out of the blue, but he accepted it with pleasure. He was eighty-four by now – on doctor's orders still taking a holiday every three months – and he got back from one of his language-learning sessions in Spain to find a surprise party at Fairways. He was due to come straight home from the airport, so it was arranged that staff from the J M Centre would do the catering, and Mrs Walther, the housekeeper, was posted as look-out to alert everyone when he was arriving. 'I opened the door and welcomed him back; he threw his hat down, and then went on into the lounge – and there were all these people; his family and one or two special people from the office. He was so overcome, he cried. It was lovely!'

The next morning there was to be a great welcome for him on the steps of the J M Centre, and for once he must have been almost overwhelmed, because he left without his Little Black Book. 'I found it on the table in the lounge,' Mrs Walther recounted. 'I thought, "Oh no!" and I fled out into the garage and got into JM2 and followed him. Of course, he went like the clappers. I saw him in the distance on the clearway and I tried to catch him. Eventually I did manage to pass him, going at goodness knows how many miles an hour, got in front of him and waved to him to stop. I said, "You've gone without the Holy Bible!" He was so pleased to have it.' He then discovered that he had left without any money, and asked to borrow some. His housekeeper lent him the two or three pounds she had with her, and then found herself lending him her handkerchief which happened to be lace. '"That's better than nothing," he said, blew his nose on it, and put it in his pocket.' As soon as he had driven off, she rushed back to Fairways and telephoned Miss Richards to tell her to be at the bottom of the J M Centre steps with a handkerchief.

If the reception he was heading for moved him to tears again, she did not want him pulling out that little lace one.

John was certainly delighted with the award, although in many ways the honours that he was most proud of were those which he received from the City of Liverpool.

He was also very pleased when later in 1980 the headquarters of the organisation received a visit from the Duke of Edinburgh. The slightly tricky decision to be made was whether Prince Philip should be welcomed by Sir John or by the chairman of the company. Owen Musther was rushed up to John's office on the eleventh floor, to vet his clothes and tell him whether he looked all right. Miss Mitchell was trying to insist that he put his overcoat on. He was 'a bit of a monarchist', that was well known. 'Adored the Queen, and the Queen Mother. Any charity that the Queen Mother was involved with, the Boss would say "Yes" – not "Maybe" or "I'll think about it."' But it was a cold day, he was a considerably older man than their visitor, and he found the front steps trying. The problem was solved; Peter, as chairman, went out to the Duke's car to greet him while John waited to welcome him at the top of the entrance steps.

John was still very much the figurehead of the company. If the honours conferred were intended to be on his retirement, then they were premature. Although he had stepped down from the chairmanship, John had never really left the business. Apart from his days at the J M Centre, he had also informed one of his directors, Colin Stanhope, that he was to visit Fairways every month to go through all the mail-order figures with him. His finger was still on the pulse, and his presence could still be felt 'in every corner of the company'. It was almost as though there were two power bases in the organisation, the chairman and the Old Man, and inevitably this produced a certain amount of jockeying and intrigue.

Soon after resigning from the chairmanship in 1977, John also curtailed most of his work for Everton. He was still the biggest shareholder, still interested, still on the board, but not such an active member; so he had even more time for the business. This led indirectly to a disagreement with Peter.

By 1979, John was complaining that his younger son was not giving the business *enough* time. He wanted Peter to leave the merchant bank of which he was a director and devote himself entirely to Littlewoods. Coming up to Liverpool for a couple of days a week and attending board meetings was not enough, in John's view, however much of the reading and paperwork Peter got through in his own time. But Peter felt that his own permanent presence at Littlewoods, as well as John's, would lead to even more jockeying and intrigue, and an increase in the tension this caused, so he refused. The row that followed was not as violent as the one that John had had with his elder son, but in 1980 on return from his summer holiday, Peter was summoned to a meeting of family directors, who voted not to renew his chairmanship in October. He remained on the board as a director, just as his brother had, but at the board meeting on November 7th, 1980, John was back in the chair again.

The return of a Conservative Government in May 1979 seemed to have given John a new lease of life. He was obviously hoping that it would have the same effect on the economy. But his own burst of energy did not last for long and in less than eighteen months, he had resigned the chairmanship again, for the last time. On May 28th, 1982, he was elected president for life. That same year, Philip Carter received the CBE. He was still the managing director; the new chairman was John Clement who came from the dairy business, Unigate, and had joined the board as a director the previous October.

The next few years saw recurring changes in the board's composition. Five family members remained throughout – John, Cecil and three of John's children; but there was a constant coming and going of highly professional and expert career men, as the board gradually sorted itself out and found its new identity. At the end of 1983, John Clement brought in Desmond Pitcher, a Liverpool-born man and a hightech communications expert from Plessey. Philip Carter resigned and in 1984 Desmond Pitcher took over as managing director.

At his suggestion, the post was retitled chief executive, and John endorsed his position as chief. Desmond Pitcher had not worked his way up through the organisation, and had never been on a junior level in John's 'listings'. He was coming in to run the place. He was aware, however, that a false step at the start could jeopardise the enterprise. He knew nobody in the company and nobody knew him, so he asked John if there was any helpful advice he could offer. He was told that his main problem would be the phrase 'Mr John wouldn't like that'. It was always used as an objection to any piece of new policy which did not please the particular speaker. Desmond's solution was simple: he personally would bring the first person who raised such an objection to John, who would instruct him to do as he was told. And that is exactly what happened. At the chief executive's first board meeting, the fatal words were said and the man who spoke them was taken to the life president's office. There he was informed, 'Mr Pitcher is the boss of this company.' It was John's backing that got the new boss off to the right start.

Before long, there was a honed and streamlined board which was reorganising Littlewoods' finances. Most of the old 'Littlewoody' directors had gone. Some of the changes caused John distress, but he recognised their necessity; indeed, in some ways he inaugurated them. They were a natural development from his realisation, back in the mid-Fifties, that with the tremendous growth of the business, more outside directors would have to be appointed. Even then, he must have sensed that a change in the character of the company was inevitable. But as life president, he was still very much *au fait* with what was going on, and he still gave orders.

In 1983, the recession bit deeper; there was widespread unemployment in Liverpool, and even Littlewoods was forced to make redundancies. One response of John's was immediate: all directors were informed that they must give up their company Rolls-Royces for less expensive cars. Most directors descended as far as a very slightly less expensive Mercedes or Jaguar.

John swapped his own Rolls for a Cortina, and never changed back again. Colleagues and staff were concerned because of the safety factor; he would surely be better protected in his Rolls. He was still driving a car at eighty-seven. Besides, they argued, there was his image to be considered. And there would be no point in giving up the Rolls in any case: the people of Liverpool knew that he was a billionaire. 'Yes, but do they know I *care* about them?' was John's response to that.

It was a relief to everyone when he finally stopped driving – at the age of ninety. 'He was always mounting the pavement,' according to one daughter. Or as Owen Musther put it, 'I won't say he was the world's best driver; he would talk to you and get so wrapped up in the subject matter that he'd forget to look where he was going. He mounted the pavement a number of times; it was when something was coming in the opposite direction that I used to wonder whether we were fully insured.'

John's mind was always on other things and his thoughts always racing ahead; it had tried even Ruby's patience in the past. 'He would walk out and get in the car and leave Mummy to lock up and do everything; then he'd forget she wasn't there and start driving out of the drive and down the road. She used to really swear about it.' On one occasion, when he had driven them both to a party, he was mulling some plan over in his head, forgot Ruby was with him, and drove home without her. 'She used to take her own car after that – she was very cross.'

He never treated his car particularly well; it was simply something that got him from one place to another. Owen never forgot the first time that he was the Old Man's passenger. 'He had a navy-blue Bentley Continental, a beautiful coupé, navy-blue leather upholstery, and hanging on the dashboard was a five-bob alarm clock on a chain – swinging against it and scratching all the marvellous mahogany veneer.' Owen could hardly bear it.

'Good God!' he said. 'Look what that's doing!'

'I've told the garage the car clock's not working. I can't stand clocks that are not going.'

'But – look at the damage you're doing!'

'It's my car. And it's my time.'

And it was quite clear which of the two mattered most to John.

When he did finally stop driving, there was to be no chauffeur. He had not employed a chauffeur since before the war, when his children were small and needed to be ferried about. 'And he didn't believe in fancy hired cars,' as Miss Richards said. 'I used to drive him for the last four or five years. I used to go from home to Formby, leave my own car there, pick him up and drive him into town and back.' If he was going to a football match or the theatre, it would be one of the firm's drivers whom he knew, but never in uniform, or one of the managers or even a top executive. It was always done on a friendly basis.

John may not have been keen on driving, but he still had his mind on the business. Until he resigned as managing director, Philip Carter would drive out to Fairways every Monday with the mail-order and chain-store figures. On one occasion, mail order was down against its budget, but John very quickly put his finger on the cause. The new catalogue had gone out on a Monday, instead of on the previous Friday. One day of a new catalogue is worth a couple of million pounds, and this one had lost two days and a weekend, when people would have had an opportunity to look at it. The impact of a new catalogue is immediate, and some of that impact had been lost, together with the extra business it would have generated. John never missed a detail.

After Philip Carter's departure it was Desmond Pitcher who, at John's request, was a constant visitor to Fairways. Sometimes John would telephone and ask him to call round on a Sunday morning, when they would read the papers and go over the previous day's football matches together. Sometimes on a Saturday at 5 p.m., Desmond would join John in his favourite meal of egg and bacon before watching a football match live on TV; more often than not they would meet one evening during the week. John wanted someone to talk to and the stimulation of new interests and activities.

He took a keen interest in changes in the running of the company, in its restructuring and in particular in planning expertise. According to his chief executive, 'the idea of this logical analysis and planning process to reach long-term decisions, objectives and goals was something new to him. He had a very sound and comprehensive database, but fundamentally if you asked him to explain a decision he wouldn't want to, or he wouldn't be able to.' (Long explanations for past decisions would certainly not interest him.) 'His instinct was his great driving force.' It was, of course, an instinct founded on the 'database', on those vast and carefully-maintained mental 'lists' of his. Now he became intrigued by the new approach. As Desmond said, 'He would spend a lot of time going over the plans. I would sit at his house with him. We had pages and pages of notes questioning the reasonings, the "whys" and "wherefores". He took it on himself to study it all, and even to challenge it as well. He was the most challenging member of the board, not in an aggressive sense, but in his thinking.' And he was no doubt testing other people's thinking and their ability at the same time.

The two men had a relationship of mutual respect, without being personal or close. 'I always called him Sir John and he called me Mr Pitcher, and over the years that never changed.' Mutual respect, however, did not stop John's straight-from-the-shoulder remarks. On one occasion, when on his way in at Goodison, Desmond was mugged in the car park and his wallet was stolen. 'How d'you expect to look after *my* money, if you can't even look after your own?' was John's greeting when they met in the directors' sanctum.

He enjoyed going to football matches with Desmond in London as well as in Liverpool; they would sit in Hyde Park for a couple of hours beforehand, watching the ducks, while John reminisced about his early years. 'He never liked people to intrude on him. If they tried to ingratiate themselves, he would resent that. If they were trying to be friendly and helpful, that he would accept.' He accepted Desmond. And above all, he wanted to talk about the business; interestingly it was 'not about how the business was going, but about what was going on inside the business'. He still knew what was happening everywhere.

By 1984 there were 108 chain-stores. In 1985, a new division was started. Index is a series of shops, some stand-alone, some in-store, where catalogues can be consulted and goods ordered over the counter, already packaged and ready to be taken home. It proved so popular that within five years there were nearly a hundred of them.

Then, in 1986, Fairways was burgled.

Thieves broke into the house, tied up the housekeeper and her husband, and found John upstairs in his bedroom. What they wanted from him was the combination of the safe. John gave them a number. Whether it was the correct one or not, they could not make it work. They ordered John to open it for them. 'I can't!' he protested. 'I'm an old man, my secretary always does it *for* me.' Apparently they believed him – he was ninety – for they trussed him up and left. As they were Liverpool burglars, one of them rang the police to say that John Moores was tied up in his bedroom and they had better get round there quickly to make sure he was all right. There is a strong theory that the wrong house had been burgled and that the intruders were taken aback to discover who their victim was. They may have been more shaken than John himself, who recovered from the ordeal remarkably quickly. Soon afterwards, he made what was probably an unwise decision.

Some time previously John's Achilles tendon had gone, and he had not immediately realised. Now he insisted on having it attended to. 'The doctors begged him not to have the operation. He had an enlarged prostate and they knew that it would cause trouble.' John had his own way, as usual. 'It's the quality of life that counts,' was his argument. 'I want to walk on the shore again, and the golf-links.' The top specialist in this type of operation worked in South Wales, so John flew down for it in May. Carbon fibre was used to repair the tendon and the operation was successful, but it did – as anticipated – affect his prostate gland. It was suggested that he have an operation to rectify this while he was there and already in hospital, but John refused. He wanted to go home. Three weeks back at Fairways, in a certain amount of discomfort and needing to use a catheter, was enough to persuade him. This time he went into the local nursing home, Park House. 'He was so ill, we didn't really think he'd come out,' Miss Richards remembers. 'But he's got a very strong constitution, and out he came. He went back to the office, too. But he was never quite the same.'

In December of that year, at a private meeting with the family directors, John suddenly realised that he was not going to get his own way in a decision which they were about to make. It was the first time in his life that he would not have carried the motion. He therefore refrained from voting. His two operations, so close together, had started a physical decline but this reversal had even more of an emotional impact.

In 1988, at the age of ninety-two, he presided at the AGM but he did not speak as much as usual. When he finally started a succinct summing-up of a particular point, he suddenly lost the thread of his argument and his voice trailed off. The second of disbelieving silence which gripped the assembly will never be forgotten by those who were there. It was his last AGM; he never went back.

Now he stayed at home at Fairways; well looked after, with a housekeeper, nurses, his faithful secretary, and with constant visits from family. His ninety-year-old sister, Ethel, always remembered his words the last time she called on him. She was the sister who had struck out and run her own business; after the goodbyes were said and as she was leaving, he suddenly grinned at her and said, 'You and I have to learn to do what we're told now.' The idea seemed to entertain him.

His mind was still working clearly, even when his grip on words began to fail. Two grandsons who were sitting with him and recounting some incident, wondered – as he was so silent – whether he was taking it in. One of them stood in front of him and said, 'Grandpa, if you can understand what we're saying, put your hand up.'

'His hand was up before I'd finished speaking,' the young man remembered.

Then, in 1989, Cecil died. He had been battling against ill health for some time, to be there for his beloved wife, Doris, and for John. But Doris had died the previous year after a long illness, and John no longer needed him. Cecil had gone to his favourite loch for a holiday with his youngest sister and his personal secretary. The day before he died was a good one; he caught two trout. He was eighty-seven. His death was difficult to take in. It was not just the end of a lifetime; it was the end of an era.

Miss Mitchell, the faithful 'Mitch', had died in the April of 1988, just before that last AGM. She was the only person, apart from Ruby, who had been capable of telling John off; during an argument, each would cheerfully refer to the other as 'that bloody woman' and 'that old fool'. John missed her. All the old faithfuls were going, family included. Arthur had died in 1984, and Hilda's husband, George, in 1985, eighteen years after his wife's death and at the age of a hundred; Lou a long time previously, in 1972; and in 1990 Ethel died, aged ninety-two.

John still had his children and his grandchildren, but he may have been lonely for all that. The old days were going; perhaps he was lonely for the shared experiences that went with them. Perhaps he missed the constant attention that absolute power always brings. Even a few years previously, while he was still going into the office, a personal secretary remembers taking him some papers from her immediate boss. It was August – 'always a dead month in the J M Centre' – and as she was leaving, he suddenly said, 'Sit down a moment. I need your advice.' She was very surprised, but did as she was told. 'He was reading through the papers and he said, "I need somebody to talk to about this, maybe you can suggest someone. Archie's away. Desmond's on his yacht in the Mediterranean. If I ring up so-and-so I might get the wrong house and the wrong wife" – he always knew what was going on, even if people thought that they had kept it from him. So I went and got somebody for him who might help.'

Now, at ninety-seven, he is surrounded by constant care and attention, but he does not speak any more. He seems happy. He does as he is told. Perhaps he is back again as that good little boy, his mother's first son and her pride and joy. Looking at this small, frail, very old man, it is difficult to comprehend his achievements.

He has founded and funded an important international art exhibition. He has given millions to charity. He has had a university named after him; the Liverpool Polytechnic has evolved into the Liverpool John Moores University (the name of the J M Centre even had to be changed to 100 Old Hall Street to avoid any possible confusion). 'And it is the first university in the UK to be named after a living person, an emphatic and sincere expression of respect and admiration for the region's best known and most successful entrepreneur.' And he has built, from scratch, an enormous business empire. In 1992, the home shopping division – now a highly automated credit system, depending increasingly on telephone ordering – had a turnover of £974m. the 127 chain-stores £696m.; Index £228m. Including pools, the organisation had, in that one year, a turnover of £2,709m., and made a profit of over £97m. What is more, John has – against all opposition – kept the heart of this gigantic undertaking in Liverpool, providing some relief from the unemployment rife there since it lost its place as a major port. Throughout a long business career, he has always been concerned with staff welfare and he has always provided opportunities for people where he could and wherever they were needed.

It is a changed business in the last few years. The days when total loyalty was given to a boss are gone. 'I think he relied upon me to a great extent and I enjoyed it. I feel a better man for having known him. It was a wonderful part of my life. I've never been sorry, never.' How many newly-retired employees would speak like Eric Barker today? How many will retire after forty years' service in the future? Priorities have changed. Long service is no longer the credit mark that it was. 'There's a feeling of – why haven't you moved on? Haven't you got the ability? Are you frightened of the outside world?' Other developments have taken place; there is enormous efficiency, automation, speed, scale, and global interaction; all the things that John saw on the horizon and switched track to reach. But Littlewoods still has a unique character of its own. Many staff still have a feeling of 'belonging' to something. It is still a private company, owned by family shareholders. There are still family directors on the main board. Grandchildren of John's and of Cecil's sit on divisional boards. The family feel has still not quite gone.

And his family itself, on a family scale, is equally enormous. Four children, each with their partners; twenty grandchildren, many with theirs; twenty-seven great-grandchildren; countless nephews, nieces, great-nephews, great-nieces, and great-great-nephews and nieces too.

John once said in an interview, 'The business is more important than my sons.' There were 30,000 people depending on him for employment in Liverpool alone. Many of them had worked for him for years. 'They've given me their lives. You can hardly repay that.'

On the other hand, in many ways his business and his family were interchangeable. They got very similar treatment. His insistence on competitiveness was the same in both. 'The Old Man always treated the men – the managers in particular – in a competitive way. He always had two people jockeying for one position. We had Watts and Sawyer, Carter and Worsnop, Hedges and Watts. There were always two competing for a position. It was the same with store managers; there was no deputy manager in those days, it was straight from assistant manager to manager. There would be one vacancy and two men would be sent for the interviews. The best one on the day got it.' If that was how he treated directors and managers, it was also exactly how he treated his sons. And although the competitiveness he encouraged between them may not have produced as good a relationship as the one they might have enjoyed, it also prevented them ever uniting against their father.

He thought he was leaving his children and grandchildren to order their own lives. He was very generous in many ways; he distributed his shares very early. 'I try never to put my dead hand on my children and grandchildren.' In other words, 'They do not have to do what I say because I might cut them out of my will.' But then, the 'dead hand' was not necessary; the live hand was quite powerful enough. It took each of his sons over forty years to break free.

This ability to achieve two results at the same time, to give and yet to get, to have one's cake and eat it – there is always this double edge to John's actions. There is always this dichotomy in his character. He was a staunch Conservative, but at the same time he was admired by a grandson for 'his socialist capitalism'. He was in many ways a self-centred man, but his life was geared to looking after and providing for other people. He had an eye for a pretty girl, but a steadfast belief in the importance of marriage and of the family. He could give as good as he got in a cut-throat and competitive world, but honesty and integrity were his watchwords. Perhaps it was due to the part of him that still held to 'the old Victorian principles'. Mentally, he was innovative, far-sighted – he could look ahead to the end of the twentieth century and probably beyond; his emotions and his values remained largely fixed in the era of his boyhood. The Victorians are criticised now for their hypocrisy, but they had almost unrealistic standards to live up to. Perhaps the two things inevitably go together. If standards are too high, it can be very difficult to adhere to them, and just as difficult to admit to failure. Our age is much less hypocritical; but then the standards which we set ourselves are much lower.

Perhaps, also, it was not simply the time that John was born into, but also the place. He is a North Country man, with a North Country man's faults as well as his virtues. There is still a north/south divide in Britain. The two cultures were described by Donald Horne in a book he wrote in 1969, and his words still apply. He called them the Southern and the Northern Metaphors. 'In the Southern Metaphor, Britain is romantic, illogical, muddled, divinely lucky, Anglican, aristocratic, traditional, frivolous, and believes in order and tradition. Its sinful excess is a ruthless pride, rationalised in the belief that men are born to serve' – a belief that was certainly not John's. 'In the Northern Metaphor, Britain is pragmatic, empirical, calculating, Puritan, bourgeois, enterprising, adventurous, scientific, serious, and believes in struggle. Its sinful excess is a ruthless avarice, rationalised in the belief that the prime impulse in all human beings is a rational, calculating, economic self-interest.' John to a T; but he would have qualified the word 'self-interest' with the word 'enlightened', and he would have called it a virtue. After all, was that not one of his maxims? 'An enlightened self-interest is the best interest anyone can have.' It was best because it allowed him to go on looking after people; he was truly paternal. That was his role: knowing what was best for people and fighting to get it for them; taking responsibility. He was paterfamilias to his work-force as well as his family; more than that, as a grandson said simply, 'He was a hero.'

And he never forgot his roots. His daughter remembers looking for something with him in the attics at Fairways once, and coming across a battered old Gladstone bag. She suggested throwing it out, but her father would not hear of it.

'When I was about eight or nine, there was a hundred yards' race,' he said. 'And this bag was the prize. The other boys had running shoes. I only had the boots I was wearing, so I took them off and tied them round my neck and I ran the race barefoot. And I won. I always keep this, to remind me that I was a poor boy once – who couldn't afford running shoes.'

It seems an amazing distance from that boy to the ninety-seven-year-old billionaire. His mother would not have thought so; she always had faith in him. And that young man – just past his twenty-first birthday and writing to his family in the middle of the First World War – he had faith in himself.

This is how he ended his letter:

'After the extreme pleasure which your cards have brought, I can at last appreciate that God *is* good. I take leave of you, therefore, as your big brother and son; a little nearer manhood's estate, but feeling smaller and more subdued; *and yet strangely confident.*

John

My train is due at 3.22 p.m. Allowing for the usual slight delays, I should reach Manchester about 3.40 p.m.'

He was starting out on a much longer journey than that.

Acknowledgments

I would like to thank John Moores' four children for entrusting me with the biography of their father, and for their help and interest. To write an impartial and truthful life story is always difficult, especially when one very much admires the person whom it is about. To write accurately about John Moores has been even more difficult because there are very few records of any sort to refer to. I have checked facts wherever possible, but most of the information I have gleaned has been from word of mouth.

I am particularly grateful to Harry Thomas and his PR team for arranging for me to talk to so many retired employees of Littlewoods, at every level. Without them this book could never have been written. It was a great experience to meet them: many had more than a dash of the John Moores spirit in them.

I am also very grateful to those members of the family who offered their help, particularly to Polly, June, Geoffrey, Charles, Matthew and Jeremy.

I would like to thank Elsie Arnold, Barbara Gardiner, Sarah Clarke and my editor, Celia Levett for their advice and encouragement; Philip Waller for vetting some of my historical references; Archie Hutchison and Sir Desmond Pitcher, two directors who worked with Sir John, for their reminiscences; Malcolm Davidson for his company research on my behalf; and Enid Richards for allowing me to see the few treasured letters and diaries.

Last, but not least, I am very grateful to my children and to my friends, who for over a year have put up with my total obsession with someone else's life.

The author and publishers would like to acknowledge the following for their kind permission to reproduce the quotations contained in this book:

Donald Horne for the extract from his book, *God is an Englishman* by Donald Horne

Chambers Publishers for the extract from Florence Desmond's autobiography, *Florence Desmond*

Faber & Faber Ltd for the extract from 'East Coker' from T S Eliot's *The Four Quartets*

Some of the quotations attributed to John Moores in this book are taken from *How to Become a Millionaire* by John and Cecil Moores which appeared in a series of articles in the *Empire News* in the 1950s

Index

JM stands for John Moores

Appleton, Clifford, 43
Arnold, Tom, 138
Ashton, Bunty, 117, 198
Ashton, Dick, 197–9
Askham, Colin Henry (né Littlewood),
  26, 27, 28, 38
  and the pools, 28–9, 31–2; still a
  friend, 61, 129, 148
Australian football, pools on, 141

Bagley, Mr, 129
Bailey bridges, 98–9
Barker, Eric, 142, 143, 156, 226
Barnard, John Jervis, 28
Barrage balloons, 86, 95, 102
Baseball, 74
Benner, Colonel, 98
Bermuda, 129–30, 148
Betting *see* Gambling
Betting and Lotteries Act, 1934,
  66, 116
Bettle, Harry, 69
Black, Tom Campbell, 71–2
Bonds Pools, 47
Bottomes, Mr (B & P Press), 29,
  31, 34, 41
Boxing of vehicles, 99, 101–2
Braddock, Bessie, MP, 134, 204
Breen, Helen, 138
Bretherton, Revd John, 116
Brian Mills of Sunderland, 142, 164
British Broadcasting Corporation, 35–6
Burlington Credit Mail Order, 142
Buying, 68–9, 117–18, 153, 154

Carey, John, 184–5
Carnegie, Dale, 110
Carr, Miss, 55
Carrickfergus, 93
Carter, Philip, 215, 220, 222

Catterick, Harry, 185
Cézanne, Paul, 174
Chain-stores, 74, 75
  see mainly Littlewoods Stores
Charities, and JM, 176–8, 189
Clare, Clifford, 43
Clark, Joe, 43
Clement, John, 220
Club system, in mail order, 52–3,
  55, 57–8
Commercial Cable Company, 19, 21,
  24–5, 25–7, 33, 34
  and formation of Littlewoods,
  28, 29, 30
Computers, introduction, 161–2,
  188, 199
Cooke, Mr, director, 133
Credit, 141, 164–5, 199
  squeeze on, 164–5

Deacon, Stuart, 38
Dean, Dixie, 73
Desmond, Florence, 71–3
Dew, Miss, 89
Dickinson, Bill, 185
Dinghies, wartime, 97
Direct-mail testing, 52
Disney, Colonel, 84, 98
Dog-racing, and pools, 44
Dunlop, and barrage balloons, 86

Eccles, JM's birthplace, 14
Edge Hill Boys' Club, 189
Edinburgh, Prince Philip, Duke of, 219
Elbow Beach Hotel, Bermuda, 130,
  170, 194, 200
Empire Pools, 46
Everton Football Club, 183–8, 212, 219

Fairways, house, 48, 49–50

Farrar, George, 173, 211
Fell, Mr, chauffeur, 77
Ferranti, 95
Fisher, Mr, financial adviser, 193
Football, and JM, 43, 49, 183
  see also Everton Football Club
Football League, anti-pools, 66
Football pools, 38–9, 46, 67, 141
  advisory service for large winners,
  164; attacked, 37, 66, 116; Australian
  football, 141; and the law, 38, 39,
  66; panels in bad weather, 188;
  prizes, 141, 163–4; ready-money
  betting, 150; rivals, 46–7; treble-
  chance pools, 117, 150, 163, 188
  see also Littlewoods Pools
Formby Golf Club, 49
Frith, Mr, 130
Furlong, Eric, 155, 217

Gambling, forces against, 37, 66, 116
Garry, Dr, 125, 129
Gaskin, Miss, 42, 44
Gemmell, Harry, 55
General Strike, 1926, 35
Geodetics, 96, 100–1
George, Arthur, 216
Germany, JM's wish to operate in,
  199–200
Golf, and JM, 26, 49
Great Universal Stores, 51

Hamilton-Sugden, Theresa, barrister,
  136, 187
Harrington, Mr, artist, 148–9
Hedges, Cyril, 95, 103, 196
Henderson, Arthur, MP, 69, 70
Herbert, A P, MP, 66
Heydler, John, 74
Hinde, Mr, gardener, 179
Hoare, Frank, 177, 209–10, 211
Hodkinson, Cyril (cousin), 84, 98
Horne, Donald, 228
Horse-racing, 44, 47, 141
Hotels owned by Littlewoods, 170
  see also Elbow Beach Hotel
Hubbard, Reg, artist, 149, 173, 202
Hughes, Bill, 28, 29, 31–2, 38
Hughes, Holland, solicitor, 66,
  125, 187
Hutchison, Archie, 196, 199

Incentive systems, 102–3
Index shops, 223, 226
Interest rates, effect on credit, 164
Irving, Dr, 201, 202

J M Centre, 192, 196–7
  now 100 Old Hall Street, 226
Jackson, Eddie, 36, 40, 43
Jackson, Frank, 36, 40, 43, 44
Janet Frazer (company), 189
John Moores Home Shopping,
  formerly Littlewoods Mail Order
  (qv), 189
John Moores Liverpool Art Exhibition,
  174–6, 189
Jones, Jimmy, 71
Jones, Tom, singer, 173

Kennerley, George, 175, 176, 194, 202
Knowles, Annie Maria Margaret
  (mother-in-law), 30
Knowles, Ruby see Moores, Ruby
Knowles, William (brother-in-law), 30
Knowles, William Albert (father-in-
  law), 30, 40

Labone, Brian, 185, 186
Legge, Ingram, 74
Lindsay, Alec, 118, 119
Little Woody Club, 179
Littlewood (H) Ltd, horse-racing, 44,
  47, 141
Littlewoods
  assessment, 227; board, 196, 220;
  computers, 161–2, 188, 199; and
  decimal currency, 210; gifts for long
  service, 211; in Northern Ireland,
  93; owners of loch and hotels, 170;
  postal strike, 209–10; premises
  (Liverpool unless stated otherwise)
    Bold Street, 91; Brownlow
    Hill, 47; Canning Street, 86,
    87, 88, 91–2, 93; Carrickfergus,
    Northern Ireland, 93; Chapel
    Street, Manchester, 90; Crosby,
    92, 93, 94, 102; Edge Lane, 47, 96,
    119; Hanover Street, 85, 90, 91;
    Hart Street, Southport, 92; Hood
    Street, 47, 91; Irlam Road, 88, 91,
    93; J M Centre, 192, 196–7, 226;
    Leeds Street, 47, 90–1; Longford,

Index

Ulster Works, 92; Old Hall Street, 91, 92, 226; Oldham Place, 90, 91; 34 Pall Mall, 47, 56; Walton Hall Avenue, 47, 93, 95, 96; Williamson Street, 47; Woolton, Eclipse Works, 92
private company, 200; redundancies, 221; in Second World War, 91–100; damage in, 91–2; turnover in 1992, 226

Littlewoods Mail-Order Stores, 53–4, 57
clubs, 55; turnover in 1934, 57; at Crosby, 67; staff pensions, 79; Second World War trade, 103; post-war, 117; catalogues post-war, 118, 135, 150; development in 1950s, 141; credit introduced, 141–2; 21st anniversary in 1953, 149; and rail strike, 150–1; buying amalgamated with stores, 153; computers introduced, 161; development in 1960s, 188–9, 199; re-christened John Moores Home Shopping, 189; postal strike in 1971, 209; 40 years anniversary, 211; turnover in 1992, 226

Littlewoods Pools
foundation, 29–30; early days, 31–4, 36; growth, 38–9; court case, 38; security systems, 40; own printing works, 41; life at, 42–3; growth in 1930s, 46, 67; rivals, 46–7; new premises, 47; treatment of staff, 50, 61, 79; Second World War, 83; post-war, 116, 119, 134; a family business, 126; Summer Pools, 141; growth in 1950s, 163; computers introduced, 188; changes in stakes and pools, 188; postal strike in 1971, 209; first £1m. winner in 1972, 212

Littlewoods Songsters, 138, 170–1

Littlewoods Stores, 75, 103
post-war, 118–19, 135; new openings, 119, 135, 142, 151, 164, 199; growth in 1950s, 142, 151; Liverpool No. 1 store, 152; headquarters moved from London to Liverpool, 153; management, 156, 157–8; computers introduced, 162; credit squeeze, 164–5; two shops in

St Petersburg, 192; number of stores in 1984, 223; turnover in 1992, 226

Littlewoods Warehouses, 188–9

Liverpool
JM's first work there, 24–5; JM Councillor in, 71; air raids, 90–2; Gold Medal for Achievement in 1978, for JM, 217

Liverpool Corporation, Freedom of the City for JM, 203–4

Liverpool John Moores University, 226

Liverpool Motorists' Annual Outing for Handicapped Children, 177

Liverpool University Business Management Studies School, 189

London, life in 1930s, 59

McCarthy, Senator Joseph, 140–1

Mail-order business, 51–2
art of buying, 68–9
see mainly Littlewoods Mail-Order Stores

Mailing lists, 52

Maltz, Maxwell, 110

Management and JM, 155–9

Manchester, 13

Medaillon Mode (company), 199–200, 205–6

Message to Garcia, 127–8

Miss Littlewood competitions, 138, 173

Mitchell, Miss, secretary, 89, 143, 147, 155, 171, 197, 201, 202, 204, 207–8, 219, 225

Moffat, Cocky, boxer, 73

Montgomery Ward, Chicago, 57

Moore, Sam Appleton, 138

Moore, Sheila (wife of John Junior), 138–9, 190, 207

Moores family
history, 12–14; support for the pools company, 33, 34; upward mobility, 48–9, 59; holidays, 59–60; during Second World War, 89–90; social life, 113–14

Moores, Arthur (brother), 15, 17, 24, 39, 169
in Littlewoods, 41, 42, 53, 54, 67; out of the company, 126; death, 225

Moores, Betty (daughter), 33, 77, 105, 193

schooling, 89, 105–6; university,
107; advice from father, 108–11; and
Kenneth Suenson-Taylor (husband),
107, 123, 129; children, 138, 148;
director of Littlewoods, 215
Moores, Cecil (brother), 15, 16,
    160, 169
    and the pools, 34, 36, 38, 39, 53;
    security system, 40; wife Doris,
    48, 62, 166, 205, 225; supports
    brother on mail-order idea, 51;
    holidays in France, 60; and sport,
    43, 62; personality, 68, 159; doubts
    on chain-stores, 74; agrees with JM
    on munitions production, 84; in
    Second World War, 88, 90–1; and
    engineering, 94–5; post-war pools,
    116, 126, 207; death in 1989, 225
Moores, Charlie (brother), 15,
    39, 78, 84
    in Littlewoods, 41, 42; out of
    company, 126; illness and death,
    129, 130–1; children looked after by
    JM, 131
Moores, Doris (wife of Cecil), 48, 62,
    166, 225
Moores, Edna (sister) *see* Moores, Joy
Moores, Ethel (sister), 15, 19, 193
    working, 21, 23, 24; husband Bert,
    39, 77, 89, 114; war work, 89;
    second marriage, 180; on JM as an
    old man, 225; death in 1990, 225
Moores, Hilda (sister), 14, 21, 24,
    48, 132
    in Littlewoods, 36–7, 39, 42;
    husband George, 40, 41, 225;
    holidays, 62, 123–4, death in
    1967, 207
Moores, J & C, printers, 41, 47, 83
Moores, Janatha (daughter), 75, 78,
    111, 123, 129, 205
    holidays, 173, 202; wedding to
    Patrick Stubbs, 179; at Ruby's death,
    193; looks after JM, 194
Moores, John (grandfather), 12–13,
    13–14, 18
Moores, John
    birth in Eccles, 14; childhood,
    15, 16, 18; first work, 18, 19;
    Commercial Cable Company
    telegraphist, 24–5; to Droylsden,

20; substitute father in family,
21–2, 24; Navy telegraphist, 24;
to Ireland, 25–7; bulk supply
company, 26; to Liverpool, 27;
starts Littlewoods Pools, 28–9;
marriage to Ruby Knowles, 30;
buys out partners in Littlewoods
Pools, 32–3; expands, 37;
prosecution, 37–8; social life in
company, 43; starts horse-betting
company, 44; house Fairways in
Freshfield, 48, 49–50; millionaire,
51; mail-order idea, 51–2, 53, 57;
motto, 51; the clubs, 55; to USA
to see mail-order firms, 57; double
millionaire, 58; fly-fishing, 59;
holidays, 59–61; skiing, 62; to
Germany and Austria, 62–3; lack of
languages, 63–4; interest in art, 64;
supervises pools business, 66; main
interest in mail-order company,
67–8; stands for Parliament,
69–71; Councillor, Liverpool, 71;
and Tom Campbell Black, 71–3;
aid to sportsmen, 73; attempt to
launch baseball, 74; interest in
chain-stores, 74; and Ruby, 76–7;
    family, 77; home entertainment,
77; to London for 1937 Coronation,
78; family matters, 78–9; pension
scheme for staff, 79; first Rolls-
Royce car, 79; JM1 numberplate,
80; and Second World War, 82;
work with ambulance service, 82,
83: munitions production idea, 84;
parachutes, 85–6; belief in time
study, 86, 101; barrage balloons,
86–8; escape from bomb, 88; turns to
engineering contracts, 94, 95, 96–7;
on Littlewoods war success, 100;
Star Operator system, 102–3;
    post-war plans, 103–4; family
during war, 105–15; relations with
his children, 106–7; and Betty,
107–8; philosophy expressed in
letter, 108–11; sons at Eton, 111–13;
relations with John Junior, 112–13;
relations with Peter, 113; post-war
Pools, 116; and suppliers, 118; rules
for managers, *Preparation for Business*,
119–20; interest in training, 120–1;

Little Black Book, 122; and family, 123, 129–33; meets Betty's in-laws to be, 123–4; ill with meningitis, 124, 125; makes arrangements for time after his death, 125–6;

the family in the business, 125–7; the *Message to Garcia*, 127–8; business as the centre of life, 128–9; to Bermuda, 129–30; buys hotel there, 130; gifts for merit, to family, 132; work after illness, 133; use of wartime factories, post-war, 135; critical of Government's financial policy, 135–6; reunions of staff, 138; and family, 138; first grandchild, 138; speech on future in 1950, 140;

view of credit, 141–2; visits his stores, 142–4; preference for low stock and selling lines, 144–5; and 'shrinkage', 144, 156; aphorisms, 144, 145; on capitalism, 145–6; need to be kept informed, 146–7, 157; holidays in Bermuda, 148; tribute to mother, 150; to US about new ideas in stores, 151–2; rigid control of stores and family, 152, 153, 159, 165; training of buyers, 154; medical care for staff, 155; and managers, 155–9; quality control, 160–1; introduction of computers, 161–2; panel system of viewing goods, 162–3;

family crisis, Patricia's marriage, 166; on the business and the family, 166–7; recalls Peter, 168–9; shooting and fishing, 169–70; encouragement of singing etc, 170–1; John Moores Liverpool Art Exhibition, 174–6, 189; charitable work, 176–8, 189; in wheelchair, 178, 213; and road safety, 178–9; nine grandchildren by late 1950s, 179; and mother's illness and death, 180–1; chairman of Everton Football Club, 183–8, 212; end of direct involvement with pools, 188; youth clubs, 189; family discord, 190–2, 195;

and Ruby's death, 193–4; friction on family holidays, 194; bad fall, 194, 201; and children, 194–5; installs IBM 360 system, 199; major business decisions in 1960s, 199–200; expands into Germany, 199–200; physical illness, 201, 202–3; holidays, 201–2; Freedom of the City of Liverpool in 1970, 203–4; clothes, 204–5;

Wimbledon, 205; quarrel with John Junior, 206; succession problem, 210; awarded CBE, 211; sponsors sports, 212; strong interest in the stores, 212–13; instructions on kidnapping, 214; resignation as Chairman, 216; but still working, 217, 222–3; honoured by Liverpool Gold Medal for Achievement in 1978, 217; awarded KBE, 217–18, 219; and royalty, 219; Chairman again 1980–1, 220; President of company, 220; and 'new brooms', 220–1; still working in his 80s, 222–3; and still driving, 221–2; burgled, 224; operations, 224; declining influence at 92, 224; an old man, 225–6; assessment of life, 226, 228–9; treatment of managers and family, 227

aspects of life and personality
ambition, 19–20, 21–2; anxiety to learn, 61; and art, 64, 148–9, 171, 174–6, 189; bridge player, 61–2; a catnapper, 197, 213; anti-Communism, 140; competitiveness, 76, 114; demonstrativeness, 17, 160; desire to be 'one of the boys', 186–7, 188; dominance, 127, 152, 153, 159, 165; football, 43, 49, 183; frugality, 191–2, 210; golf, 26, 49; hatred of waste, 97, 120; health, obsession with, 201; honesty, 38, 68–9; humility, 173–4;

idealism, 12; impracticality, 176; and languages, 63–4, 171, 213–14; leadership, 45, 55, 68, 97, 102; Little Black Book, 218; love of Liverpool, 71; and management, 155–9, 227; mental control, 110; and music, 113, 148; as Northerner, 228–9; and painting, 64, 148–9, 171, 173–4; paternalism, 50; reading including philosophy, 110; and religion, 131–2; anti-Roman Catholicism, 27; ruthlessness, 67; and 'shrinkage',

144, 156; anti-snob, 172–3;
anti-Socialism, 133–4, 136, 214, 215;
sporting interests, 26, 29, 59, 62,
73, 74, 169–70; sternness, 16; time
and punctuality, obsession with, 61,
109, 155, 194; unostentatiousness,
49; willingness to pitch in, 56; and
women, 76, 136–7
Moores, John, junior (son), 41
at Eton, 105, 106, 111; good at
sport, 112, 189; works at Sears
Roebuck, 112; relations with father,
112–13; works for firm, 120–1;
marriage to Sheila Moore, 138–9;
director, 146; house, Random
House, Freshfield, 146; children,
146, 148; and stores, 151–3; visits to
US, 151–2; chief buyer for stores,
154; charitable work, 178, 189;
anti-discrimination, 189; divorce
from Sheila, marriage to Jane
Stavely-Dick, 190; child by Jane,
191; car accident, 192–3; at mother's
death, 193; to Germany to run
Medaillon Mode, 200–1; relations
with father over work, 199, 206;
resignation from company, 206; later
life, 207
Moores, John III (grandson), 148
Moores, John William (father),
12, 14, 15
personality, 14, 16–17, 18; drinking,
18, 20, 21; death from TB, 22, 23
Moores, Joy (née Edna, sister),
15, 23, 49
and Littlewoods, 36–7, 39, 541,
43, 47; organiser of mail-order
company, 54–5; leaves Littlewoods,
61; holidays, 61, 62; marriage to
army officer, 78–9
Moores, Louisa (née Fethney, mother),
14, 20–1, 48, 182
as mother, 14–15, 16; character, 16,
17, 18; encouragement of JM, 19, 20;
businesses, 20, 23–4, 39; holidays,
59–60, 61; centre of family, 77, 123,
131, 150; in London in 1937, 78;
in Second World War, 90; religion,
131–2; at mail-order anniversary,
149; bungalow, 180; cancer and
death, 180–1

Moores, Louise 'Lou' (sister),
15, 20, 23
in Littlewoods, 39, 43, 47; new
house, 48; husband Len, 48, 125;
war work, 88, 89; holidays, 62, 64;
in Second World War, 89, 90; at
Ruby's death, 193; social life with
JM, 207; death in 1972, 225
Moores, Nigel (nephew), 214, 215
Moores, Patricia (niece), 166
Moores, Peter (son), 53, 111, 113
in business, 121, 147–8; work at
Glyndebourne, 148; comparison
with JM, 158; at Oxford, 168; back
in chain-stores, 169; on his father,
176, 177; marriage to Luciana Pinto,
182–3; anti-discrimination, 189;
interest in arts, 189–90; charitable
foundation, 189–90; gifts for 40th
wedding anniversary, 191; at
mother's death, 193; director in
1965, 196; relations with father, 199,
219–20; deputed to run Medaillon
Mode, 200; runs down Littlewoods
interests, joins Sothebys, 200; and
father's illness, 202; Vice-Chairman,
215; Chairman, 216
Moores, Ruby (née Knowles, wife), 31
personality, 30–1, 49, 190, 191, 221;
supports JM in pools venture, 33;
holidays, 61, 62, 148, 173, 181; and
Florence Desmond, 72–3; fishing,
76; in Second World War, 90; and
the family, 111; religion, 132; cancer,
180–1, 192; jewellery from son,
191–2; death in 1965, 193
Moores, Selina (née Rogers,
grandmother), 13, 14, 18
Moores, Sidney (great-grandfather), 13
Moores, Sidney (uncle), 15
Mumford, Frank, 55–7
Musther, Owen, 162, 201, 221, 222
restyles JM, 204, 219

National Government, 69–70
Neary, Joe, 68
Nixon, Major, 86

Oak, Freddy, 143, 156–7, 160

Pacific packs, 100

Page, Stanley, 158, 160, 213
Panel system of goods judgement, 162–3
Panels, pools, 188
Parachutes, 85–6, 90, 92
Parliament, JM stands for, 69–71
Peale, Norman Vincent, 110
Penny Points pool, 67
People competition, 34
Peter Craig (company), 199
Phillips, Bert, 36
Pinto, Luciana (Mrs Peter Moores), 182–3
Pitcher, Desmond, 220–1, 222, 223
Pontoons, war-time, 98, 101, 117
Pools Betting Act, 1954, 150, 188
Pools betting duty, 134–5, 188
Pools *see* Football pools; Littlewoods Pools
Pools panels, 188
Pools Promoters Association, 66, 103
Post Office, security for Littlewoods mail, 40
Price, Miss, 43, 87, 97, 117

Quality control, 160–1

Ready-Money Betting Act, 38, 150
Reece, James, 177
Rice, Mr, 155
Richards, Miss, secretary, 89, 122, 147, 197, 201, 202, 204–5, 207–8, 214, 222, 224
Rimmer, T, 98
Ritchie, Alan and Jack, 74
Ritson, Max, 51, 52, 53
Road safety, 178–9
Roberts, Len, 172, 173, 192
Roberts, Rosetta, 171–2, 192
Roberts, Tommy, 74
Rootes, 95–6
Royal Commission on Betting, 66
Russell, R J, MP, 66
Ruth, Babe, 74

Sawyer, Eric, 95, 133, 166, 193, 196
Scott, 'Scotty', 93
Scrutton, Hugh, 175
Sears Roebuck, 57, 112, 148
Second World War, 80–1, 107–8, 115

Sergeant, Bob, 73, 84
Shells, explosive, 95
Sherman's Pools, 199
Simpson, Willie, 36
Slump 1929–34, 46
Smith, Mr, bookmaker, 44
Soccer Pools, Leicester, 46
Stanhope, Colin, 219
Stavely-Dick, Jane (Mrs John Junior), 190–1, 207, 216
Stevenson, Bill, artist, 149, 173
Storm-boats, wartime, 99
Stubbs, Jessie, 154
Stubbs, Patrick (son-in-law), 179, 194
Suenson-Taylor, Kenneth, 2nd Baron Grantchester (son-in-law), 107, 123, 129, 169–70
Suez crisis, 164

Tarleton, Joe, boxer, 73
Temple, Derek, 186
Thomas, Harry, 163, 212, 213
Treble Chance Pool, 117, 150, 163, 188
Tucker, Sir Henry, 130
Turns Clubs, 53
Twenties, characteristics, 35–6

Unity Pools, 103, 116, 176

Vernons Pools, 46, 175
Vickers, 95, 96

Walker Art Gallery, Liverpool, 175–6, 189
Walther, Mrs, housekeeper, 194–5, 205, 218
Waterville Supply Company, 26, 28, 51
Watts, George, 151, 152, 157
Managing Director, 196, 197, 207
Webster, David, 168
Welfare, aspects of, 50, 79
Wellington bombers, 96, 100–1
Williams, Arthur, 94
Worrall, Mr, 21, 122

Young, Alec, 185–6

Zetters Pools, 46